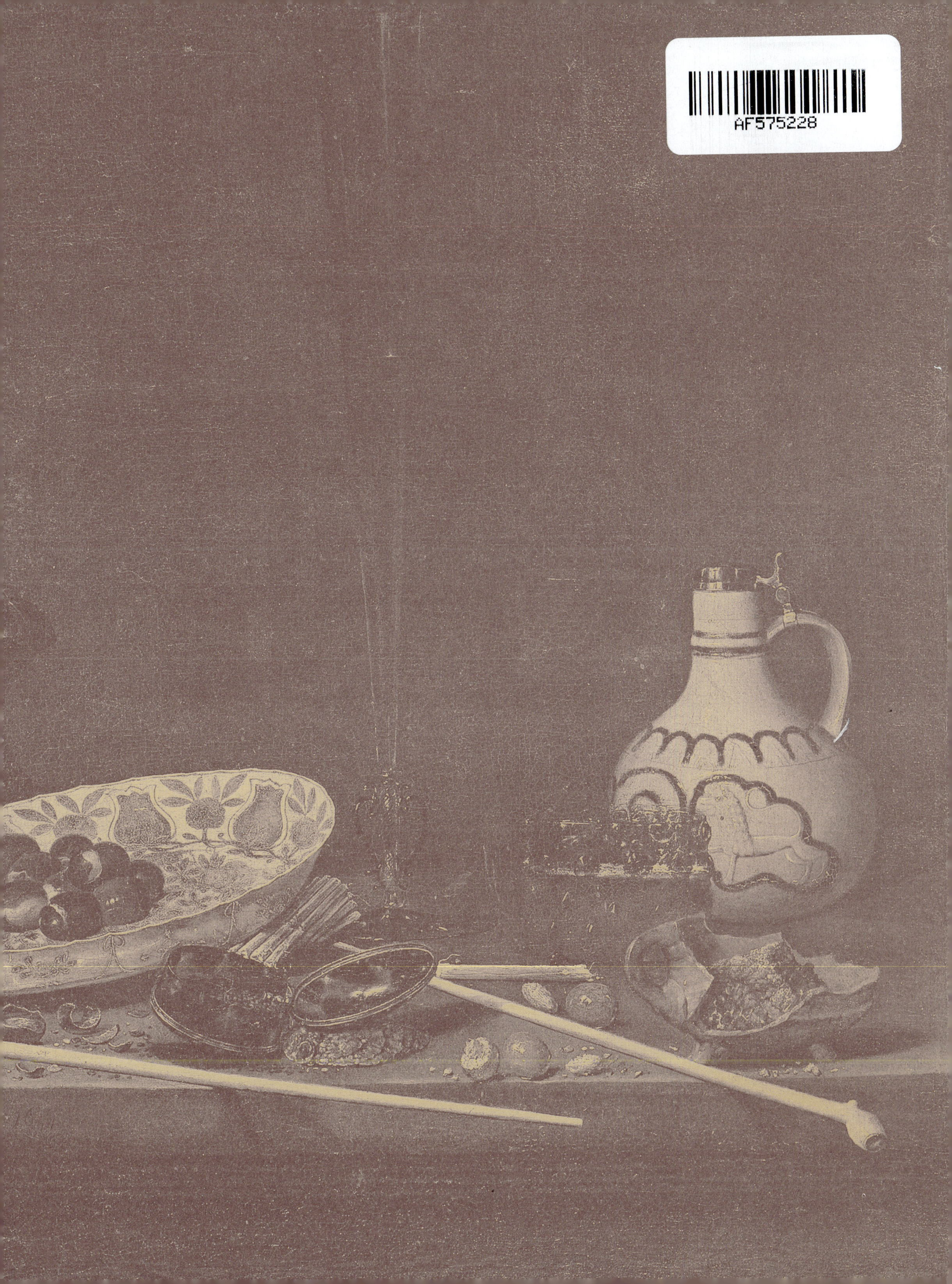

AF575228

# REMBRANDT AND THE GOLDEN AGE OF DUTCH ART

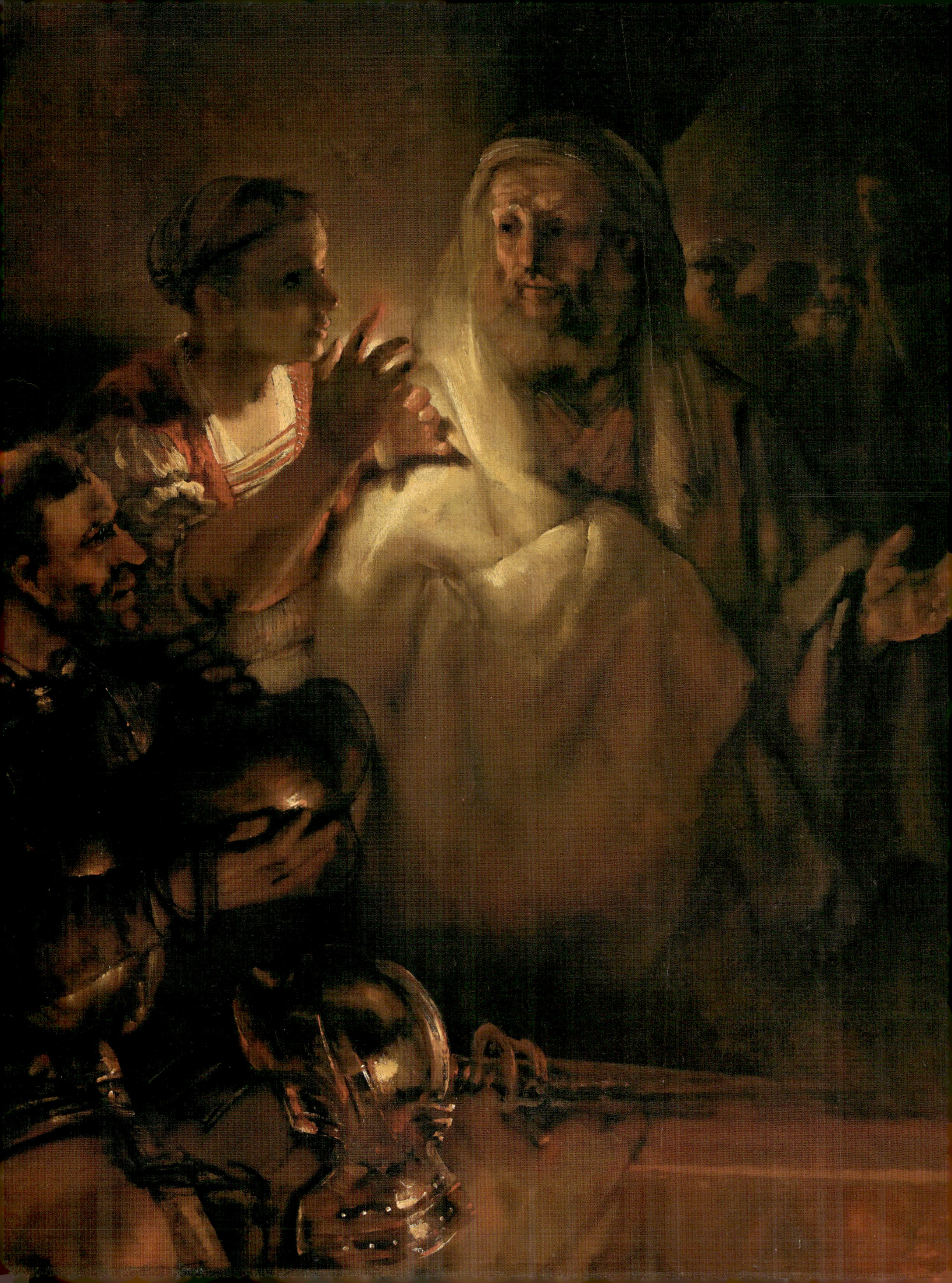

# REMBRANDT AND THE GOLDEN AGE OF DUTCH ART

*Treasures from the Rijksmuseum, Amsterdam*

RUUD PRIEM

EDITED BY PENELOPE HUNTER-STIEBEL

DAYTON ART INSTITUTE, OHIO

PHOENIX ART MUSEUM, ARIZONA

PORTLAND ART MUSEUM, OREGON

*in association with*

THE RIJKSMUSEUM, AMSTERDAM

Published in conjunction with the exhibition *Rembrandt and the Golden Age of Dutch Art: Treasures from the Rijksmuseum, Amsterdam*

**Exhibition Itinerary**

| | |
|---|---|
| Dayton Art Institute | September 30, 2006–January 7, 2007 |
| Phoenix Art Museum | January 27–May 6, 2007 |
| Portland Art Museum | May 26–September 16, 2007 |

"Rembrandt and the Golden Age of Dutch Art" copyright © 2006 by the Rijksmuseum, Amsterdam. Images copyright © 2006 by the Rijksmuseum, Amsterdam (except pages 10, 12, 13–15).

All rights reserved.

Library of Congress Cataloging-in-Publication Data
Priem, Ruud.
Rembrandt and the Golden Age of Dutch art : treasures from the Rijksmuseum, Amsterdam / Ruud Priem ; edited by Penelope Hunter-Stiebel.
p. ; cm.
Published in conjunction with the exhibition 'Rembrandt and the Golden Age of Dutch art: treasures from the Rijksmuseum, Amsterdam' to be displayed at the Dayton Art Institute, Sept. 30, 2006–Jan. 7, 2007, the Phoenix Art Museum, Jan. 27–May 6, 2007, and the Portland Art Museum, May 26–Sept. 16, 2007.
Includes bibliographical references and index.
ISBN-13: 978-1-883124-23-6 (hardcover : alk. paper)
ISBN-10: 1-883124-23-9
1. Art, Dutch—17th century—Exhibitions. 2. Art—Netherlands—Amsterdam—Exhibitions. 3. Rijksmuseum (Netherlands)—Exhibitions. I. Hunter-Stiebel, Penelope. II. Dayton Art Institute. III. Phoenix Art Museum. IV. Portland Art Museum (Or.). V. Title.
N6946.P75 2006
709'.49207477173—dc22 2006014746

Details: pp. 2 and 16, Rembrandt van Rijn, *The Denial of Saint Peter,* no. 56; pp. 6–7, Govert Flinck, *The Governors of the Kloveniersdoelen,* no. 28; p. 8, Frans Hals, *Portrait of a Man, Possibly Nicolaes Hasselaer,* no. 63; p. 18, Rembrandt van Rijn, *Self-Portrait, Etching at a Window,* no. 2; p. 32, Abraham Mignon, *Still Life with Fruit and Oysters,* no. 15; p. 46, Gerrit Berckheyde, *The Town Hall on the Dam, Amsterdam,* no. 29; p. 66, Paulus Potter, *Hilly Landscape with Herders and Animals,* no. 46; p. 82, Govert Flinck, *Isaac Blessing Jacob,* no. 54; p. 102, Rembrandt van Rijn, *Saskia van Uylenburgh,* no. 72; p. 120, Pieter de Hooch, *Man Handing a Letter to a Woman,* no. 90; pp. 136–137, Jan Davidsz de Heem, *Still Life with Books,* no. 12.

All images courtesy Photography Department, Rijksmuseum, Amsterdam, except pages 10 and 12, courtesy Portland Art Museum (Paul Foster); pages 13 and 14, courtesy Phoenix Art Museum (Craig Smith); and page 15, courtesy Dayton Art Institute.

Distributed by
University of Washington Press
PO Box 50096
Seattle, WA 98145-5096
www.washington.edu/uwpress

Project coordination: Portland Art Museum
General editor: Penelope Hunter-Stiebel
Manuscript editor: Suzanne Kotz
Proofreader: Jessica Eber
Designer: Jeff Wincapaw
Color separator: iocolor, Seattle
Produced by Marquand Books, Inc., Seattle
www.marquand.com
Printed and bound in China by C&C Offset Printing Co., Ltd.

# CONTENTS

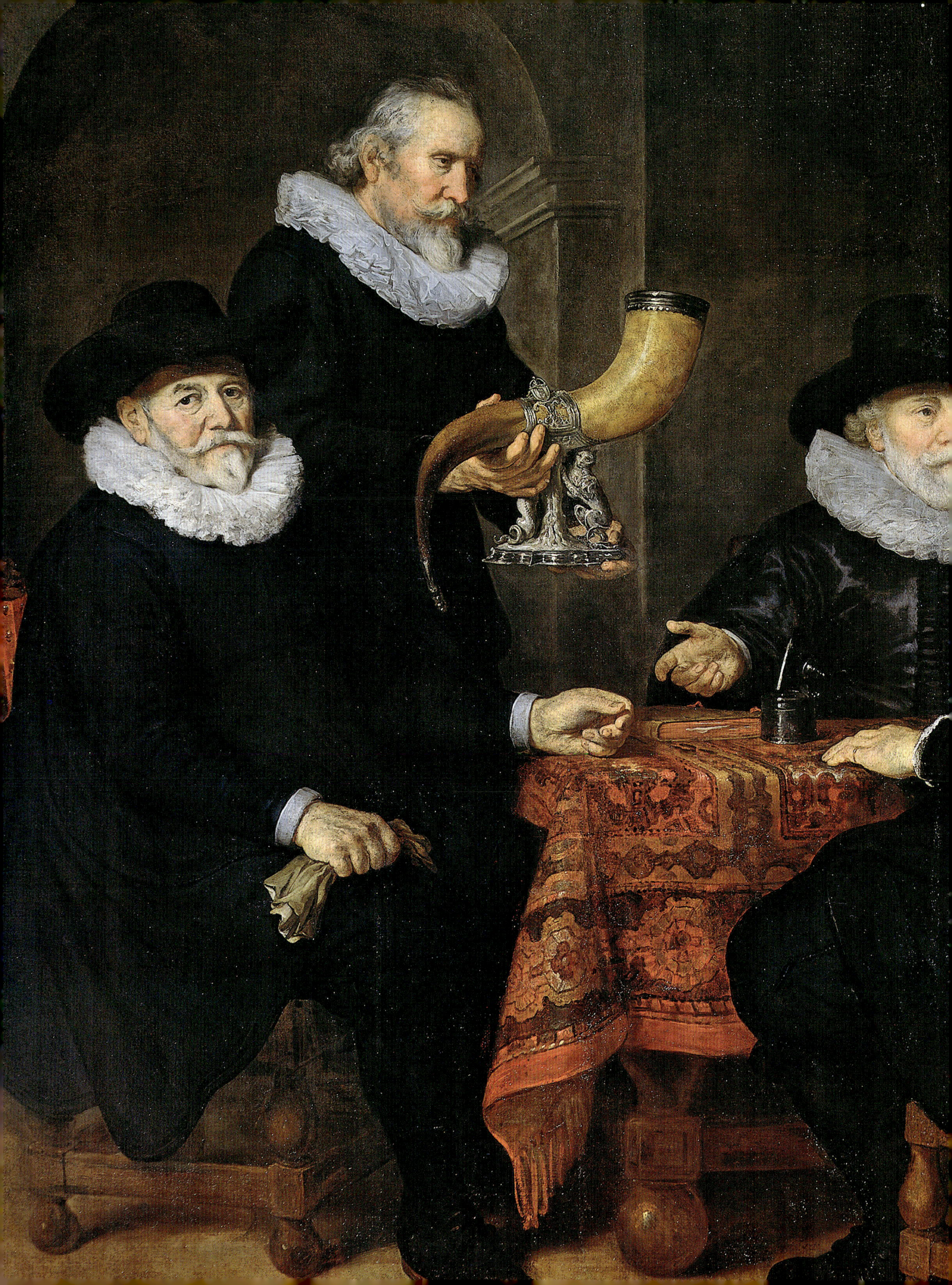

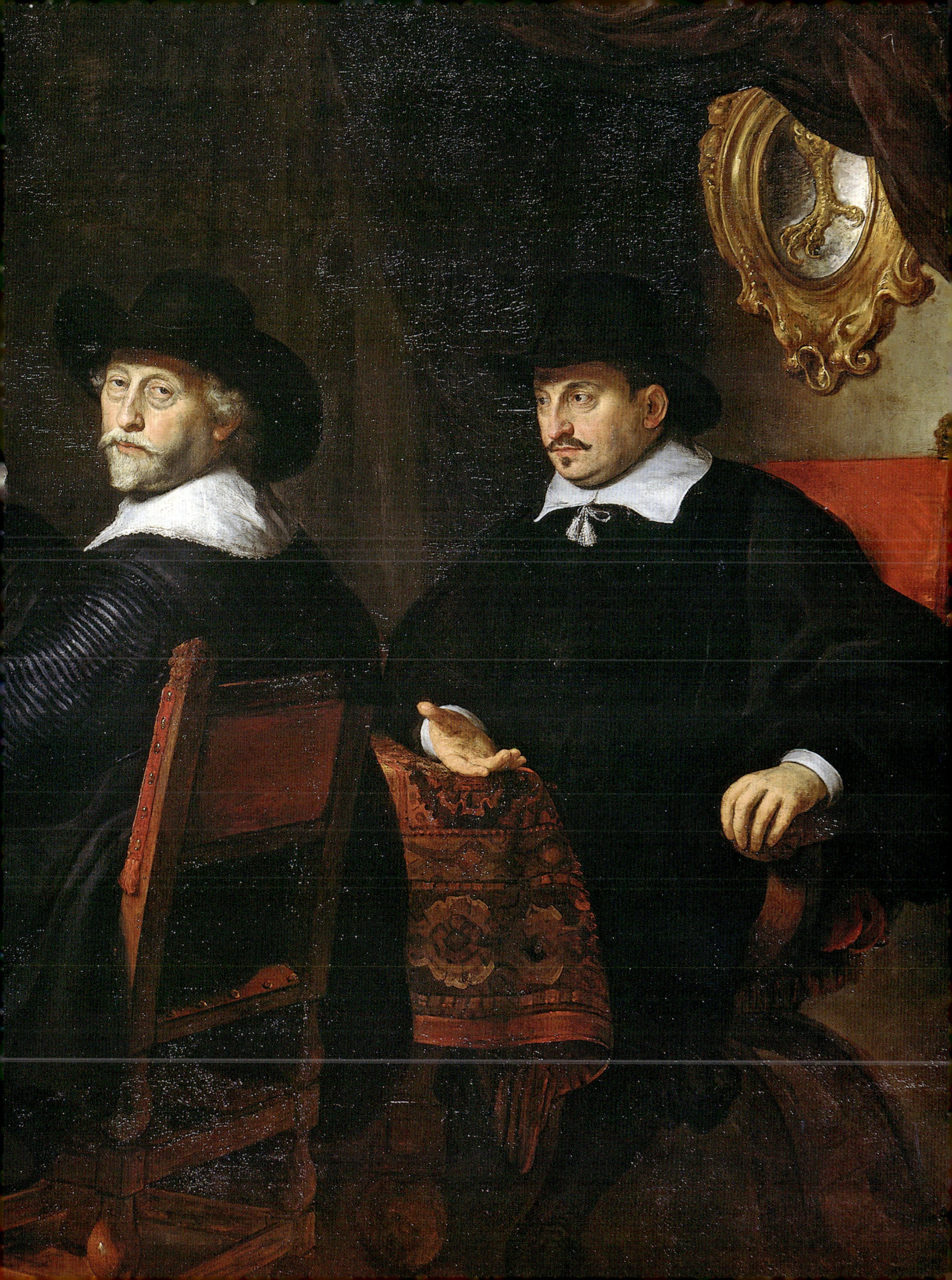

# DIRECTORS' FOREWORD

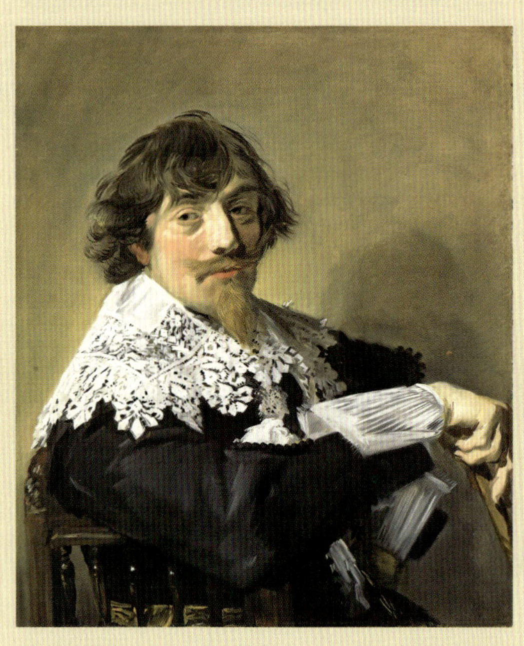

IT HAS BEEN A GREAT HONOR FOR OUR FOUR INSTITUTIONS to collaborate on the first American touring exhibition of masterpieces from the Rijksmuseum in Amsterdam. Housed in the same imposing building since 1885, the Rijksmuseum is the Dutch national museum of art, history, and the decorative arts. *Rembrandt and the Golden Age of Dutch Art* celebrates the richness and versatility of the paintings, prints, and decorative objects produced in the Netherlands in the 17th century. Rembrandt van Rijn, Frans Hals, Jacob van Ruisdael, Pieter de Hooch, and Jan Steen are painters featured in almost every art history textbook. Equal to their paintings in quality and artistry are superb *objects d'art* in silver, glass, and ceramics, especially those from Delft. Rembrandt was unparalleled as a printmaker and as a painter, and at the core of this project are eight prints and six paintings that demonstrate the full range of his talent. In all, ninety spectacular works of art clearly convey a sense of 17th-century Dutch culture, thus fulfilling the missions of our three American institutions: to bring the world's greatest art to the people of Dayton, Phoenix, and Portland.

At the Rijksmuseum, special acknowledgment is owed to Peter Sigmond, Jan Rudolph de Lorm, and Taco Dibbits, whose initiative was central in bringing the exhibition to life. Guest curator Ruud Priem conceived the organizing principle of the exhibition as "the world seen through the artist's eye" and made the selection of objects from the Rijksmuseum's collections. We thank him for his discerning scholarship as curator and as the author of the catalogue. Jan Piet Filedt Kok, Ger Luijten, Dirk Jan Biemond, Jan Daniël van Dam, and Manja Zeldenrust and her team of conservators were instrumental in the preparations for the exhibition, while Wendela Brouwer and Paulien Retèl played pivotal roles in the realization of the exhibition and catalogue.

In the United States, curators Penelope Hunter-Stiebel and Tom Loughman along with staff members in Dayton, Phoenix, and Portland worked tirelessly to create this breathtaking exhibition. Ms. Hunter-Stiebel demonstrated enthusiasm and patience throughout the project, and her thoughtful oversight of the catalogue greatly enhanced the final product. We thank Marquand Books for the elegant design of the book and Suzanne Kotz for her careful editing.

Dutch art has had great popularity in America since the middle years of the 19th century. The flowering of American landscape and genre painting was significantly influenced by earlier Dutch art. Following the American Civil War when the country's economy rapidly expanded there developed great similarities between the cultures of America in the 19th century and the Netherlands in the 17th. Societal freedoms thrived in an expanding merchant middle class. A cultural self-confidence encouraged artists to capture everyday life in finely delineated genre paintings, to celebrate their native landscape, and to memorialize important individuals through sensitive portraiture, often at a large scale. Interestingly, in both countries the emerging merchant class developed a hunger for collecting art. Painters created pictures for these new markets at a smaller scale to reside in homes rather than churches and other public buildings.

Each of our American institutions houses a number of beautiful works by Dutch masters, many by artists represented in this exhibition. In presenting *Rembrandt and the Golden Age of Dutch Art,* it is our desire to enrich the lives of visitors to the exhibition and to reveal to them one of the world's great treasure houses of art, the Rijksmuseum, Amsterdam.

Alexander Lee Nyerges
*Director, Dayton Art Institute*

James K. Ballinger
*The Sybil Harrington Director, Phoenix Art Museum*

Judith L. Poe
*Interim Director, Portland Art Museum*

Ronald de Leeuw
*Director General, Rijksmuseum, Amsterdam*

# AN AMERICAN AFFINITY

PENELOPE HUNTER-STIEBEL

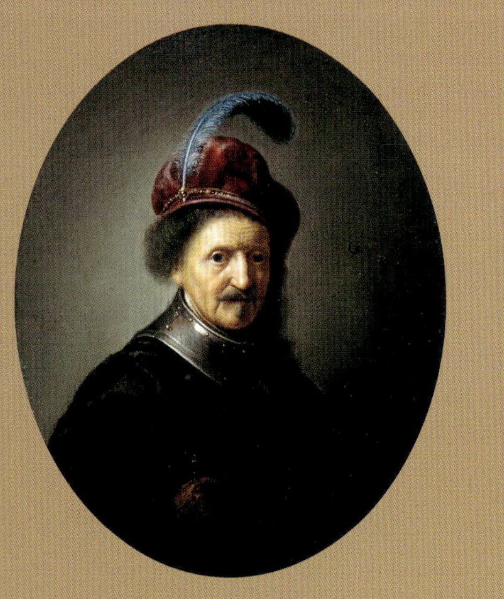

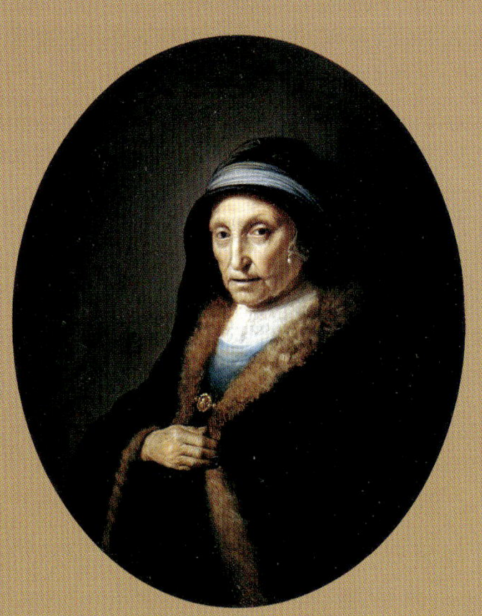

IN THE JOURNEY WE START BY TURNING THE PAGES of this book, re-creating the experience of the exhibition it documents, we discover a long-standing affinity between America and the Netherlands. A Dutch scholar, Ruud Priem, conceived this journey at the behest of the Rijksmuseum in Amsterdam. Its purpose is to lead the American visitor through the Golden Age of Dutch art with examples from the famed Rijksmuseum collection. We begin face-to-face with the artists themselves, in revealing self-portraits and likenesses made by colleagues. Entering the artists' studios, we see how they created works of extraordinary beauty by arranging and painting everyday objects. We even view a selection of period objects like those depicted in the paintings. From the studio, we emerge into the bustling streets of the cities the artists inhabited and the countryside they traversed and recorded. Through their interpretations, we discover the uniquely open religious life of the Netherlands, and we meet the newly moneyed burghers of the Republic's upper class, outfitted in the regalia of their fancy-dress portraits. Finally we are invited to relish the fabric of daily life in artfully orchestrated scenes so realistically detailed that we feel we can touch, smell, and hear as well as see the world of the 17th-century Dutch.

The more we look, the more the gap of centuries diminishes between the artists and ourselves. The 17th-century Dutchman's world seems not so different from our own. His society is more affluent than any of his contemporary neighbors. Religion takes a backseat to commerce in his concerns. Financial success and civic service, not noble birth, define his aristocracy. He dotes on the intimacy of home life and touts its virtues above the glamour of courts and celebrity. He harbors a Protestant fear of overindulgence that the historian Simon Schama has so aptly dubbed "the embarrassment of riches."

Paintings in particular filled the same niche in the Dutch social structure as they do in America today. The Dutch broke with the tradition of commissioned images that fulfilled dictates from leaders of church and state. In the Netherlands of the 17th century, private collectors bought pictures produced for sale on the open market and displayed them in their homes for personal enjoyment and to demonstrate their social status. Much like today's art market, a few artists commanded big prices and had a waiting list of collectors, while the rest struggled to make ends meet and often supported themselves with other occupations.

## A HISTORY OF ATTRACTION

Today 17th-century Dutch paintings generate more enthusiasm among private collectors and museum visitors than any other European Old Masters. No name in the history of art has more resonance with the American public than that of Rembrandt, and none sparks the imagination like that of Vermeer. The runaway success of Tracy Chevalier's novel and subsequent film *The Girl with the Pearl Earring* are just the latest expressions of this popular interest.

FIG 1 Monogrammist GAR (n.d.), *Portraits of an Old Man and an Old Woman (Called Rembrandt's Father and Mother)*, 1630–1635, oil on panel, each 8¾ × 6¾ inches. Portland Art Museum, museum purchase, funds provided by the bequest of Dr. Francis J. Newton, 2005.65.1–2.

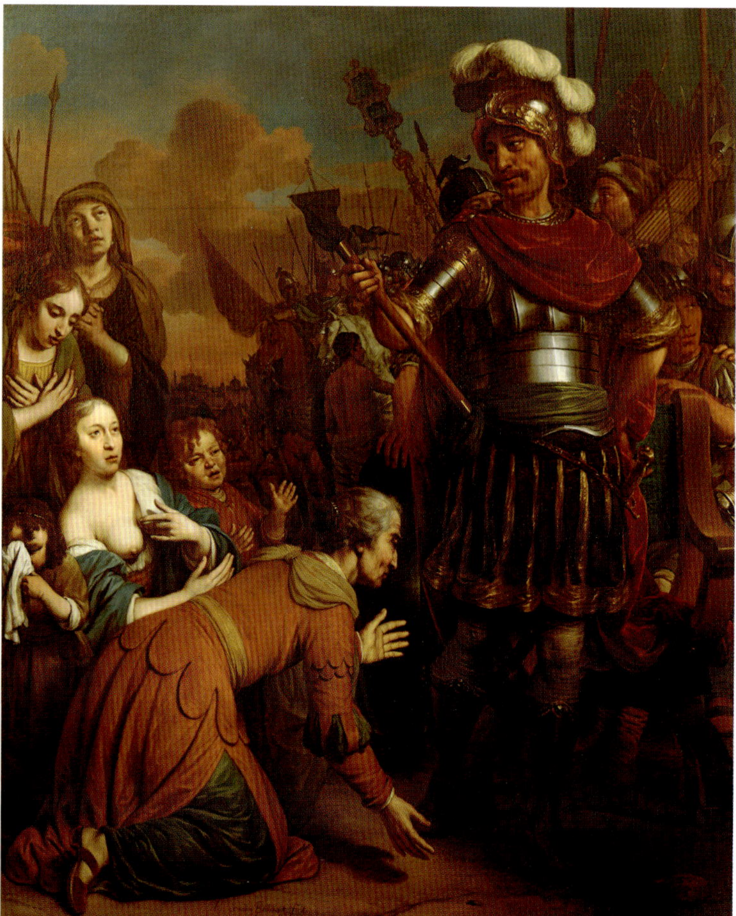

FIG 2 Gerbrand van den Eeckhout (1621–1674), *Volumnia before Coriolanus,* 1674, oil on canvas, 81½ × 67 inches. Portland Art Museum, museum purchase, 2005.19.

The exhibition *Great Dutch Paintings from America,* organized by the Royal Picture Gallery Mauritshuis in 1990 and presented in The Hague and San Francisco, revealed the astonishing wealth of American collections in this field. In the exhibition catalogue, scholars traced the American appetite for Dutch pictures to the United States' own Gilded Age, from the 1870s to the advent of income tax in 1916. The country's first generation of captains of industry eagerly imported European culture through the purchase of art. Above all they aspired to own a painting by Rembrandt, but they also admired other Dutch masters who celebrated ethical virtues in their depictions of everyday life and realistic landscapes. The pleasures of private ownership eventually gave way to the moral belief that exposure to art would elevate the broad public. In a pattern of benefaction, American collectors gave or bequeathed works of art originally purchased for their homes to museums built in their communities. The trend established by American millionaires before World War I was renewed in the era of prosperity and civic pride following World War II. Public enthusiasm for Dutch painting had already been made abundantly clear in the 1909 exhibition of 150 Dutch paintings, all drawn from American collections, presented at the Metropolitan Museum of Art. In just two months the show attracted 288,103 visitors, making it the first museum blockbuster of the 20th century.

## DUTCH MASTERS IN PORTLAND, PHOENIX, AND DAYTON

Like so many institutions in the United States, the museums of Portland, Phoenix, and Dayton that welcome the treasures of the Rijksmuseum in *Rembrandt and the Golden Age* have a history of interest and involvement in the field of 17th-century Dutch art.

The Portland Art Museum, founded in 1892, is the oldest art museum in the Pacific Northwest. In 1927 the museum acquired a still life by the Dutch painter Willem Kalf, purchased from the estate of a founder's widow. When board members feared incendiary bombings during World War II, the Kalf was selected as one of three treasured works from the collection (along with a Renoir and a Delacroix) to be sent in 1942 for safekeeping to the Rockhill Nelson Gallery in Kansas City for the duration of the war. Over the years, the museum added a range of prints by Dutch masters as it built its expansive graphic arts collection.

Portland inaugurated a new focus on Dutch painting in 2004 with *The Mauritshuis Project.* Loaning a selection of paintings representing the specializations of Dutch artists of the 17th century, the Royal Picture Gallery in The Hague collaborated with the Portland Art Museum in crafting an introduction to the values and qualities of the Golden Age of Dutch painting. *The Mauritshuis Project* was the starting point of an overall program, leading up to the present exhibition, through which the museum would strengthen its holdings in this area. In 2005 the museum made two purchases. The first was the history subject *Volumnia before Coriolanus* of 1674 by Rembrandt's student and lifelong friend Gerbrand van den Eeckhout (fig. 2). In this monumental work the artist dressed contemporary Dutch men and women in the garb of classical antiquity in a parable of civic virtue. Subsequently the museum purchased a pair of painted character studies (*tronies*) whose models are traditionally identified as Rembrandt's mother and father (fig. 1). Although signed with a cryptic monogram that has been read as "GAR," the author has not been identified. The studies can be dated between 1630 and 1635, when a group of artists in Leiden in the circle of the young Rembrandt and his first pupil, Gerard Dou, repeatedly portrayed these same elderly models with the loving attention to detail that would become known as the fine painter, or *fijnschilder,* style.

The Phoenix Art Museum is the largest museum of its kind in the Southwest. Its expansion has reflected the rapid postwar development of the population and economy of this burgeoning metropolis

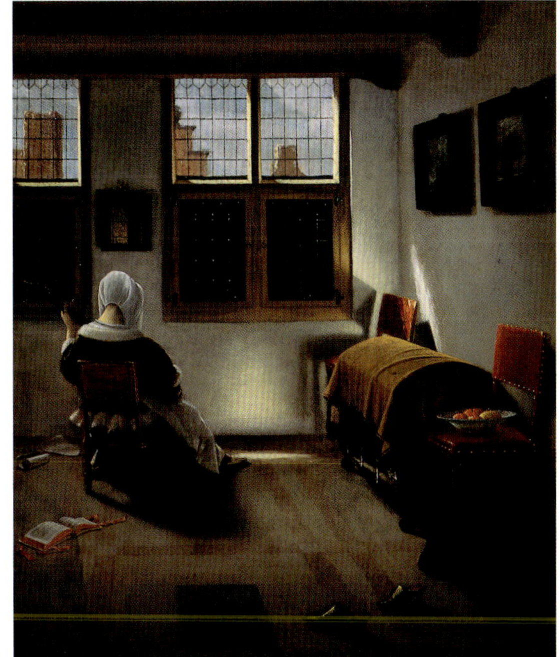

FIG 3 Pieter Janssens Elinga (1623–c. 1683), *Interior with Girl Playing Guitar,* 1655–1665, oil on canvas, 28⅞ × 24¾ inches. Phoenix Art Museum, gift of Mr. and Mrs. Donald D. Harrington, 1964.235.

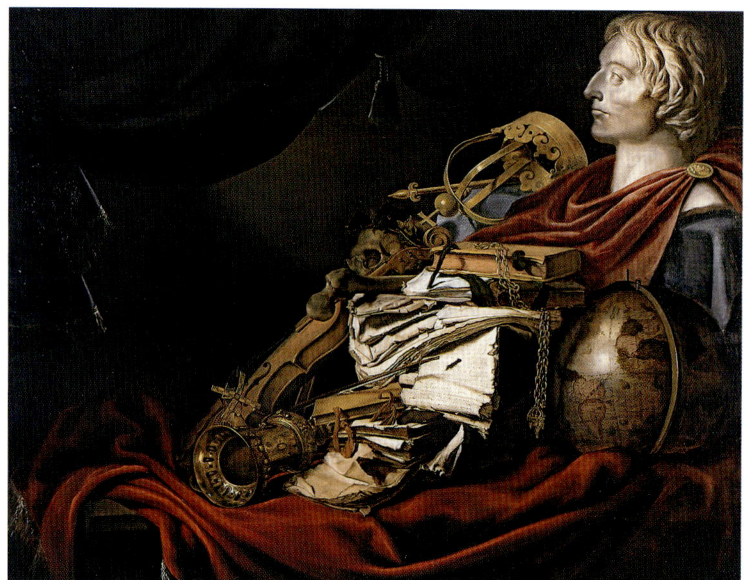

FIG 4 Jan van Dalen (c. 1611–1677), *Still Life: Vanitas,* c. 1665, oil on oak panel, 42⅜ × 54 inches. Phoenix Art Museum, museum purchase with funds provided by Friends of European Art, 2004.33.

in the Arizona desert. A concerted effort to build a collection for the art museum occupied community leaders even before the 1959 opening of the building. In 1957 the estate of Phoenix department store owner E. W. Edwards donated the first Old Master painting to enter the museum's collection, Salomon Koninck's *The Old Philosopher.* In this fine representation of the Leiden school, dating from the late 1640s, an elderly sage diligently sharpens his quill before a pile of manuscripts, dramatically illuminated by a ray of light penetrating the surrounding darkness.

Among forty-six paintings donated in 1964 as a lifetime-retention gift by Donald and Sybil Harrington are Balthasar van der Ast's *Still-Life with Seashells and Insects* (1630s) and *Interior with Girl Playing a Guitar* (c. 1660) by Pieter Janssens Elinga. In this haunting genre scene (fig. 3), which is the pendant to a work in Munich's Alte Pinakothek, Janssens elicits a moment of intense quietude in a sunlit room. A woman, seen from the rear, has thrown off her shoes and the concerns of reading scripture to find solace and freedom in her music. More than one hundred Dutch Golden Age prints and drawings now supplement the museum's growing collection of paintings.

The Phoenix Art Museum in 1998 organized *Copper as Canvas: Two Centuries of Masterpiece Paintings on Copper, 1575–1775,* which traveled to Kansas City and The Hague. The exhibition and its catalogue, the first investigation of painting on copper, advanced scholarship on a medium historically linked to painters in the Netherlands. Similar ingenuity and initiative can be found in the recent acquisition of an exceptionally large still life by Jan van Dalen (fig. 4), a little-known master from Gorkum, near Dordrecht, active in the 1660s. The museum's purchase of this powerful work, rife with *vanitas* symbols ranging from a classical bust to a globe and toppled crown, exemplifies the important buying opportunities still available to ambitious regional institutions.

The Dayton Art Institute was founded as a museum in 1919 but renamed in 1930 to reflect the importance of its art school. It turned serious attention toward the building of its Old Master collection under the directorship, from 1957 to 1975, of Thomas E. Colt Jr. The moment was opportune on the art market, and civic-minded donors were generous. As a result, Dayton's collection today boasts a rich representation of European Baroque art, including major paintings from the Netherlands as well as examples of Dutch graphic arts.

Trustee Elton F. McDonald and his wife, Ruth F. MacDonald, donated numerous masterpieces to the art institute, among them works by Rembrandt's student Ferdinand Bol and the Caravaggist Hendrick ter Brugghen. The acquisition of the latter's *Boy Violinist* spurred the

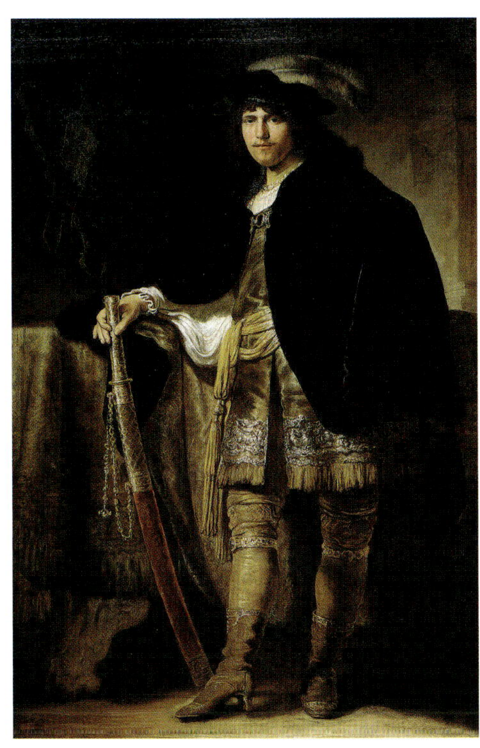

FIG 5 Ferdinand Bol (1616–1680), *Portrait of a Young Man with a Sword,* c. 1635–1640, oil on canvas, 81 × 51½ inches. Dayton Art Institute, gift of Mr. and Mrs. Elton F. MacDonald, 1962.18.

institute to organize the 1965 exhibition *Hendrick ter Brugghen in America,* which traveled to the Baltimore Museum of Art.

In the portrait by Bol, a young man stands larger than life, leaning on a long sword (fig. 5). Given by the McDonalds in 1962, the painting ranks as the most impressive of several exotic figures in similar costume and pose executed by members of Rembrandt's studio and the master himself. Scholars have long debated whether this remarkably ambitious work is a self-portrait, and current thought holds it to be a fantasy of a Turkish prince based on a model, who might be the artist himself.

Since 1957 the Art Ball has actively engaged the Dayton community in enhancing the institute's collections. Attendees vote on works for acquisition, preselected by the curators, which the ball's proceeds will fund. In 1980 the winner was Gerard van Honthorst's *Flea Hunt* (fig. 6), a work in which the artist used the Caravaggist device of blocking the light of a candle, in this case by the figure of an old crone, who illuminates the assets of a comely young woman for two brothel patrons on the pretext of hunting fleas in her bedding. In 2000 Art Ball patrons selected a Dutch Italianate landscape by Bartholomeus Breenburgh.

Convinced of the deep roots of cultural affinity, the directors of museums in the wide geographic swath from Ohio to Arizona to Oregon took up the opportunity to bring to their audiences the treasures of the Dutch Golden Age from the Rijksmuseum's incomparable holdings. What follows belongs to the history of America's long love affair with Dutch 17th-century art. If you have read this far, you are already part of it.

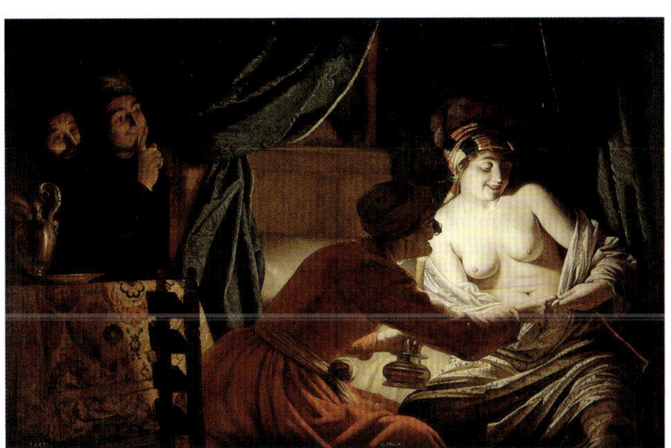

FIG 6 Gerard van Honthorst (1590–1656), *The Flea Hunt,* 1628, oil on canvas, 52¼ × 78½ inches. Dayton Art Institute, museum purchase with funds provided by the 1980 Associate Board Art Ball, 1980.2.

# REMBRANDT

## AND THE GOLDEN AGE OF DUTCH ART

RUUD PRIEM

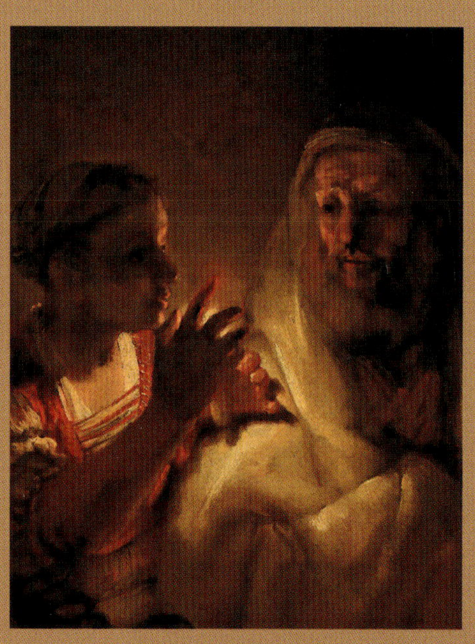

THE 17TH CENTURY IS OFTEN REFERRED TO as the Golden Age of Dutch painting—the era of Rembrandt van Rijn, Frans Hals, and Johannes Vermeer. These great artists are household names, but behind them an extraordinary number of artists produced paintings of exceptional quality in such diverse areas as portraiture, landscape, seascape, genre, still life, flower pieces, and architectural interiors. This varied and energetic artistic tradition flourished under the particular political, economic, and religious conditions that defined the unique phenomenon of the Netherlands in the 17th century.

The Netherlands freed itself from Spanish domination in 1588 after a long period of religious friction. Philip II (1527–1598), king of Spain and head of its empire, was a strong Catholic, and he resisted the growth of Protestantism in the northern part of the Netherlands. Religious tensions led to a revolt against Spanish rule and marked the beginning of the Eighty Years' War in 1568, which resulted in the separation of the northern and southern provinces. The south chose to stay with the Catholic monarchy, while the north formed an independent republic in 1588. Representatives of the seven northern provinces—Friesland, Gelderland, Groningen, Holland, Overijssel, Utrecht, and Zeeland—formed the new government. Rather than adopt the aristocratic power structure typical of the rest of Europe, these merchants, traders, and civic officials governed the Republic of the United Netherlands according to relatively modern democratic principles. Military authority was vested in a stadholder (deputy), and for most of the century, princes from the royal House of Orange took this role. The year 1648 saw the end of the Eighty Years' War and the formal recognition of the Republic as an independent state.

The Dutch economy flourished in the 17th century. The center of commerce had shifted north from Antwerp to Amsterdam, and trade with the West and East Indies brought spices, gold, ivory, silk, porcelain, and sugar to the lively port city. The hugely successful United East India Company, established in 1602 and with markets in Asia, Africa, the Caribbean, and America, employed a significant proportion of the population. Closer to home, the Dutch relied on industries such as fishing, the processing and export of herring, and the production of fine textiles and ceramics. In contrast to the predominantly rural social structure of the rest of Europe, the importance of trade and industry in the Netherlands gave rise to a modern, mostly urban society.

The wealth of 17th-century Dutch paintings that have come down to us were mostly made for sale on the free market, not commissioned by the nobility or for the church, the traditional patrons for art. This was the first time that the middle classes bought art on a large scale. Dutch merchants, burghers, traders, and government officials developed a seemingly insatiable demand for paintings and decorative arts to fill their homes, where adornments served as status symbols. An English visitor to Amsterdam observed in 1640: "As for the art of Painting and the affection of the people to pictures, none other go beyond them. . . . all in general striv[e] to adorn their houses, especially the outer or street room, with costly pieces. . . . Such is the general notion, inclination, and delight that this country's natives have for paintings."

While Dutch society was generating an environment conducive to a thriving arts industry, Dutch painters of the 17th century were representing that society with an accuracy rarely equaled in any other period. The people, interiors, and country and city sights are recorded so completely that the paintings provide us with a window to a world just as it existed almost four hundred years ago.

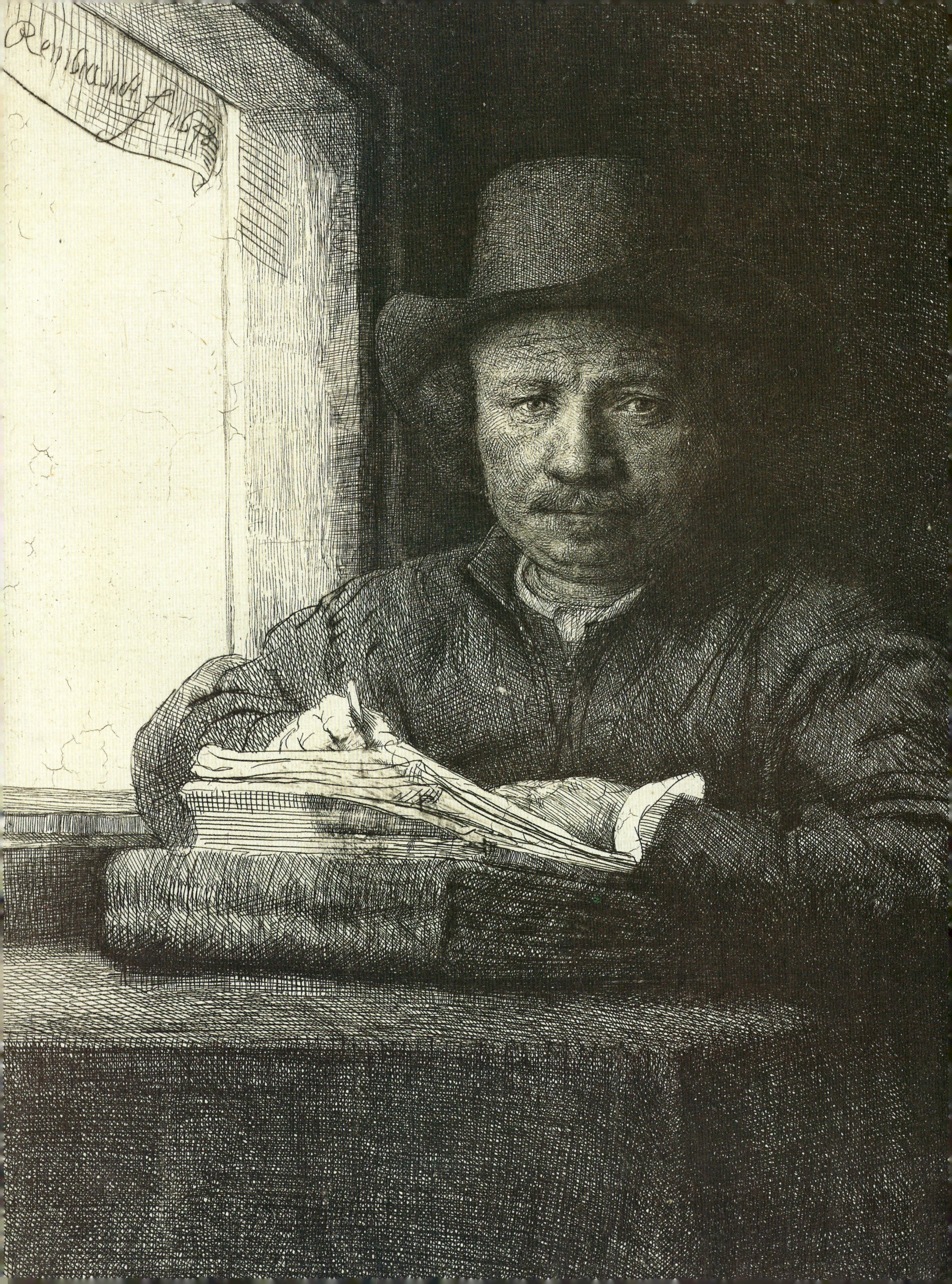

# I

## THE ARTISTS AND THEIR WORLD

THE SHEER NUMBER OF HIGHLY ACCOMPLISHED PAINTERS made the artistic environment of the Netherlands in the 17th century extraordinary, if not unique. Foreign visitors were quick to note this exceptional situation. The Italian Ludovico Guicciardini remarked in his *Descrittione di Tutti Paesi Bassi* (1567) that Antwerp had more painters working in a greater variety of specialties than several other European countries combined. Throughout the 17th century, travelers to Holland exclaimed at the amazing number of painters residing in its cities and the enormous quantity of paintings with which the Dutch burghers surrounded themselves. For example, the Englishman William Aglionby noted in *Painting Illustrated in Three Dialogues* (1686) that "the Dutch in the midst of their Boggs and ill air, have their houses full of pictures, from the highest to the lowest." By analyzing archival material, the economic historian John Michael Montias has shown that paintings were the most common art objects in the Dutch Republic between 1597 and 1638, and from 1620 on, a large and growing market for drawings and prints established itself. Those who bought art at the beginning of the 17th century appear to have been relatively young (on average, thirty-five years of age) and usually belonged to the merchant class.

Seventeenth-century publications originating in the Republic, such as descriptions of particular cities, contain numerous references to the significant contributions of painters to a town's fame and to the proud self-image that radiated from their work. In turn, members of the urban elite had a deeply rooted sense of pride in the artists of their cities. Today, some four hundred years later, a great many artists active in the Republic are known to us by name, their works are found in museums and private collections worldwide, and they fetch high prices when sold by art dealers or at auction. This is proof enough that the esteem of their contemporaries was not misplaced. Besides the handful of painters of world-class stature, there were dozens, perhaps even hundreds, of skilled artists who left behind large quantities of excellent paintings. It is not just the peaks but the high average quality of the works—especially between 1610 and 1675—that makes the phenomenon of Dutch painting unique.

Due to the considerable demand for paintings, almost every town—whether large or small—had an active group of painters. Patrons in cities like Amsterdam, Leiden, Delft, Haarlem, Middelburg, Deventer, and Zwolle commissioned work from leading local artists. The artists gained a competitive edge by perfecting their skill and specializing in a particular type of painting. This concentration on a single specialty became so pronounced that painters often chose fellow artists to complete certain features of their work. For example, Adriaen van de Velde (1636–1672) of Haarlem enjoyed a great reputation as a painter of figures in landscapes. Various colleagues, including Jan van der Heyden (1637–1712), a master of townscapes, and Jan Wijnants (c. 1630/35–1684), a landscape painter and probably Van de Velde's master, asked him to do their *staffage,* the term for the human and animal figures that animated their compositions. Adriaen's better-known brother, Willem van de Velde the Younger (1633–1707), specialized in marine pictures. Even before completing his schooling with the Amsterdam portraitist Bartholomeus van der Helst (1613–1670), Willem was filling in the backgrounds of his master's paintings when a port scene or seascape was required.

Painters were organized in guilds, which were broad-based professional organizations: artists, artisans, and house painters all belonged to the same guild. Members were more or less assured of a safety net in hard times and some degree of protection against competition from colleagues outside their own city. The first guilds for painters date from the 13th century and were named after Saint Luke, their patron saint. Without membership in a guild, an artisan was not permitted to practice his profession, and guild members were bound by standards of quality and price. But the guild also provided certain social services, such as taking care of impoverished members and their families. The system was based on apprenticeship; an aspiring painter trained in the studio of a master until he reached the level of accomplishment necessary to apply for membership in the guild and become a master himself.

Work painted for the open market found its way to a buyer by various ways. Artists often sold their paintings directly to customers who visited their studios, but they could also offer them at exhibitions or sales organized by the guild. In addition, works were raffled or sold at auctions. In some cases, paintings served to pay off debts to innkeepers and dealers. Artists made use of various structures within the art market, from street vendors to established art dealers. Art historical sources have bestowed considerable attention on the Amsterdam art dealership of Hendrick van Uylenburgh (1604–1669), an important patron and business partner of Rembrandt, and the uncle of the artist's first wife, Saskia. Painters regularly entered the art market themselves, as a kind of sideline. One example is thought to be the Haarlem couple Jan Miense Molenaer (c. 1610–1668) and Judith Leyster (1609–1660), who were both artists. They were so successful at selling their paintings that they were able to purchase several buildings in various Dutch cities, and even a country home.

In a few cases the artist could rely on a wealthy patron. For example, the estate inventory of the Delft collector Pieter Claesz van Ruijven (1624–1674) suggests that he owned no fewer than twenty paintings by his illustrious fellow townsman Johannes Vermeer (1632–1675). This is an incredibly large quantity, especially considering that today only about thirty paintings are known to be the work of Vermeer, and his entire output was probably not much larger. Vermeer's Delft colleague Pieter de Hooch (1629–1684) had a patron in the person of the prosperous local linen merchant Justus de la Grange (1623–1664). The latter is believed to have supported the painter in return for a number of paintings: in 1655 De la Grange's collection included eleven paintings by De Hooch. Several other painters, such as Nicolaes Berchem, are known to have had similar arrangements with private patrons. Distinct from commissions, this form of patronage was much like the circumstance today when a collector wants to acquire an artist's work in depth and buys up new paintings as they are completed.

Strict regulations laid down by the guild prevented artists from accepting official commissions from outside their city of residence. The portraits that Haarlem painter Frans Hals made of the Amsterdam brewer Nicolaes Hasselaer (no. 63, p. 104) and his second wife, Sara Wolphaerts, are an exception, testifying to the formidable reputation Hals enjoyed in his lifetime. The same goes for the most versatile and renowned 17th-century Dutch painter, Rembrandt van Rijn (1606–1669). In a few cases, he even received commissions from foreign collectors. Three half-portraits of famous figures from Greek antiquity, commissioned by the Sicilian nobleman Antonio Ruffo (1610–1678) between 1653 and 1663, are a case in point. Rembrandt's talents were not confined to a single specialty. He did a great many portraits, several magnificent landscapes, and one or two still lifes. But he took a great interest in history painting. This type of picture, which included subjects from mythology and the Bible as well as history, was considered the most important form of painting at the time. No doubt the challenge appealed to Rembrandt.

*Self-Portrait as the Apostle Paul* of 1661 (no. 1, p. 22) shows Rembrandt at the age of fifty-five. The familiarity of his face has to do with the eighty-odd self-portraits he made spanning his entire career. Rembrandt appears to have used his self-portraits to practice depictions of the human face and its emotions, and he is seen in many different moods and guises. Here he is dressed as the Apostle Paul. Light catches the hilt of a sword (symbol of Saint Paul) tucked into the front of his robe. The papers he holds make reference to the letters Paul wrote to the Christian community of Ephesians in his native Turkey (hence the turban). As he did in this work, Rembrandt often experimented with the dramatic effects of light and shadow on the face. He presents himself in a dark room, his head brightly lit by a strong beam of light from the upper left. Fully exploring the technical possibilities, he molded the folds in the turban, as it were, by smearing the thickly applied paint, from left to right, with a hard brush while it was still wet.

*Self-Portrait as the Apostle Paul* demonstrates Rembrandt's masterful evocation of thoughts and emotions to realize the essence of his subject, whether illustrating a story or portraying a person or everyday situation. Many of Rembrandt's first paintings, drawings, and etchings were studies of the human head, for which he himself was a convenient model. Portraiture, whether in paint or etching, remained a staple activity throughout Rembrandt's life, and some of his finest prints during the 1650s fall within this category. His engraved or etched portraits were much in demand, and Rembrandt received several commissions. In his painted portraits he tended to concentrate on the sitter, with a minimum of background detail, but in his etchings Rembrandt often depicted not only the sitters but their settings, so that we read something of their occupations as well as their characters. His *Self-Portrait, Etching at a Window* of 1648 (no. 2, p. 23) is a fine example. The artist has portrayed himself in his working clothes, wearing a plain hat.

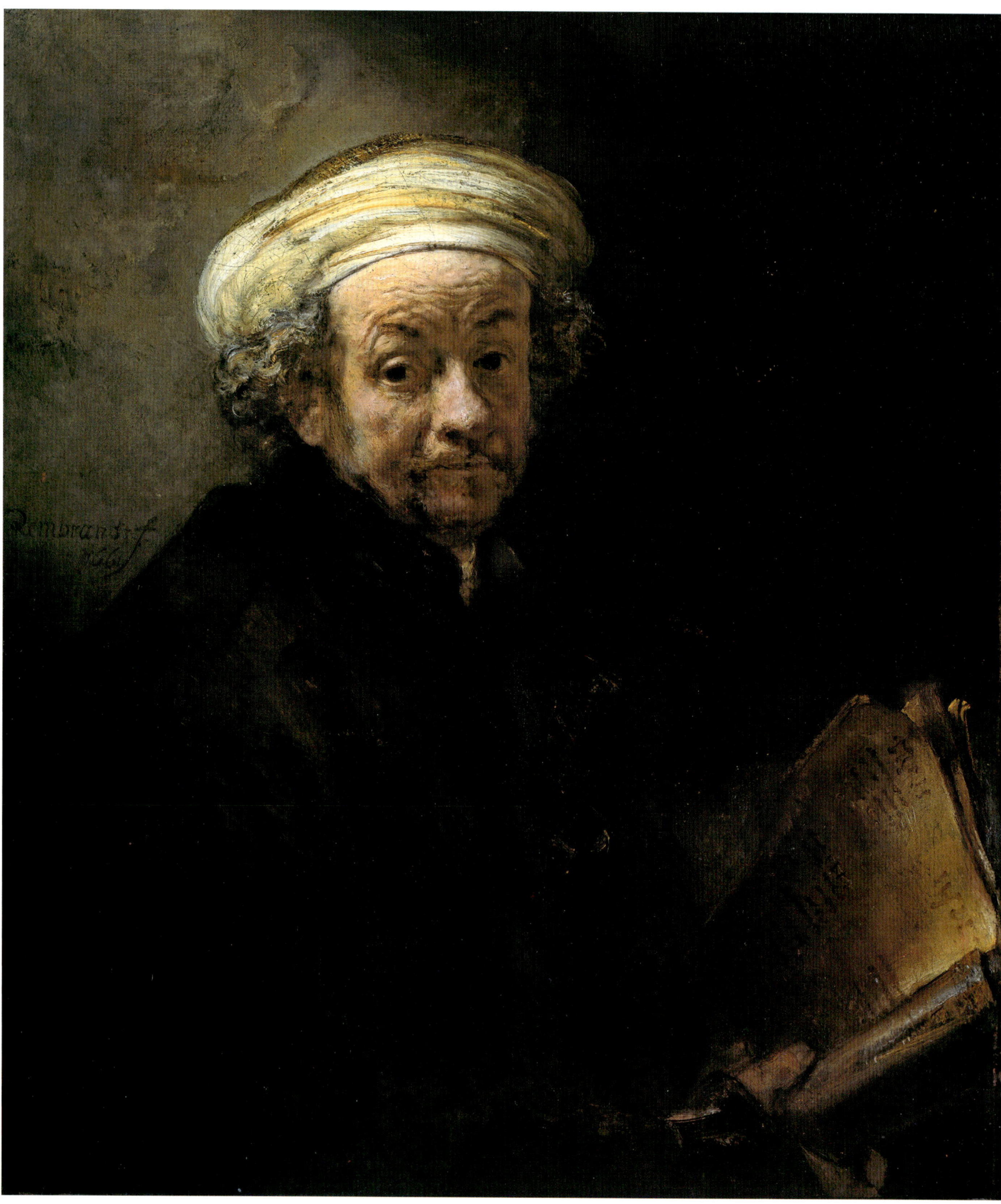

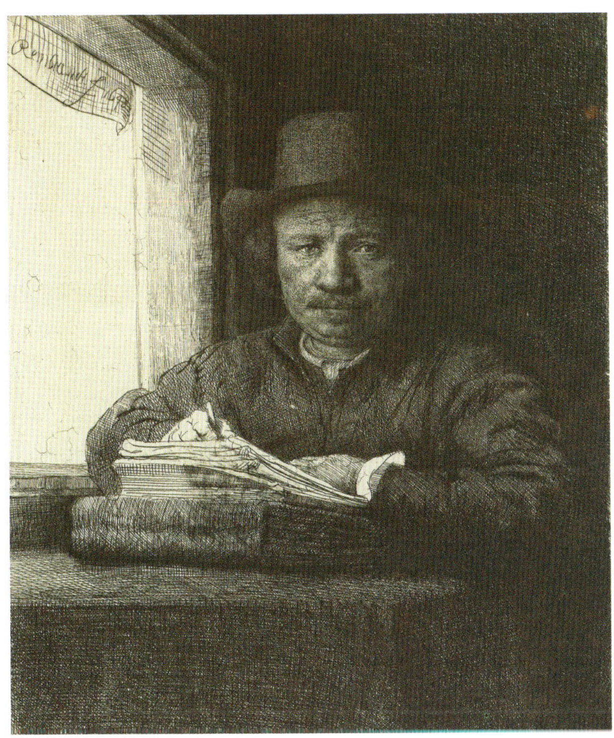

The etching tool has replaced the sword as a symbol of the sitter: the focus in this work is on Rembrandt as an artist.

Rembrandt established quite a reputation for himself during his lifetime. His etchings were very popular throughout Europe, and more consistently admired and collected than his paintings. This had a profound impact on Rembrandt's artistic status. The prints, easily reproduced and disseminated, were much more effective in publicizing the name and work of the artist than his paintings or drawings ever could be.

In that respect, it would perhaps have helped the (later) reputation of the Leiden painter Jan Steen (1626–1679) if, like Rembrandt, he had tried his hand at etching or engraving. Still, Steen is well known for his ironic and humorous vision of the world. He was long assumed to have lived just as he regularly portrayed himself in various comical roles. Although he did earn a living as an innkeeper and brewer and undoubtedly enjoyed a drink himself, he was not the irresponsible joker later biographers often have made him out to be. In fact, he acquired a reputation as a major artist early in his career and produced no less than four hundred paintings. Steen

1 Rembrandt van Rijn (1606–1669) · *Self-Portrait as the Apostle Paul* (1661) ·
Oil on canvas · 35¾ × 30¼ inches

2 Rembrandt van Rijn (1606–1669) · *Self-Portrait, Etching at a Window* (1648) ·
Etching and drypoint · 6¼ × 5 inches

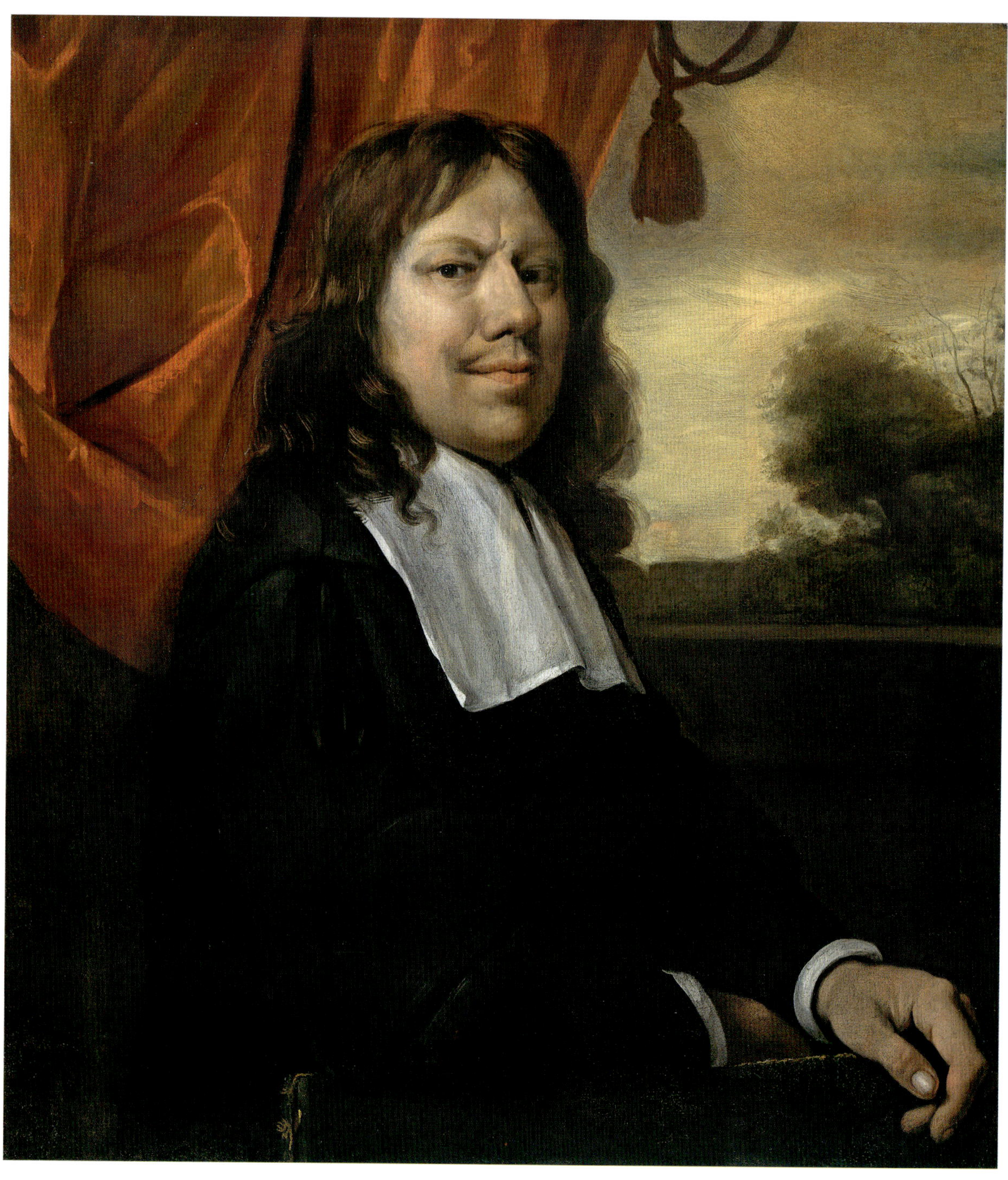

3 Jan Steen (1626–1679) · *Self-Portrait* (c. 1670) · Oil on canvas · 28¾ × 24½ inches

4 Adriaen van der Werff (1659–1722) · *Self-Portrait with the Portrait of His Wife Margaretha van Rees and Their Daughter Maria* (1699) · Oil on canvas · 31¾ × 25¾ inches

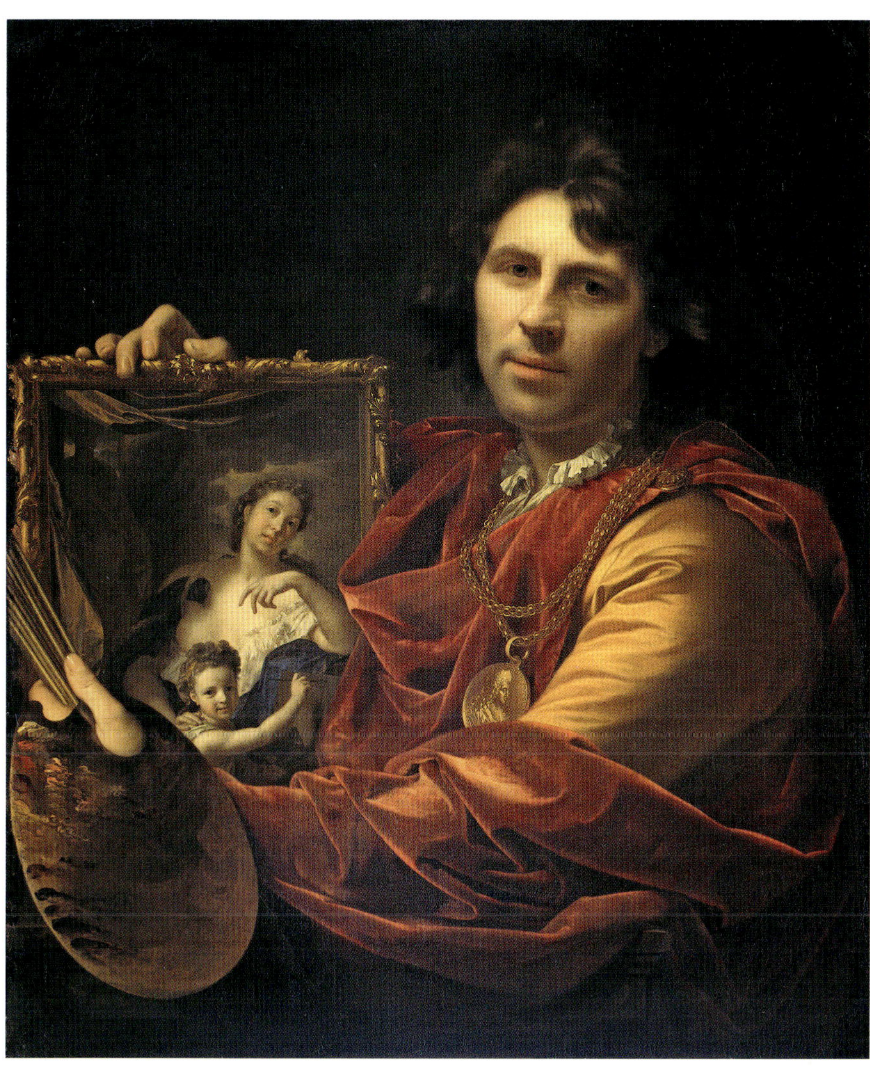

was a great storyteller and talented artist, witty, erudite, and well informed about artistic traditions. In his *Self-Portrait* of c. 1670 (no. 3) he depicted himself as a distinguished painter and a successful member of society. It stands out as one of just a handful of formal portraits he painted, and it is his only conventional self-portrait.

Adriaen van der Werff (1659–1722) from Rotterdam enjoyed a tremendous reputation among his contemporaries. Attributes of *Self-Portrait with the Portrait of His Wife Margaretha van Rees and Their Daughter Maria* of 1699 (no. 4) demonstrate his awareness of his standing. He became the most famous Dutch painter of his day, winning international success and earning an enormous fortune. The biographer Arnold Houbraken, writing in 1721, considered him the greatest of all Dutch painters, and this remained the general critical opinion for the next century. Johann Wilhelm (1658–1717), Elector Palatine of Pfalz, appointed Van der Werff court painter in 1697, two years before he painted the present work. Van der Werff received an annual salary of four thousand guilders with the understanding that he would spend six months of the year at the Elector Palatine's court in Dusseldorf. In recognition of his services he was given the gold chain

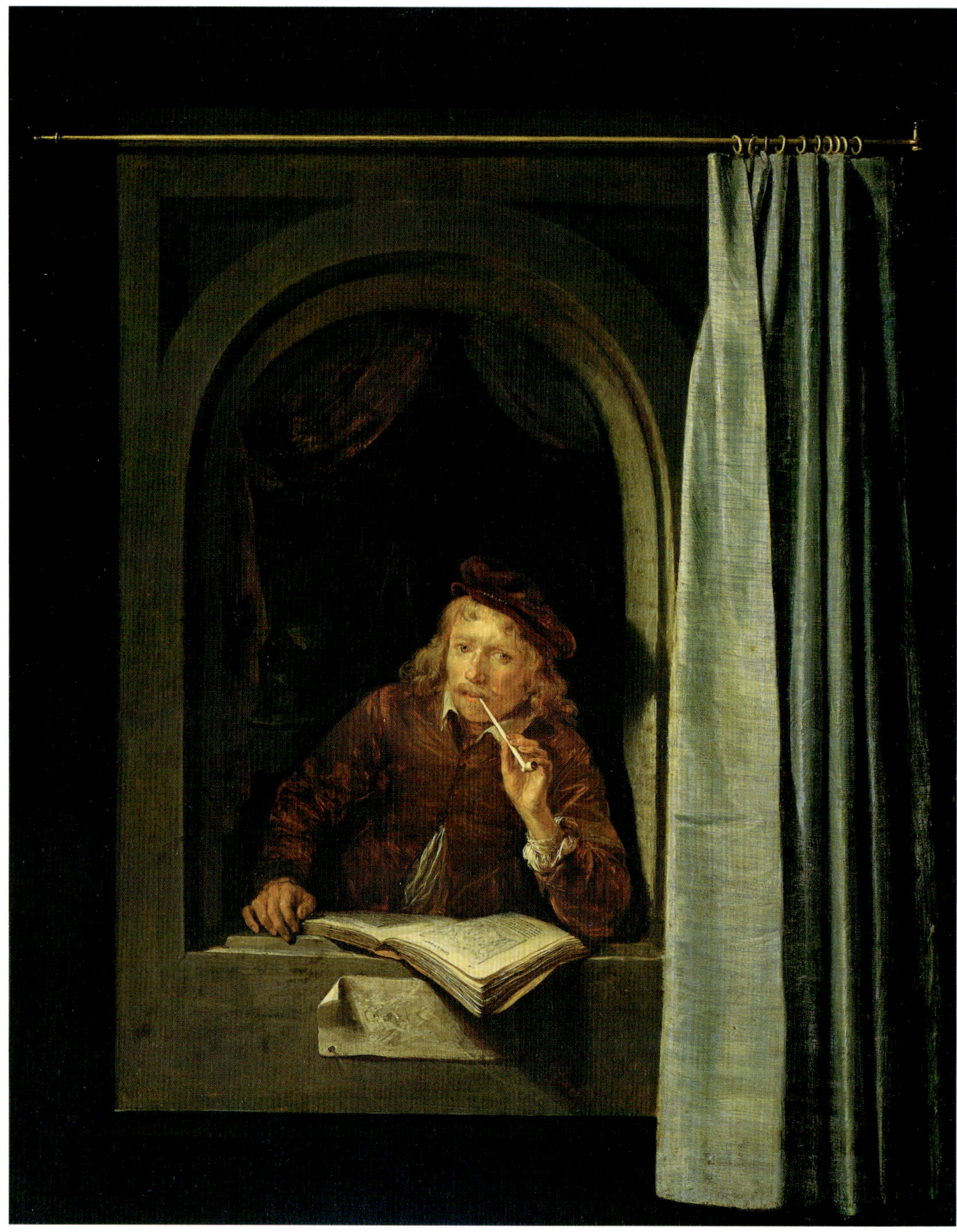

5 Gerard Dou (1613–1675) · *Man Smoking a Pipe* (formerly *Self-Portrait*) (c. 1650) · Oil on panel · 19 × 14½ inches

6 Michiel van Musscher (1645–1705) · *Michiel Comans (d. 1687), Calligrapher, Etcher, Painter, and Schoolmaster, with His Third Wife, Elisabeth van der Mersche* (1669) · Oil on canvas · 28 × 24¾ inches

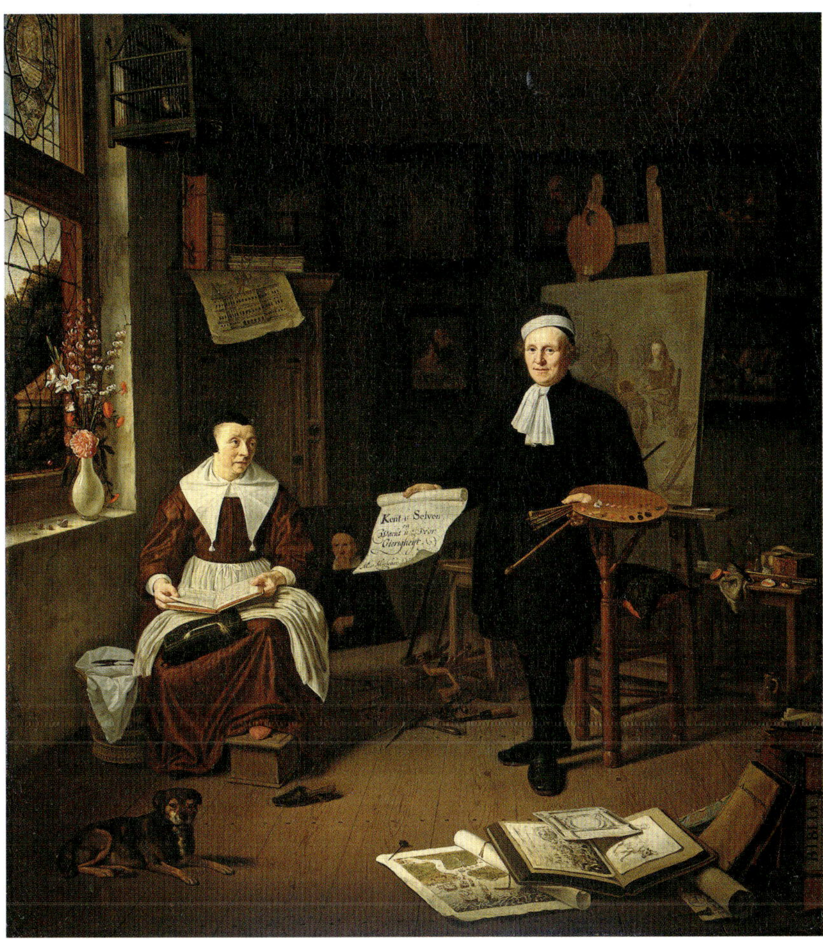

and medal, with his patron's effigy, that he proudly wears in the self-portrait. Besides the palette emblematic of his trade, the artist holds a delicate little painting in which his daughter Maria is portrayed as a young painter, working on a portrait of her mother, Margaretha van Rees. It is not known whether such a painting ever existed. Possibly, Van der Werff portrayed his allegedly talented seven-year-old as a personification of genius, practicing on a portrait of her mother, who in turn is seen as Pictura, the personification of painting.

*Man Smoking a Pipe* (formerly *Self-Portrait*) of c. 1650 (no. 5) is testimony to the unrivalled skill of its author, the Leiden painter Gerard Dou (1613–1675). Dou painted a green curtain, of the sort often used to protect paintings in the 17th century, so realistically that the viewer might be tricked into trying to draw it aside. The trickery goes on, for this is in fact a painting within a painting. Dou was a highly esteemed master with an international reputation. He joined Rembrandt's atelier in Leiden as the master's first pupil in 1628. While Rembrandt's style evolved when he moved to Amsterdam in 1631, Dou stayed in Leiden to perfect the precise, meticulous style characteristic of the so-called *fijnschilders* (fine painters). The biographer Houbraken described Dou as a slow and careful painter, who would not pick up his brush until the dust had settled in his studio. He would begin painting only when he was sure no particles could settle in the wet paint to spoil the illusion of realism.

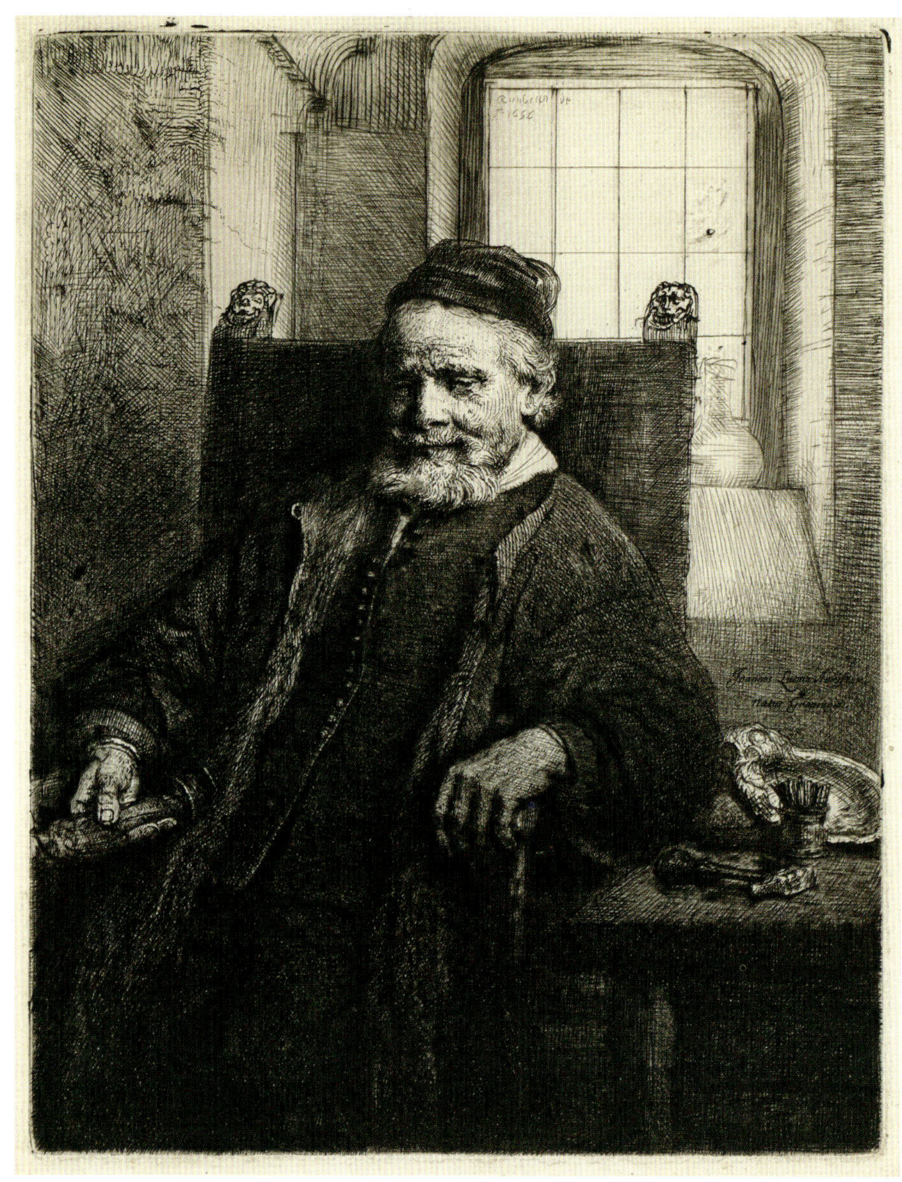

7 Rembrandt van Rijn (1606–1669) · *Johannes Lutma I (1584/85–1669), Amsterdam Silversmith* (1656) · Etching and drypoint · 7¾ × 6 inches

8 Johannes Lutma I (1584/85–1669) · *Salt Cellar* (1639) · Silver, partly gilded silver · 9½ × 5 inches

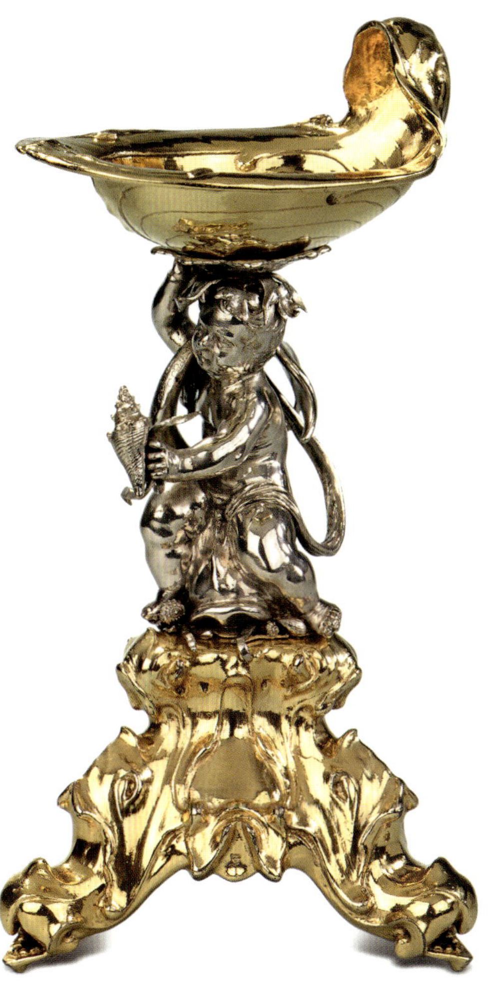

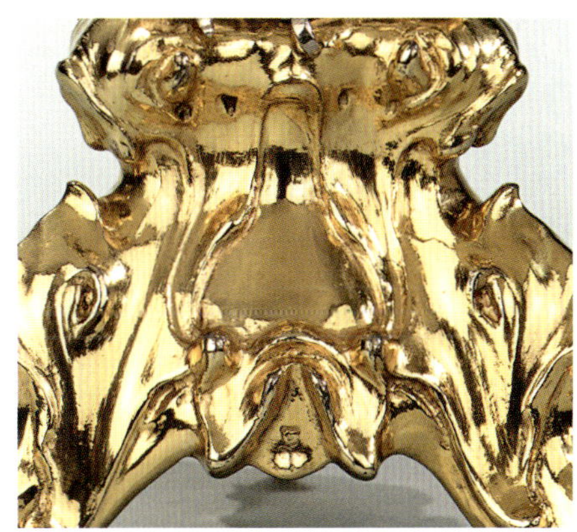

The painter and engraver Michiel van Musscher (1645–1705) was born in Rotterdam, but accord‸g to Houbraken, he received most of his artistic training in Amsterdam from 1660 onward from, among others, Gabriel Metsu. After 1668 Van Musscher settled in Amsterdam, where he made the portrait *Michiel Comans (d. 1687), Calligrapher, Etcher, Painter, and Schoolmaster, with His Third Wife, Elisabeth van der Merssche* (no. 6, p. 27). Dated 1669, it is probably the earliest painting by Van Musscher in a series of about ten depictions of artists in their studios. Although Comans chose to have himself shown as an artist, he never made his name as such. In fact, when notice was given of Comans's marriage to Elisabeth van der Merssche in 1668, his profession was recorded as a dyer. The marriage must have been the occasion for the commission of this double portrait, which was completed in the following year.

In an etching of 1656, Rembrandt portrayed his close friend Johannes Lutma (1584/85–1669), Amsterdam's foremost silversmith, in what appears to be the latter's atelier (no. 7). In his right hand Lutma is holding one of his works (probably a candlestick), and on the table beside him we see his silversmithing tools and a silver dish. The latter looks very much like a small dish Lutma chased from a single plate of silver in 1641, and now in the Rijksmuseum collection. Lutma obviously took great pride in his work. In the portrait he commissioned from Jacob Backer (thought to have been one of Rembrandt's students), he had the artist depict a salt cellar (no. 8), now also in the Rijksmuseum collection. In this remarkable example of the silversmith's mastery, organic forms flow into one another in what is termed the auricular style. The practical function of the salt cellar is subordinate to its form and decoration, which have merged completely. Lutma regarded such products of the silversmith's art as independent works of art, in effect, as sculptures. The gilt base is made up of three amorphous, fantastic creatures; the middle section is in the form of a boy sitting on a dolphin. His right hand supports the shell-shaped salt dish, while his other hand holds a shell. The dolphin and the shells refer to the source of the salt: the sea.

In contrast to Rembrandt's portrait of the aged Lutma with its token object, *Portrait of a Gold- and Silversmith* of around 1680 (no. 9) depicts a craftsman's workshop. An unidentified Dutch painter portrayed a young silversmith surrounded by a score of tools of his trade. In the window hangs a large pair of scissors, used to cut silver to the desired proportion. Strung on the wall in the background are plaster models, pairs of cutters, pincers, and other instruments. With a certain pride, the silversmith looks directly at the viewer, holding a richly ornamented bowl with his right hand. His left hand gestures toward the table and the chasing tools he used to make the object. With the hammer and iron punches of different sizes (in the box), he formed the metal, heated to be soft and pliant, into the required shapes to get a relief. With the smaller, more delicate punches, he inscribed a finer finish on the bowl.

In portraits painted by themselves and by their colleagues, Dutch artists of the 17th century have given us a window into their world, their self-image, and their status in society.

9 Northern Netherlandish School · *Portrait of a Gold- and Silversmith* (c. 1680) ·
Oil on panel · 18 × 15 inches

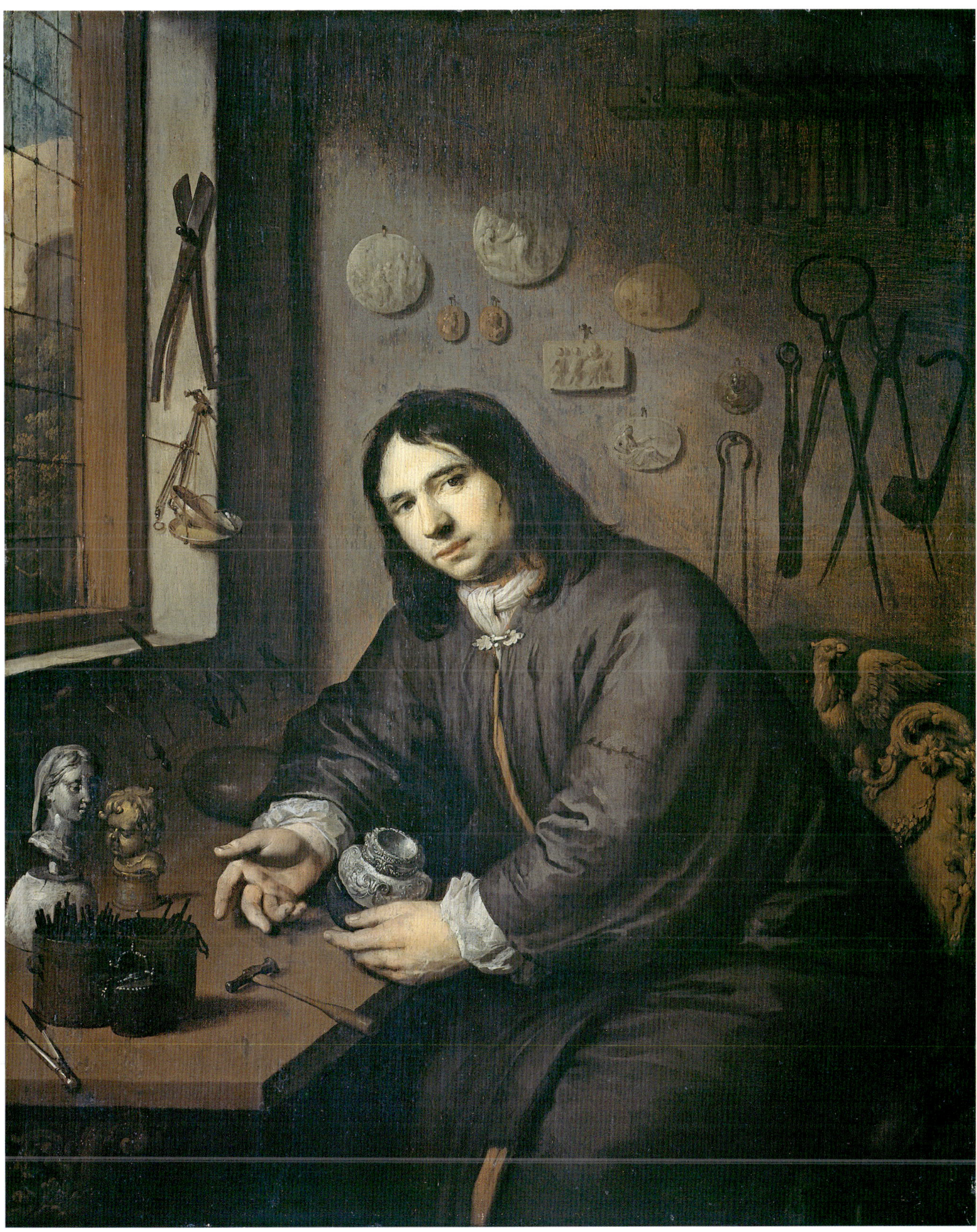

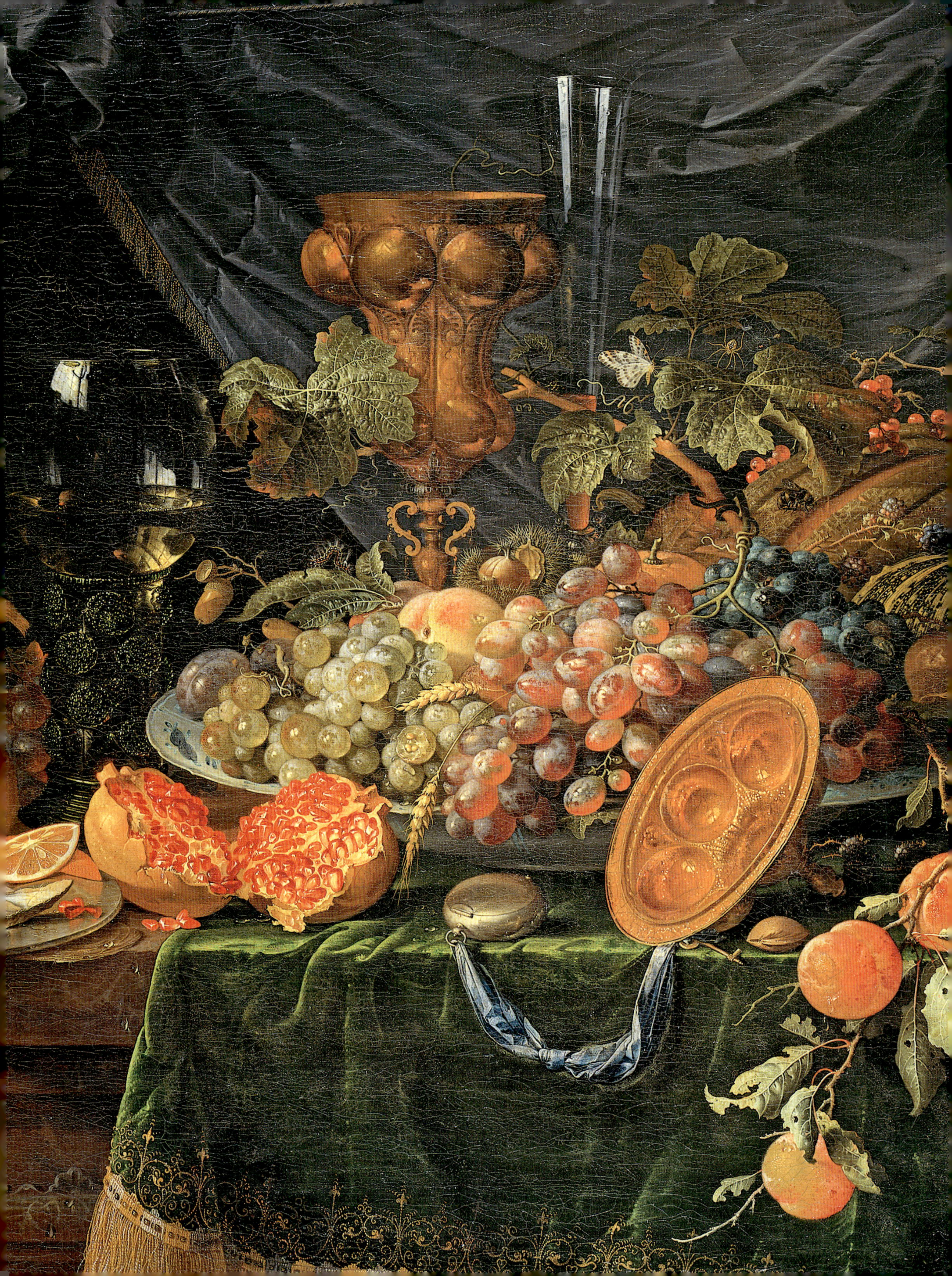

# 2

# STILL-LIFE PAINTING AND THE APPLIED ARTS

THE CONSIDERATION OF STILL-LIFE PAINTING takes us a step away from the artist as subject to the depiction of real objects in the studio. There, the painter carefully arranged objects for his compositions, sometimes also using drawn sketches to incorporate fruits and flowers that do not grow or blossom simultaneously. One of the most popular categories of Dutch 17th-century art, still life was broken down into further subcategories in which a painter would specialize; among them were flower pictures, *ontbijtjes* (breakfast pieces featuring bread, cheese, fruit, and occasionally fish), *toebackjes* (still lifes with smoking materials), *banketjes* (sumptuous banquet pieces), and *vanitas* (a skull or timepiece often combined with costly objects to symbolize the transitory nature of worldly goods).

The artist carefully combined the objects in these works to display his painting skill to maximum effect. The perfect rendering in still lifes of textures, ingenious compositions, and subtle light effects found many admirers, making them much in demand. The silver, glass, and textiles in the paintings shown here are ample proof that the applied arts were practiced on an equally high level.

The human skulls arranged in *Vanitas Still Life (Skulls on a Table)* of about 1660 (no. 10, p. 34) by the Utrecht artist Aelbert Jansz van der Schoor (c. 1603–c. 1672) may seem bizarre, but it is not difficult to deduce the idea behind this canvas: life is fleeting. The books and documents in the background seem to tell us that not even knowledge and science can alter that fact, while the wilting peonies, sputtering candle, and hourglass underscore the message of the skulls and bones. This painting, widely regarded as Van der Schoor's masterpiece, is a fine example of the so-called *vanitas* still life. It is as powerful as it is original, for this ode to the transience of things is also an anatomical study. Looking closely, we see that the painter has portrayed a skull from six different angles, a unique example in Dutch 17th-century painting.

*Still Life with Fish* of 1647 (no. 11, p. 35) by Pieter Claesz (1597/98–1660) shows all the typical 17th-century ingredients of a Dutch breakfast piece. On the left is a large green *roemer*, or drinking glass (see p. 45). Next to it is a pewter cellar, mounded with white salt. It perilously supports a

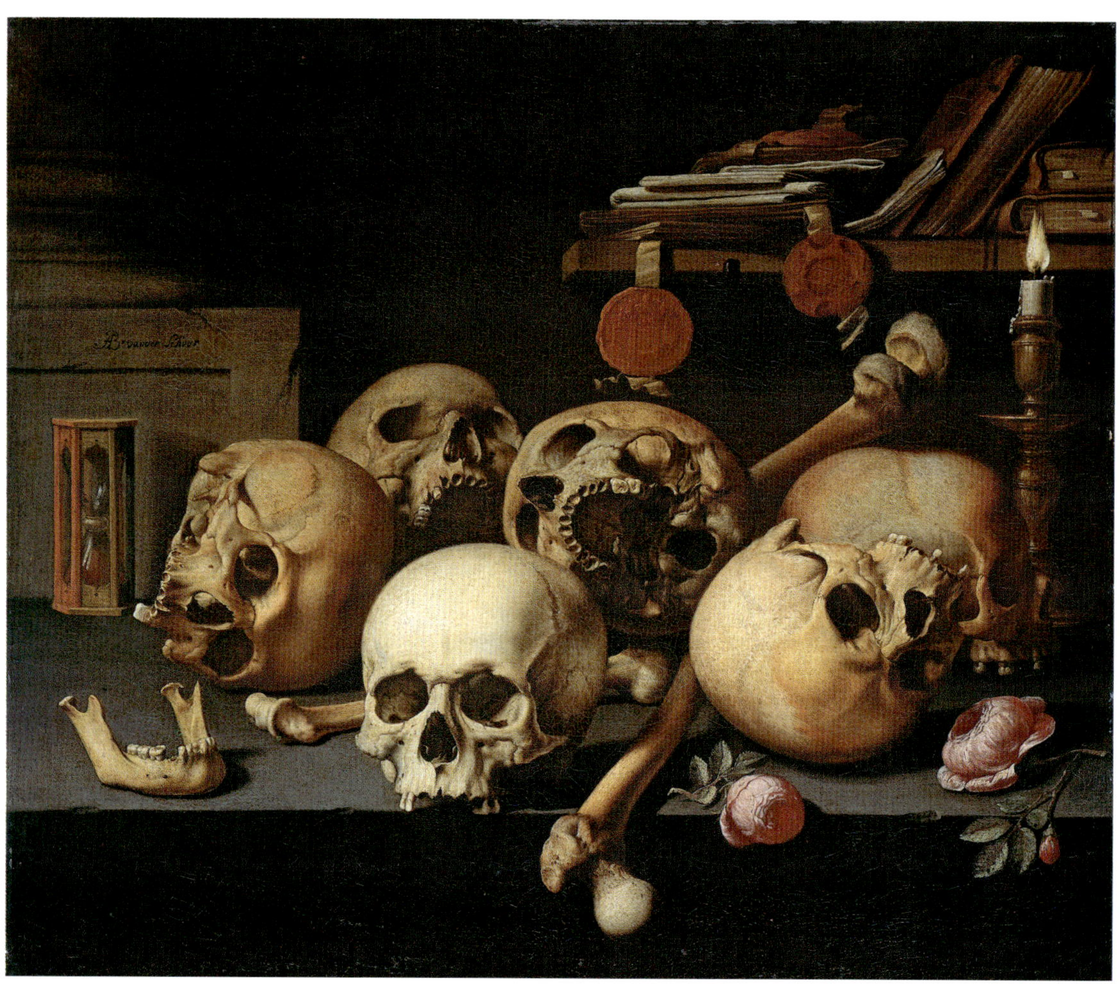

10 Aelbert Jansz van der Schoor (c. 1603–c. 1672) · *Vanitas Still Life (Skulls on a Table)* (c. 1660) · Oil on canvas · 25 × 28¾ inches

11 Pieter Claesz (1597/98–1660) · *Still Life with Fish* (1647) · Oil on panel · 25¼ × 32¼ inches

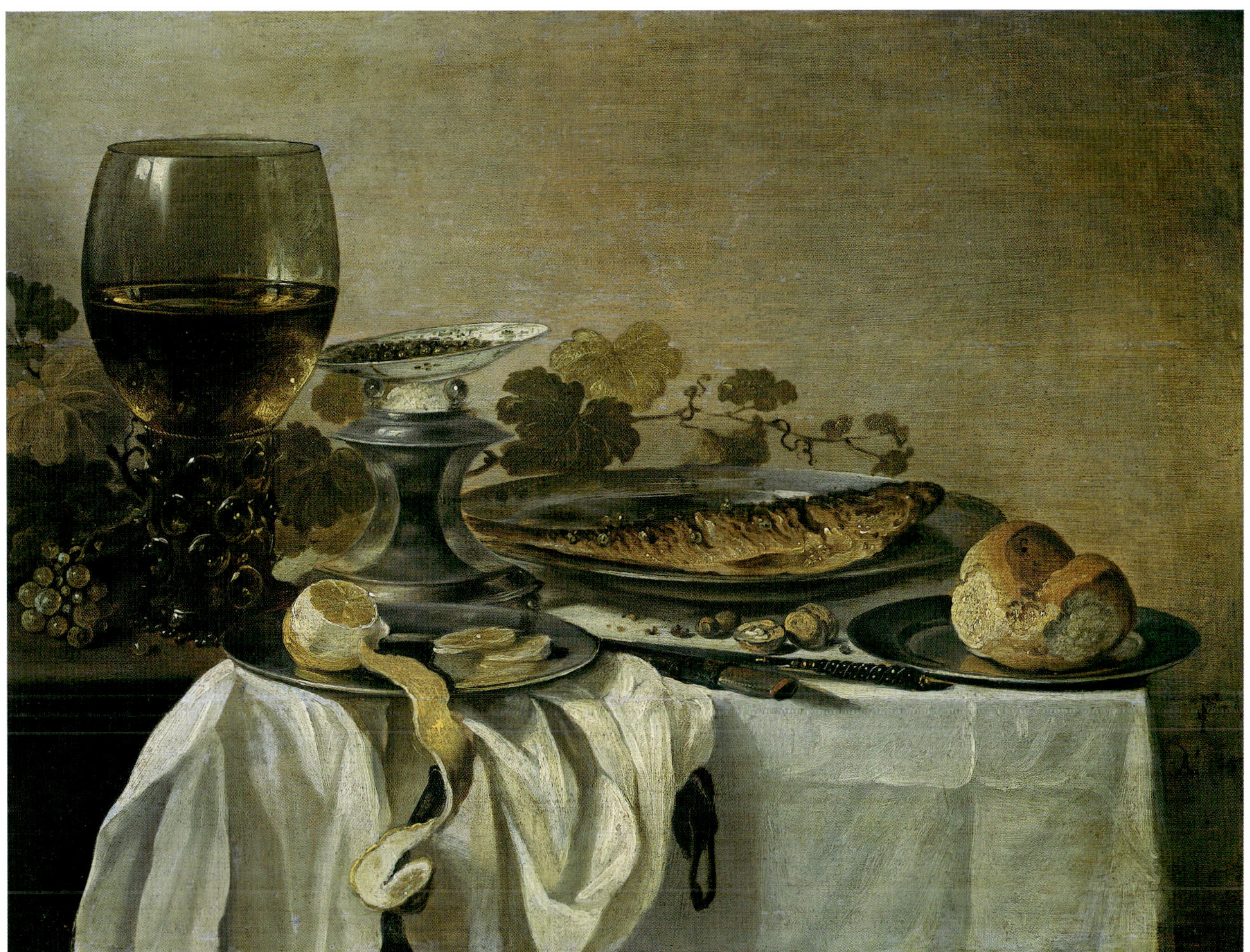

Chinese porcelain dish holding capers to go with the fish. Delightful details, such as the curling of the lemon peel and vine tendrils, and the projection of the pewter plates beyond the edge of the table, enhance the composition. Monochrome paintings were popular in the 1640s, and this still life is subdued in color, with only the yellow of the lemon to arrest the eye. Earlier in his career, Claesz had employed brilliant colors very different from the restrained palette that characterizes the almost nonchalant compositions of this and other later works.

Claesz probably came from Berchem near Antwerp (his son Nicolaes Berchem also became a painter, p. 76). He moved to Haarlem, where he married in 1617 and worked for the rest of his life. The elegance and intimacy of his tabletop still lifes are in marked contrast to the ostentation of *pronkstilleven* (sumptuous still lifes). For Pieter Claesz, the principal aim was to render materials and reflected light as accurately as possible.

*Still Life with Books* (no. 12, p. 36) is an early work in the oeuvre of Jan Davidsz de Heem (1606–1683/84). It was probably painted between 1625 and 1629, when the artist lived and worked in Leiden. There was a large market in Leiden for this type of still life, as the city's university (the oldest in Holland) drew many students, scholars, and writers who appreciated the motif. De Heem's stepfather was himself a bookbinder and bookseller, and he must have been helpful in

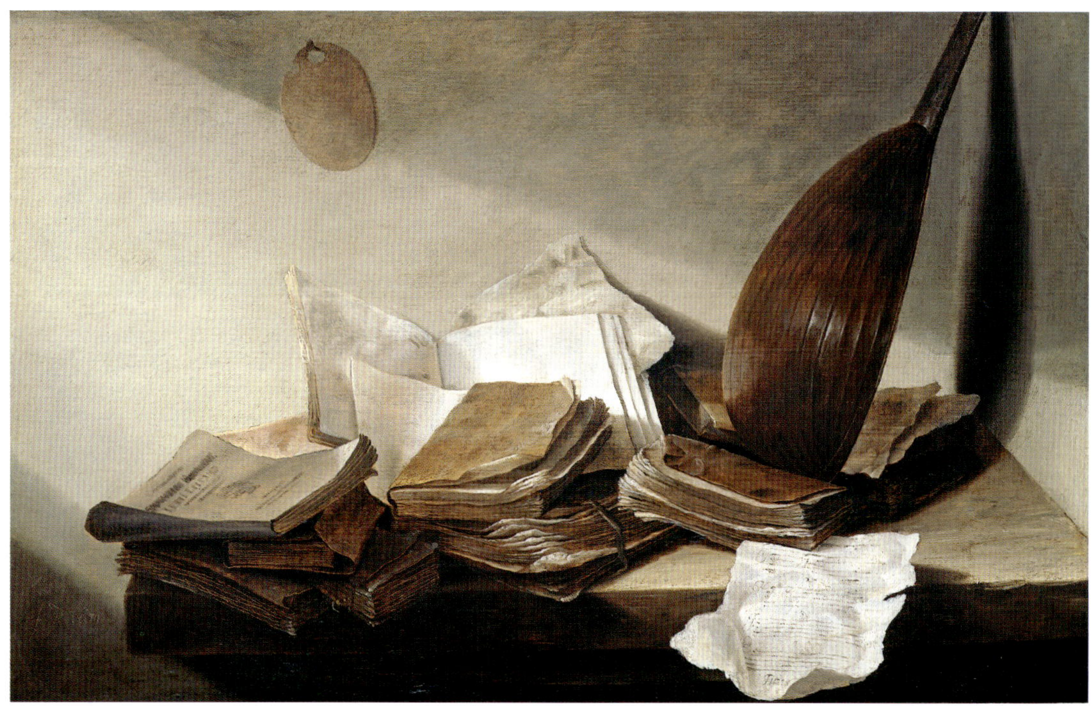

finding buyers for his stepson's paintings. The subject was tackled by the pick of Leiden painters, among them two young colleagues of De Heem who in the mid-1620s had yet to make a name for themselves: Jan Lievens (1607–1674) and Rembrandt. There are even similarities in technique: in this still life De Heem, just like his two fellow townsmen often did, scratched into the wet paint with the butt end of his brush to indicate the pages of several of the tomes. Books played an important role in 17th-century moral thought, being regarded as a source of wisdom and knowledge. In emblem books, symbolic images combined with prose or verse encouraged readers to renounce worldly goods and devote themselves to study. In De Heem's painting, the table is piled with fourteen or so volumes, arranged haphazardly on top of and next to one another. The books themselves may be understood as sources of transient knowledge; however, even books, intended to make the ideas of mortal authors immortal, are subject to decay. Those in De Heem's composition have clearly been well used—their pages are creased and torn, and some have even lost their bindings—and can thus be interpreted as a literal reference to the emphemerality of all earthly things. An explicit allusion to the painting's symbolic meaning is found on the piece of paper about to fall from the table, inscribed with the word "Finis."

12 Jan Davidsz de Heem (1606–1683/84) · *Still Life with Books* (c. 1625–1629) · Oil on panel · 10½ × 16¼ inches

13 Jan Jansz van de Velde (1619/20–1662) · *Still Life with Wineglass, Flute Glass, Earthenware Jug, and Pipes* (1651) · Oil on canvas · 27¼ × 35¼ inches

Although less obvious than the skulls of Van der Schoor and the books of De Heem, a deeper significance attaches to the objects in *Still Life with Wineglass, Flute Glass, Earthenware Jug, and Pipes* of 1651 (no. 13) by the Amsterdam painter Jan Jansz van de Velde (1619/20–1662). They refer to drinking, smoking, and the consumption of oysters, all symbols of a licentious lifestyle that one would do well to avoid. This visual warning is a fine specimen of Van de Velde's oeuvre, which includes a great many of these so-called *toebackjes:* sober, subdued still lifes featuring smoking materials. The dark background into which the objects seem to fade, making the tiny highlights on the objects stand out even more distinctly, is characteristic of Van de Velde's paintings.

In *Still Life with Dead Peacocks* of about 1639 (no. 14, p. 38), Rembrandt portrayed a girl looking through a window at two dead birds. From the pool of blood below them, it is clear the peacocks have only just been shot and left for a day or more to allow the blood to flow out, tenderizing the meat and improving its flavor. The birds seem to rest in a pantry, where other food is kept as well. The raking light, thickly applied paint, and muted colors are typical of Rembrandt. Particularly impressive is the way he painted the peacock on the table, whose head seems to protrude from the large canvas. This still life is an extraordinary painting in many respects. For one, it was highly unusual to combine an attractive girl with dead game. There are

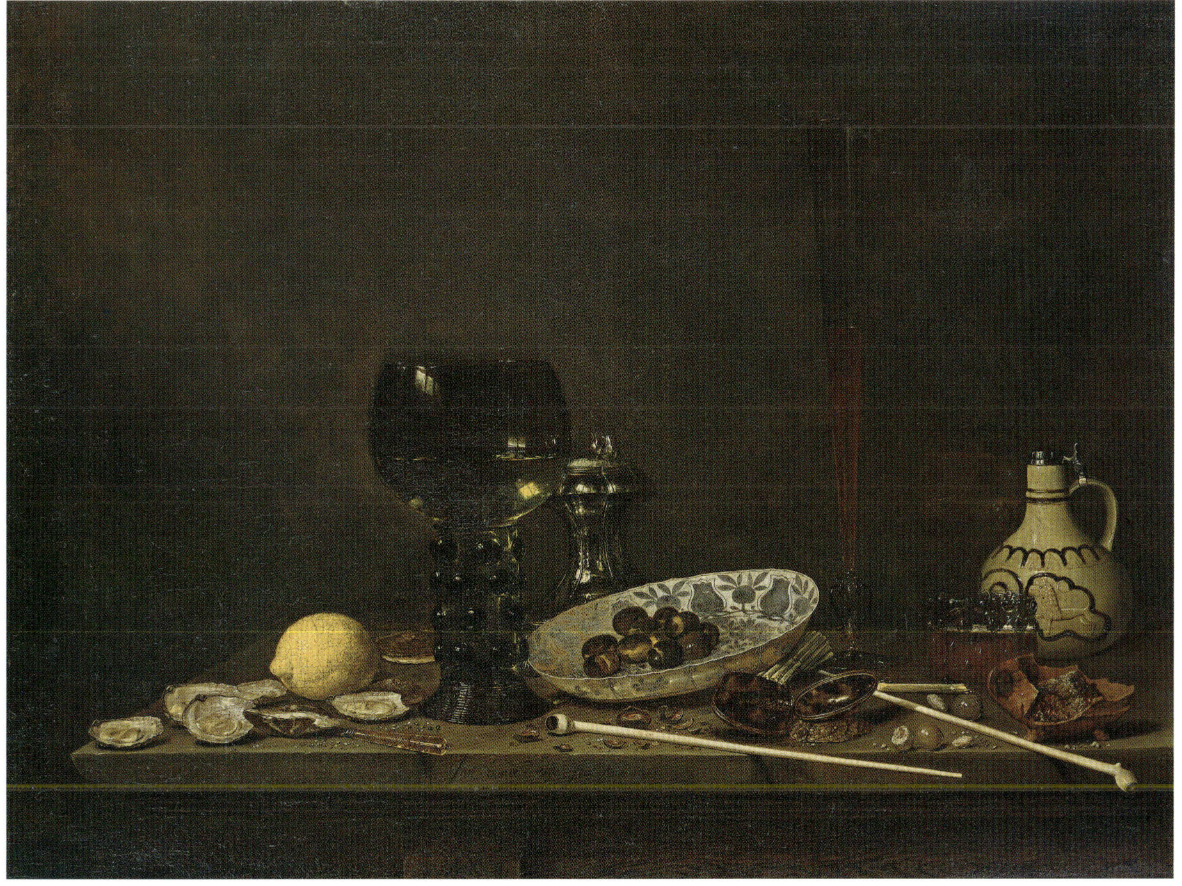

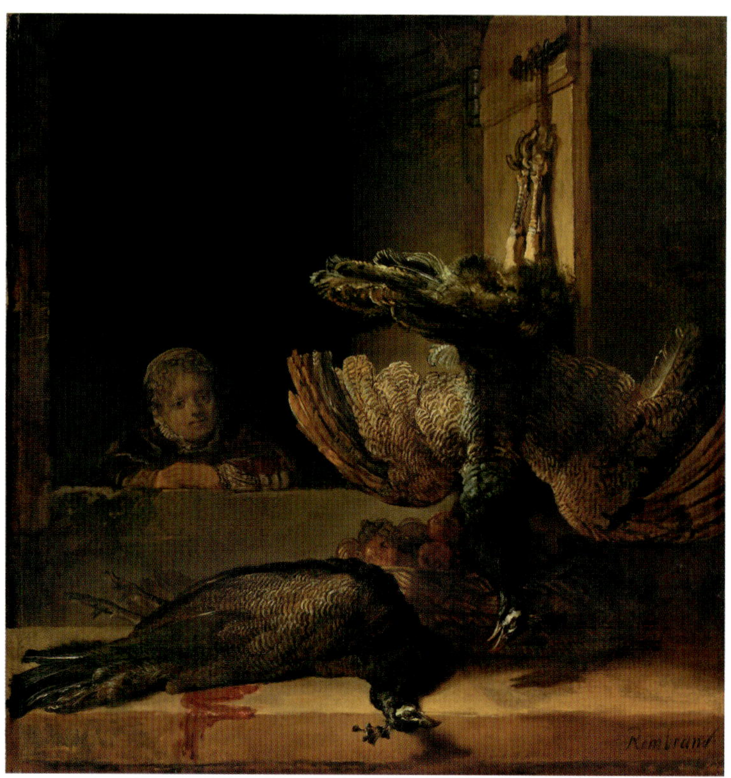

several examples of Dutch and Flemish paintings with kitchen interiors where female beauties are portrayed alongside food, but these are voluptuous adults, not young girls. Girls would also be out of place in conventional Dutch still lifes where game and hunting trophies are the main motifs. We do not know what Rembrandt's intentions with this painting were, but possibly he wanted to try his genius at successfully combining seemingly incompatible elements. It is a unique work in his oeuvre, as no other painted still life by his hand have come down to us.

Painters of the so-called *pronkstillevens* (sumptuous still lifes) chose a very different challenge in depicting colorful arrays of lavish objects in a wide range of materials and fabrics. Abraham van Beyeren (1629/21–1690) of The Hague was the leading practitioner of the style. The genre is exemplified by Abraham Mignon's opulent *Still Life with Fruit and Oysters* (no. 15, p. 40) in its rich display of luscious fruit and abundance of costly utensils, including a gold cup, gleaming *roemer,* and flute glass (quite similar to two examples on page 44). Mignon (1640–1679), a pupil and close collaborator of Jan Davidsz de Heem, was a master at rendering materials and textures. He carefully built up his compositions, in this work from small objects in the left foreground (the orange and the oysters on the plate) to larger items at the right rear (the pumpkin and gold cup). Painters of this era often showed off their skill at achieving a lifelike realism by projecting an item

14 Rembrandt van Rijn (1606–1669) · *Still Life with Dead Peacocks* (c. 1639) · Oil on canvas · 57 × 55 inches

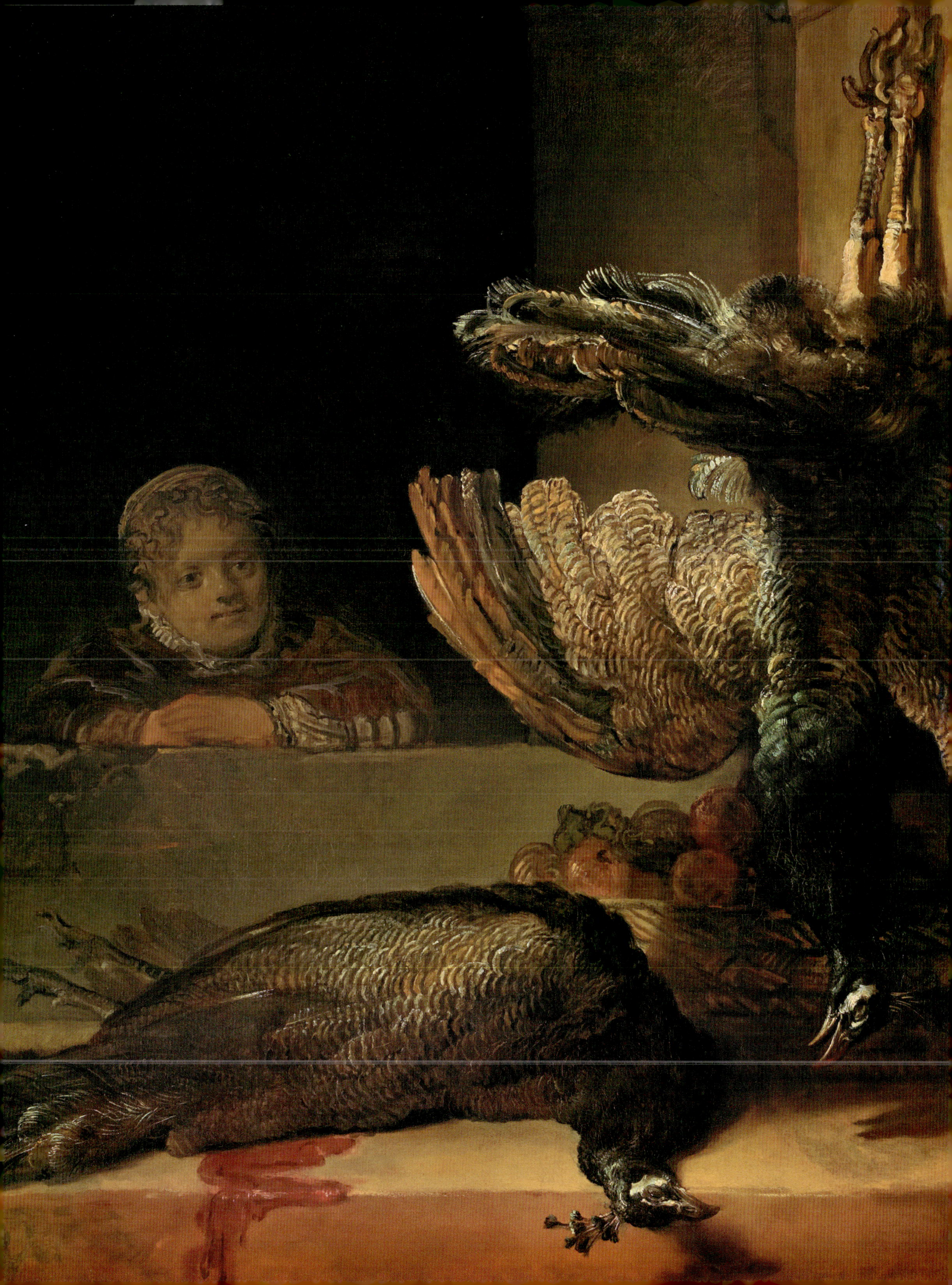

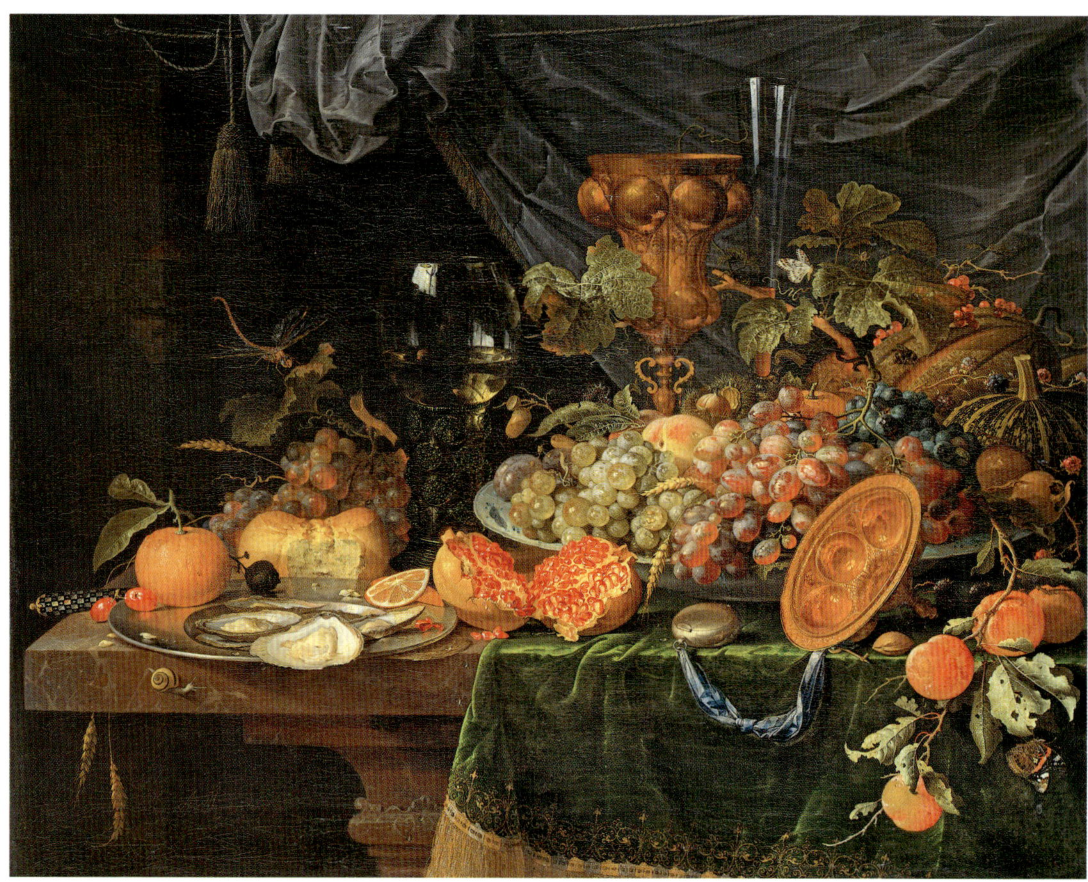

seemingly from the picture plane, as Rembrandt did with his peacock. In this still life, Mignon deftly extended a pewter plate over the edge of the table. The pocket watch on the table and the decaying leaves at the right remind the viewer that all the earthly riches seen here are fleeting and will not withstand the ravages of time. The snail and butterfly in the painting probably also refer to the transience of life.

The names of some twenty-five women painters active in the 17th century are known: a very small number in comparison with their male counterparts. They were either the daughters of painters or well-to-do ladies for whom drawing and painting were part of their upbringing. In the case of Rachel Ruysch (1664–1750), it was a combination of the two. Her mother was the daughter of the architect Pieter Post (1608–1669), while her father, Frederik Ruysch, was an amateur painter and an internationally renowned professor of anatomy and botany in The Hague. Although she married the portrait painter Jurriaen Pool (1666–1745) in 1693 and had ten children, family life did not keep her from painting. She continued to work for a distinguished international clientele until the ripe old age of eighty-three. In 1709, the date of *Still Life with Flowers* (no. 16), she had just been appointed court painter to Johann Wilhelm, Elector Palatine of Pfalz in Dusseldorf. During her lifetime, Ruysch was a much praised painter-specialist of flowers and fruit. At least eleven contemporary poets dedicated poems to her.

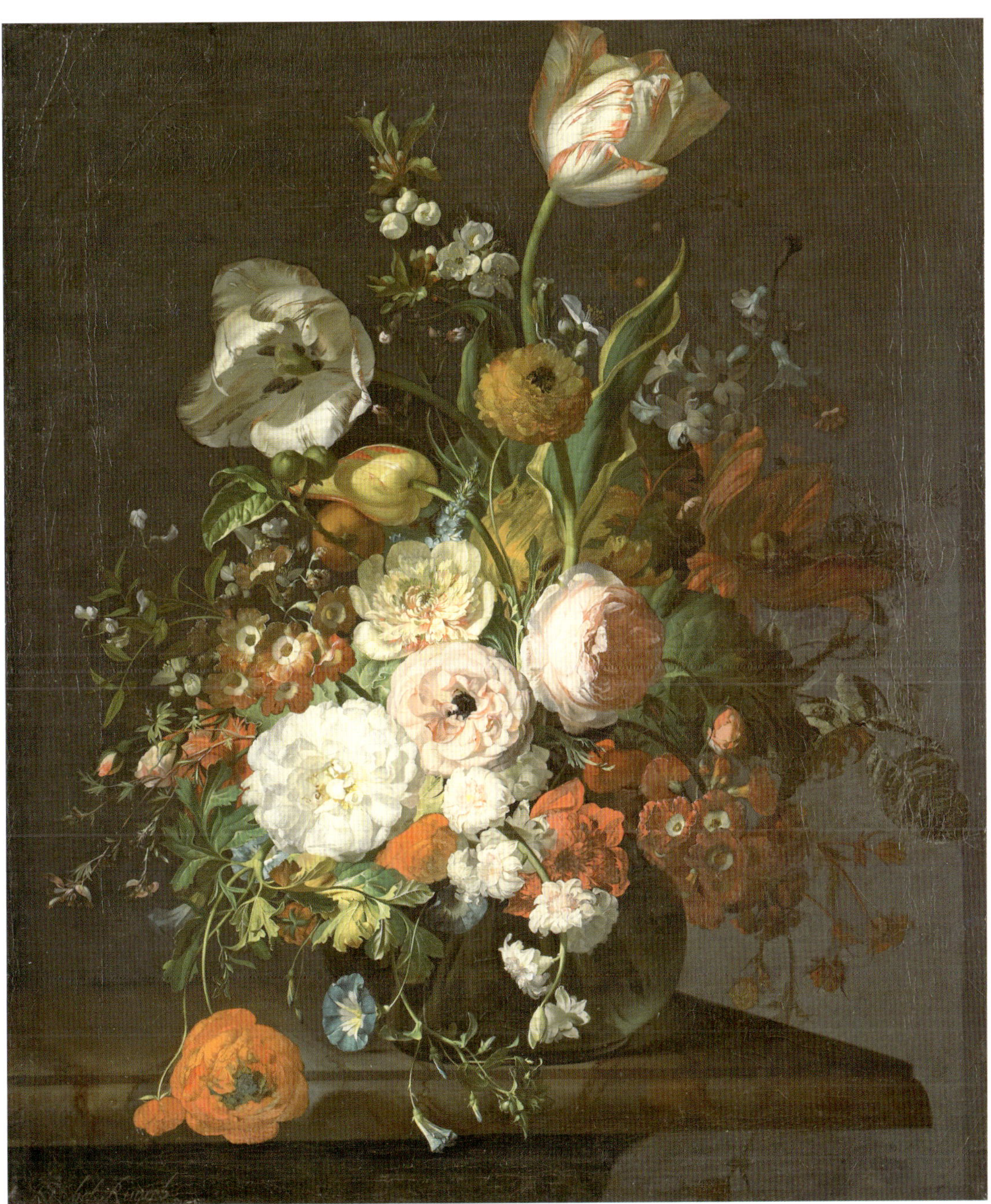

15 Abraham Mignon (1640–1679) · *Still Life with Fruit and Oysters* (c. 1660–1679) · Oil on canvas · 23¼ × 29½ inches

16 Rachel Ruysch (1664–1750) · *Still Life with Flowers* (1709) · Oil on canvas · 25¾ × 21 inches

From the enthusiasm for flowers that led to the popularity of Rachel Ruysch's paintings, it is a small step to the flower motifs that were executed in silver during the second half of the 17th century. Amsterdam and The Hague grew into major silver centers where, in the 1640s, the floral style gradually replaced the fluid auricular style seen in Lutma's salt cellar (see p. 29). Spring flowers such as the tulip, the anemone, and the carnation were eminently suitable for chasing in silver, while engraving was used to incise more delicate floral motifs on smooth, straight-sided objects. A bowl (no. 17) marked with the stamp of the silversmith Nicolaas Hoyer (active 1660–after 1676) is an exceptionally fine example of Amsterdam silver decorated in the floral style. The floral décor of the rim and figural decoration of the center are combined with auricular edging. Two infants drink together from a bowl in an idyllic landscape scene. Not only is the rim decorated with swirling leaves and flowers, but the bowl itself has the shape of a flower. Both the flowers and the pastoral scene were presumably based on prints. Bowls of this type were often depicted in 17th-century prints and paintings, where they are often shown containing fruit.

Claes Claesz Schoon, a registered master silversmith in Amsterdam from about 1666, made a pair of salt cellars dated 1668 (no. 18) in the shape called *diabolo.* The type evolved in the late 1640s, and examples with floral decoration are known from the 1660s. The rounded surfaces of this pair are embellished overall with a profusion of all sorts of flowers enlivened by several putti and birds (a pelican, stork, and heron). Usually *diabolo*-shaped salt cellars rest on plain silver balls, but these examples have feet cast in the form of two roses and an anemone.

In the last quarter of the 17th century, the exuberance of the floral style that characterized Hoyer's 1661 bowl subsided into the more restrained variant seen in a pair of candlesticks date-marked 1672 (no. 19) and attributed to the silversmith Peter Alberts (active c. 1668–before 1723). The twisting stems of the candlesticks are engraved with a flowering vine, and chasing defines the tightly packed flower swags on the knob and foot. The undecorated areas, including blank cartouches, maximize the reflection of light on the object's convex and concave parts. Even though the candlesticks are richly ornamented, the overall effect is much less opulent than in Hoyer's bowl or the salt cellars by Schoon, reflecting the late-17th-century taste in Holland for more straightforward forms.

Dutch still-life paintings often include one or two fine drinking glasses. Sometimes they are modeled after Italian, in particular Venetian, examples. In the 16th century the fame of Venice's fine, clear, hard glass inspired glassblowers north of the Alps to attempt imitations of it. Although

17 Nicolaas Hoyer (active 1660–after 1676) · *Bowl* (1661) · Silver · h. 3¼ inches, diam. 14 inches

18 Claes Claesz Schoon (active c. 1666–1702) · *Pair of Salt Cellars* (1668) · Silver · h. 6 inches, diam. 8 inches; h. 6 inches, diam. 7 inches

19 Peter Alberts (active c. 1668–before 1723), attributed · *Pair of Candlesticks* (1672) · Silver · h. 13¾ inches; h. 13½ inches

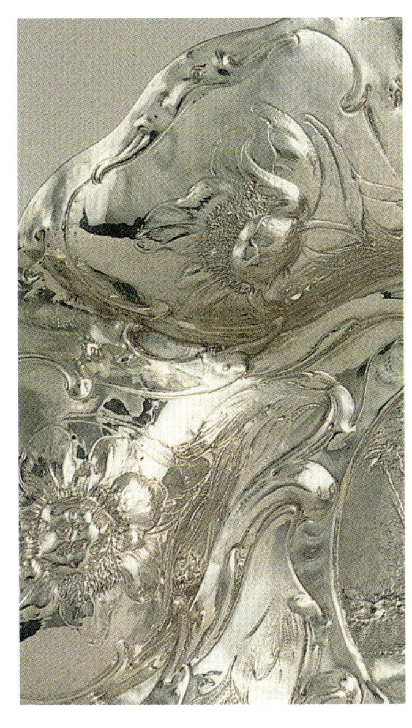
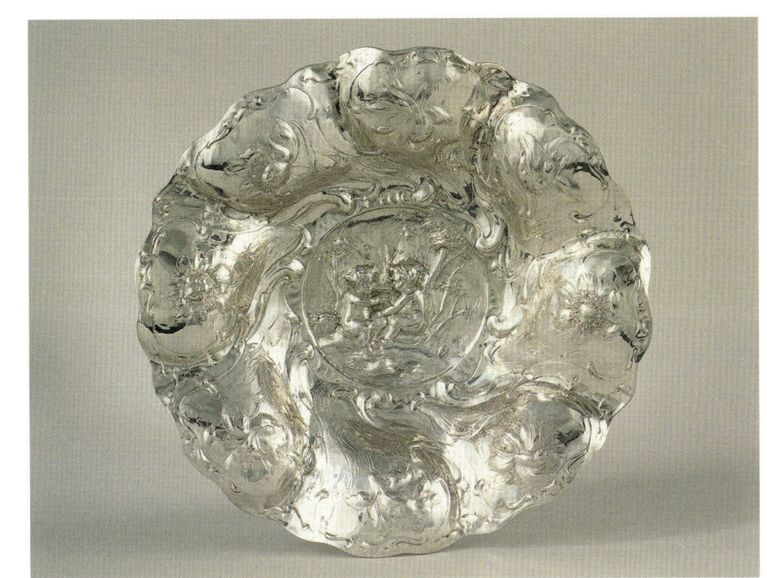
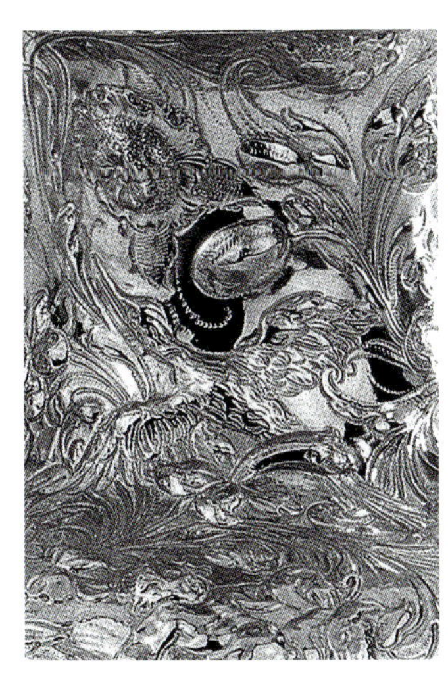
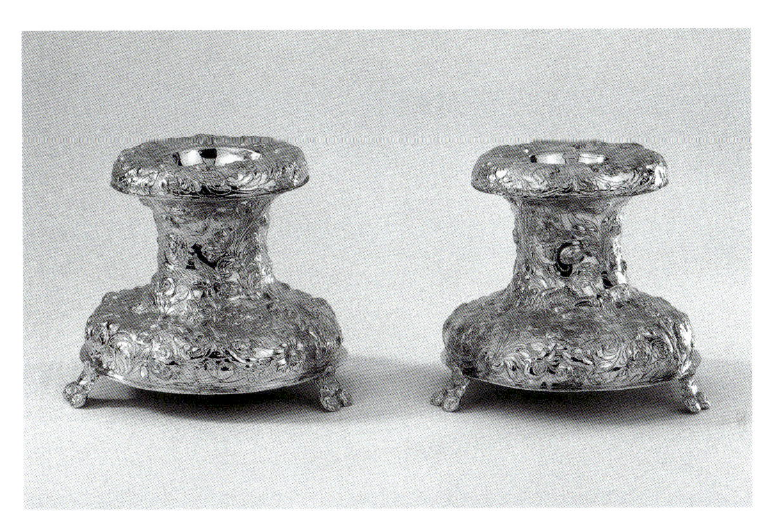
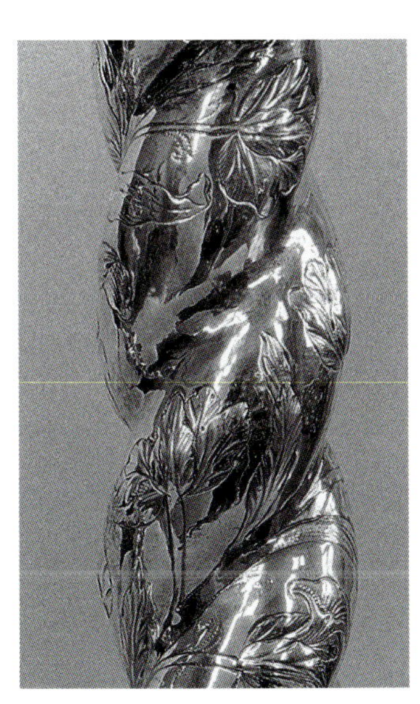
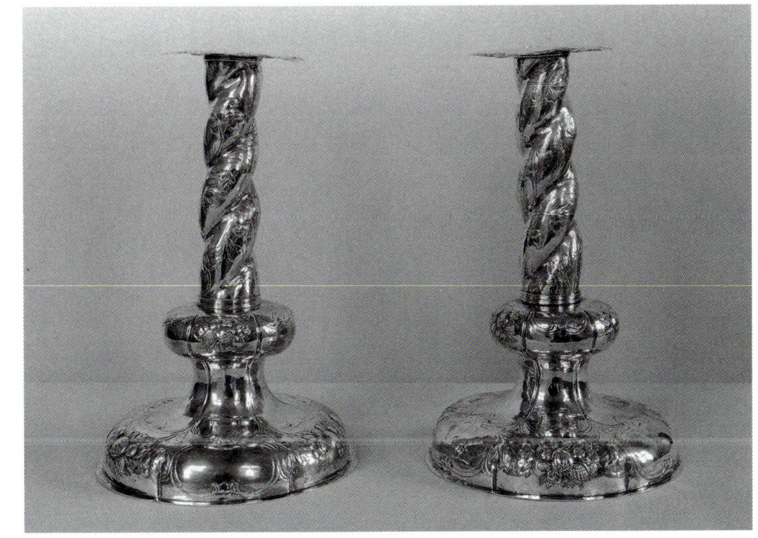

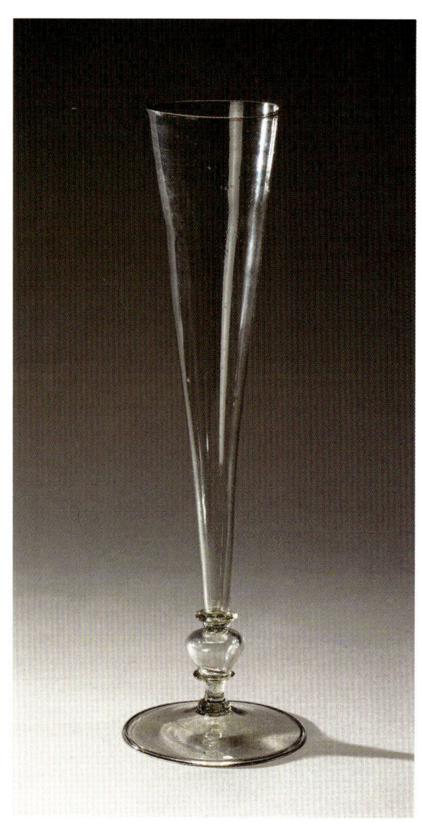

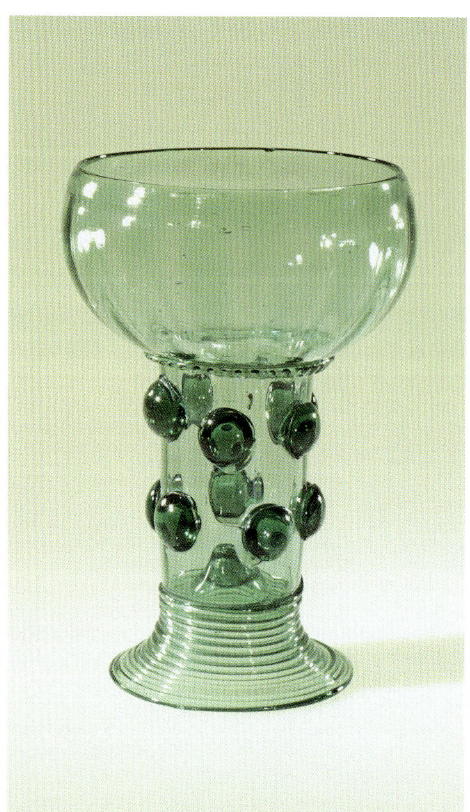

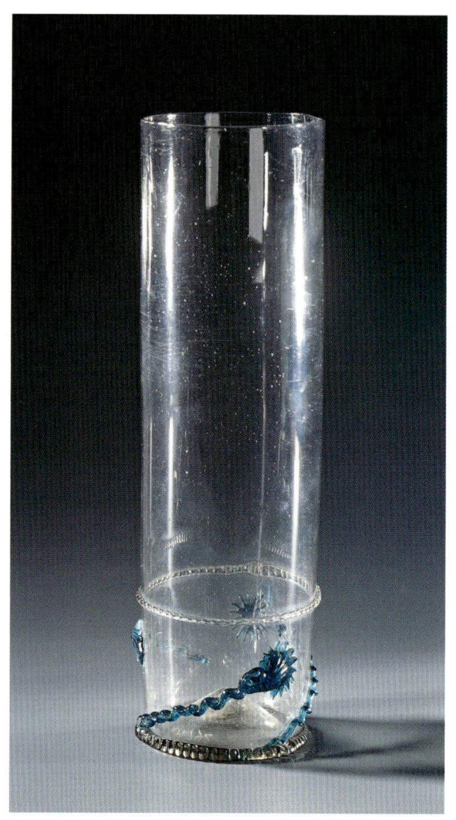

20 Northern Netherlands · *Flute Glass* (late 17th century) · Glass · h. 14 inches, diam. 4 inches

21 Netherlands or Germany (third quarter 17th century) · *Roemer* (c. 1650–1700) · Glass · h. 5¼ inches, diam. 3½ inches

22 Northern Netherlands · *Beaker* (late 16th–early 17th century) · Glass · h. 8½ inches, diam. 2¼ inches

in Venice the techniques of blowing glass were regarded as state secrets, some artisans defied the ban and risked severe punishment by disseminating their knowledge. In the Netherlands the first glass blown *à la façon de Venise* (in the Venetian manner) was made in Antwerp and Liège.

In the flute glass (no. 20) shown here, the decorative features of the stem, the thin glass wall, and the clarity of color are imitative of Venetian examples. Such tall, slender flutes were traditionally used for red wine, as can be seen from numerous genre scenes and still lifes of the period, such as Abraham Mignon's *Still Life with Fruit and Oysters* (p. 40). The elongated flute shape bridged the width of the oversized ruff collars fashionable in the early 17th century and made it easier to consume and enjoy the contents of the glass. The pure simplicity of this specimen, with its slender funnel bowl supported by a so-called *merese* (flat disc or collar), above a hollow baluster stem and spreading foot, attests to the shift in taste away from the flamboyant decoration of Dutch flute glasses made earlier in the century.

The *roemer* was the more common form of wineglass made in northern Europe. During the 17th century *roemers* were so popular in the Netherlands that domestic production could not meet demand, and large quantities were imported from the Rhineland. The glass has a green tint due to the iron oxide present in the sand used in Germany. The name can be traced to the German word *Römer,* meaning "Roman." These pieces are identifiable by a spherical bowl above a hollow stem studded with protrusions called prunts, made by applying daubs of hot glass. The hollow foot often consists of spirally wound glass filament. In the course of the century the shape altered only slightly; late-17th-century *roemers,* like the present example (no. 21), have a taller foot, and their appearance is more slender than *roemers* from the beginning of the century. The prunts decorating the stem presumably served as hand grips, and impressed stamps were often used to give them the shape of blackberries. Many Dutch paintings of the third quarter of the 17th century feature *roemers* with smooth spherical prunts like this example, but only a handful have survived.

Equally few are intact examples of the fragile cylindrical beakers of clear, colorless glass made in the Netherlands during the second half of the 16th and early 17th centuries (although many fragments have been excavated in Holland and Belgium). The beaker seen here (no. 22) dates from precisely this period and belongs to a group known as "comet beakers," a name that refers to the decoration of applied spiral threads of blue and clear glass. Comets were first recorded in the skies of the Dutch Republic in the 16th century, and from 1558 onward the veritable comet fever that swept across Europe was reflected in the applied arts.

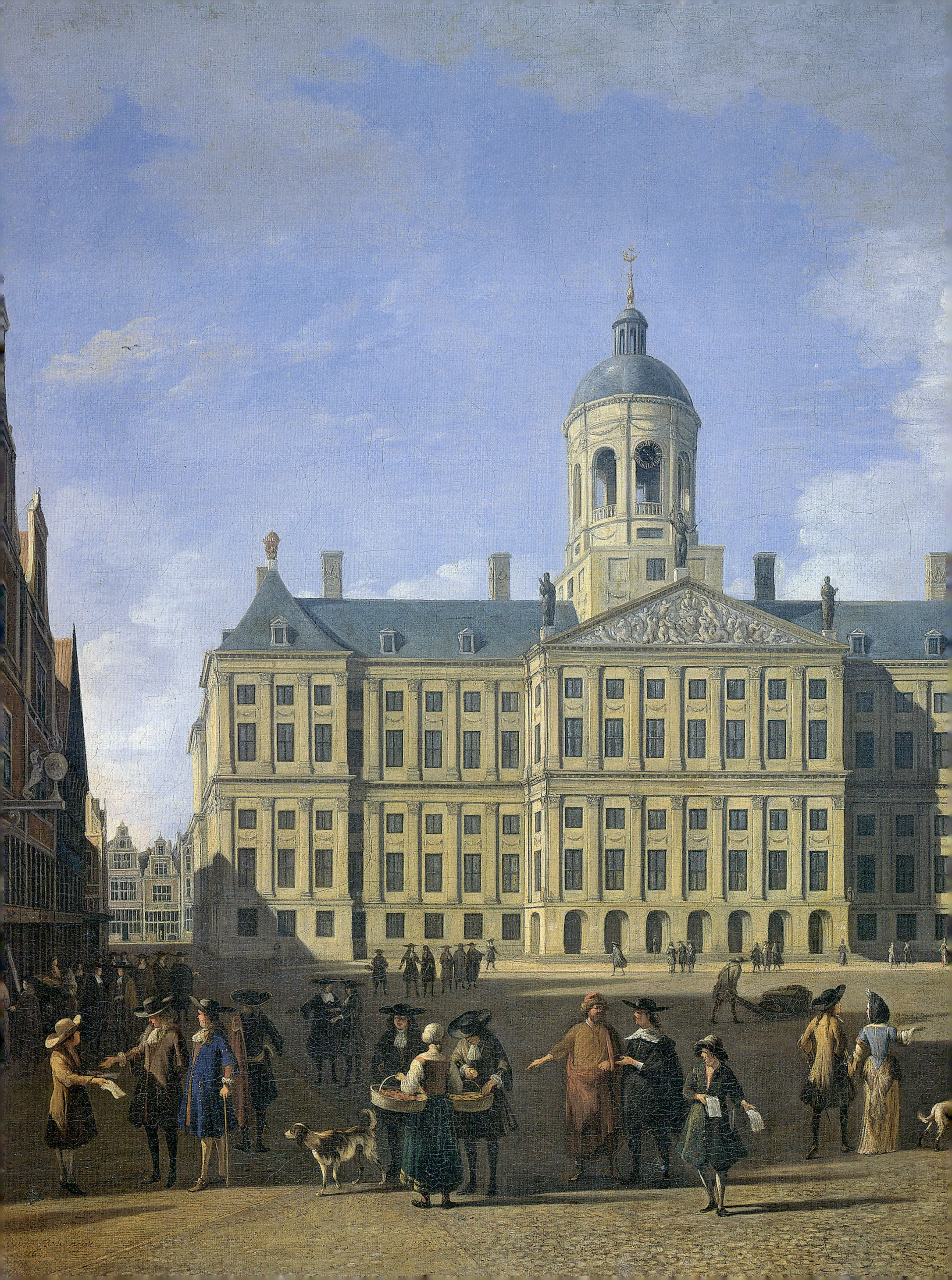

# 3
# THE CITY

ABUNDANT INSPIRATION LAY OUTSIDE THE ARTIST'S STUDIO in the rich matrix of urban life in Dutch towns, enriched by thriving trade and the industries of the Republic. The rebellion against the Spanish had not interfered with the economic development of the northern Netherlands. Since the beginning of the 16th century, trade with the Baltic region had steadily grown, and over the following two hundred years it came to form the largest source of income within the Dutch economy. Ships from cities bordering the Zuyder Zee participated in that trade, and Amsterdam became the main entry point for imports. After the Spanish captured the important port city of Antwerp in 1585, many of its wealthier citizens fled. Almost half of them ultimately settled in the Republic, and those who moved to Amsterdam brought with them not only their capital but their knowledge of, and contacts with, various European banks and businesses. Their arrival reinforced the city's position within the European trading network and triggered a new period of prosperity for Amsterdam and other cities in the region. The skills of Flemish tradesmen and artisans, who formed a large segment of the enormous stream of immigrants, had a considerable influence on the arts.

In 1585 northern rebels had blocked the mouth of the river Schelde with a flotilla of ships, cutting off access to Antwerp, then under Spanish control. This effectively transferred the center of Dutch commerce to the port of Amsterdam, to the north. In 1611 the Amsterdam Commodity Exchange was opened, and it quickly became the economic heart of the Republic. The English writer Daniel Defoe noted the commercial activity of the Dutch in 1728: "The Dutch are the carriers of the World, the middle persons in Trade, the Factors and Brokers of Europe; they buy to sell again, take in to send out; and the greatest part of their vast commerce consists in being supplied from all parts of the World, that they may supply all the World again."

Many exotic products—such as Asian porcelain, ivory, and spices—had previously reached the north via Lisbon, after Pope Alexander VI in 1493 granted trading rights to half the world to Portugal, a Catholic colonial power. Because of the war with Spain, however, maritime traffic into Lisbon was impossible, and a number of trading companies sponsored by investors in Amsterdam, Rotterdam, and Zeeland equipped their own merchant ships and successfully undertook the risky journey to the Far East. The companies fiercely vied with one another, which resulted in rising prices and declining profits. To better compete with the Spanish and the Portuguese, the States of Holland and the States General (the central organ of the Republic) joined forces as shareholders in a new enterprise called the United East India Company, or VOC (for its Dutch name, Verenigde Oostindische Compagnie). In 1602 the States General granted the newly formed company a trade monopoly for the area east of the Cape of Good Hope and west of the Straits of Magellan for a period of twenty-one years.

The VOC was empowered to enter into trade agreements and to maintain diplomatic relations in the name of the States General. Moreover, the company was allowed to wage war and make peace, and to take all appropriate measures to that end. The VOC soon proved a resounding success, and spices, gold, ivory, silk, porcelain, and sugar filled the warehouses of Amsterdam. The largest multinational concern active in the 17th and 18th centuries, the VOC employed some thirty thousand people at a time when the entire Republic had fewer than two million inhabitants. Over a period of two hundred years, the company sent more than a million company officials and their families, agents, soldiers, and sailors from Europe to Asia, and traded in an area stretching from the Red Sea to Japan. Spanish, Portuguese, and English trade was dealt a crushing blow. The VOC acquired exclusive trading rights in Asia via its posts there. In 1609 it set up the first Western trading station in Japan on the island of Hirato, and in 1619 the Dutch city of Batavia was founded on the Indonesian island of Java, which then served as VOC headquarters. The Dutch West Indies Company, or WIC (Westindische Compagnie), played a role in the notorious slave trade from 1635 on. African slaves were shipped from West Africa to plantations in the Caribbean and South America.

The journeys of the Dutch to distant destinations contributed in no small measure to the flourishing of knowledge worldwide. Initially in Europe this took the form of globes, cartographic materials, and travel stories, but these were soon followed by books and pamphlets covering a wide variety of subjects. All manner of strange knickknacks came to Holland in the sea chests of the VOC. Wealthy burghers installed so-called cabinets of curiosities in their homes to display the various specimens of flora and fauna brought back from the East. The contents of these collections also served as study objects for early amateur scientists. This new scientific knowledge was imparted to students at the universities of Leiden, Utrecht, Amsterdam, and Harderwijk.

The ready availability of capital made it possible to undertake such costly enterprises as the draining of the country's large lakes to reclaim land. The burghers who funded such projects reaped great profits by leasing the fertile lands (known as *polders*). But not all new money was invested in the country's economy. The lack of pretension that initially characterized most Protestant merchants gave way to an increasing focus on outward appearances. In Amsterdam, then the prosperous and influential center of the Republic, work started on an extremely prestigious building project, an impressive new town hall, which was to be a symbol of the grandeur of the city. All over Amsterdam, large sums of money were being spent on expensive houses, furniture, clothing, and artworks. Paintings by Dutch artists, such as those seen here, graced the elegant interiors of the canal houses and country homes of the well-to-do. Sculptors, cabinetmakers,

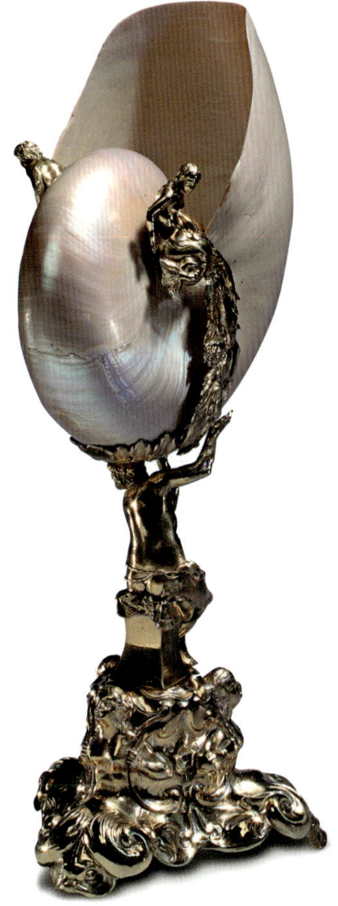

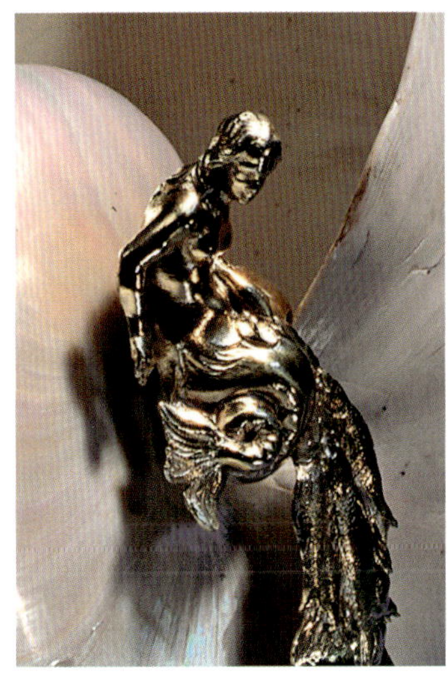

and silversmiths also contributed to the often colorful extravagance that was characteristic of the taste of upper-crust Dutch society in the Golden Age.

The *Nautilus pompilius* is typical of the precious specimens of flora and fauna the Dutch brought back from the East. These mollusks live in the waters of the South Pacific, and when a VOC base was established on the Indonesian island of Ambon in 1605, the nautilus shell became a popular prestige item. The shells were often given precious-metal mounts, ingeniously crafted with decorations of marine motifs. In the silver-gilt mount of a Nautilus cup (no. 23) made by a Dutch silversmith in the first half of the 17th century, the shell is held in place by mermaids and supported by another mermaid poised above the base, which takes the form of waves filled with dolphins and other sea creatures. The cup would have been a showpiece in a wealthy merchant's collection of curiosities, but it could have been used for drinking on special occasions when presented at the dining table.

A silver-gilt cup made by a Delft silversmith in 1603 (no. 24, p. 50) is one of a pair which for over three hundred years formed part of the silver treasury of the archers' guild of Gorkum (Gorinchem) near Dordrecht. The impressive covered cup is richly decorated in the Renaissance

23 Northern Netherlands · *Nautilus Cup* (c. 1600–1650) · Mounted in gilded silver · h. 12½ inches

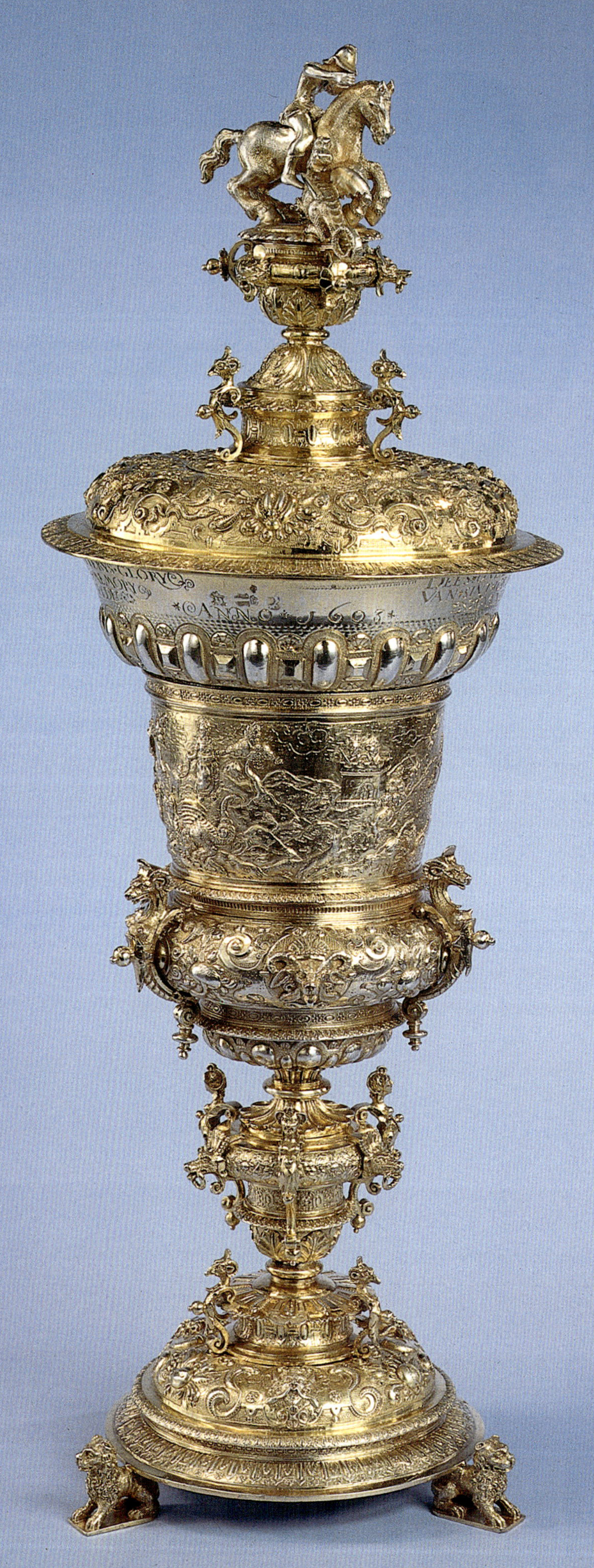
ANNO 1603

style with small-scale strapwork enclosing masks and bunches of fruit, with gadrooning and other ornamental moldings, and applied scrolls cast with the heads of beasts and monsters. The main decorative theme is the life of Saint George, the patron saint of archers. The finial on the cover (from which his sword has been lost) and scenes on the sides show the saint slaying a dragon and rescuing the princess who had been surrendered to the monster. The cup is of a traditional type that had been developed by the first half of the 16th century and was still popular in all parts of the Republic around 1600, as is apparent from extant pieces from The Hague, Dordrecht, Middelburg, and Nijmegen. By that time, there was no master working in Gorkum skilled enough to make such a cup, so the chief officers of the city's archers' guild were obliged to entrust its important commission to a silversmith in another town. The hallmarks on the cup show that it was made in Delft by a silversmith who used the mark of a bird's claw. Accomplished as he was, he has not been identified, and only two other footed cups with his mark, made in 1604 and 1606, are known.

Around 1600 the richly detailed ornament of the Renaissance style began to be supplanted by the soft organic shapes of what is known as the auricular style. The Utrecht goldsmiths Paulus van Vianen (c. 1570–1613), who worked for Emperor Rudolph II, and his brother Adam (1568/69–1627) were the originators of these novel, fanciful forms, which were shown off to great advantage in embossed silver. The auricular style became increasingly popular from the 1620s, reaching its high point around 1650. Initially the Van Vianens used auricular ornament for cartouches and borders, but soon they developed it into the three-dimensional forms that had such a strong influence on the work of their contemporaries. It was Adam who took the style to its fullest extent in 1614, when the Amsterdam silversmiths' guild commissioned him to make a memorial jug in homage to his celebrated brother Paulus, who had died the year before. Instead of limiting the style to the decoration, Adam made the whole object one large auricular lobe, chased from a single sheet of silver. The auricular style itself thus formed the main theme of the jug. The object, now at the Rijksmuseum, was admired by contemporaries as much for its craftsmanship as for its artistry. It was on public display at the premises of the silversmiths' guild, and it appears in many paintings, particularly by artists of the Rembrandt school, including Salomon Koninck's *The Idolatry of King Solomon* of 1644 (no. 53, p. 90).

The bold irregular, organic forms for which the 1614 memorial jug became famous also characterize a delightful silver ewer with scenes from Roman history made by Adam van Vianen around 1620 (no. 25, p. 52). The ewer gives the impression of having been molded from a treacle-like mass, suggesting masks in various places, from which various creatures emerge. The foot is decorated with dolphins, and winged female figures appear between auricular ornament on either side of the body. The face with closed eyes on the neck of the jug and the strangely shaped handle, resembling a snake, are particularly striking. Van Vianen gave the ewer's decoration an

24 Delft · *Cup of the Gorkum Archers' Guild* (1603) · Gilded silver · h. 15¾ inches, diam. (foot) 4¼ inches

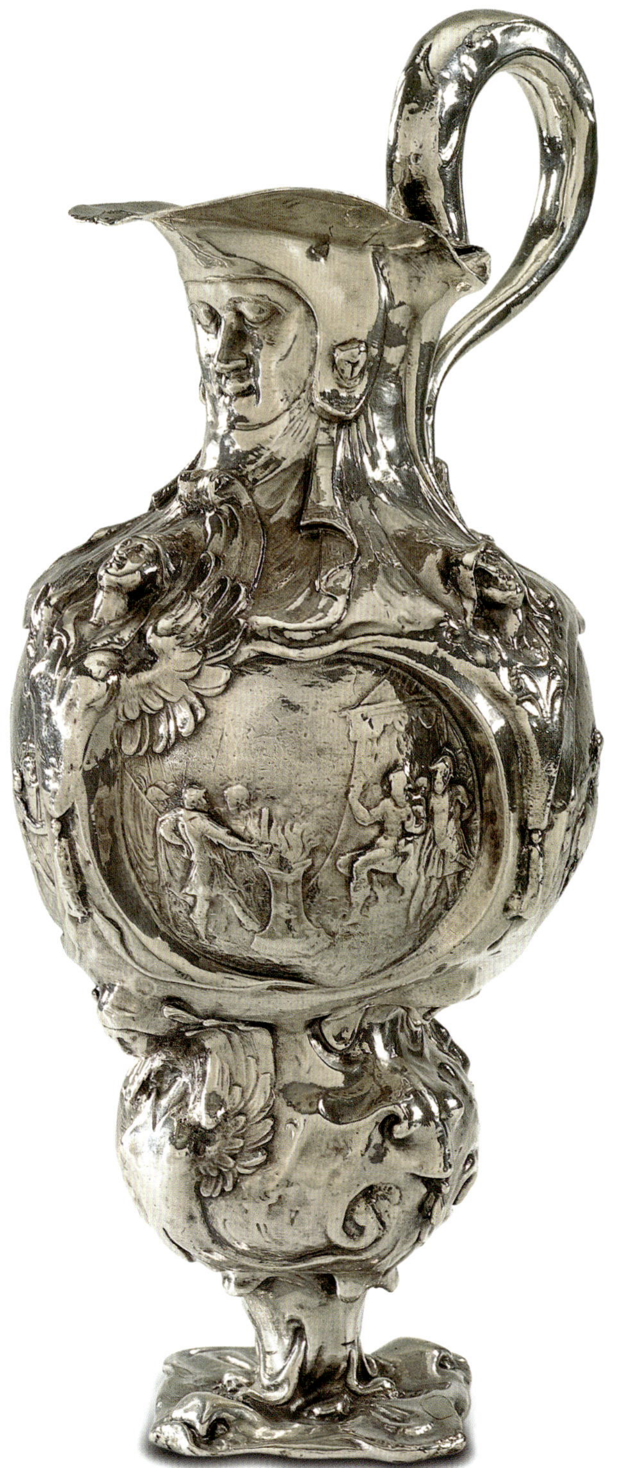

25 Adam van Vianen (1568/69–1627) · *Ewer with Scenes from Roman History* (c. 1620) · Silver · h. 11¾ inches

26 Delft · *Spice Pot* (c. 1660–1680) · Faience · h. 7¾ inches, w. 8¼ inches

27 Delft · *Beaker Vase* (1693) · Faience · h. 10¾ inches

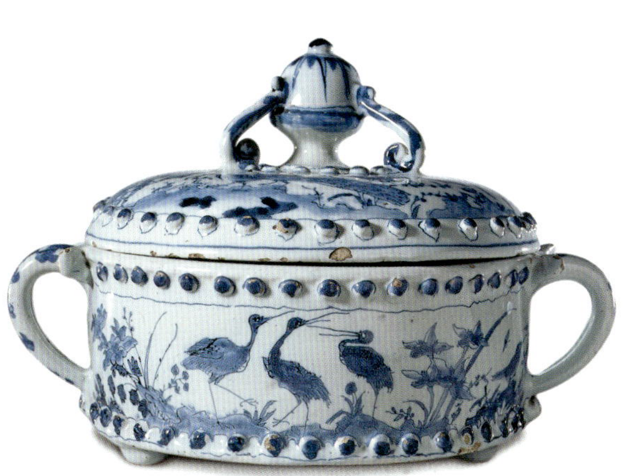

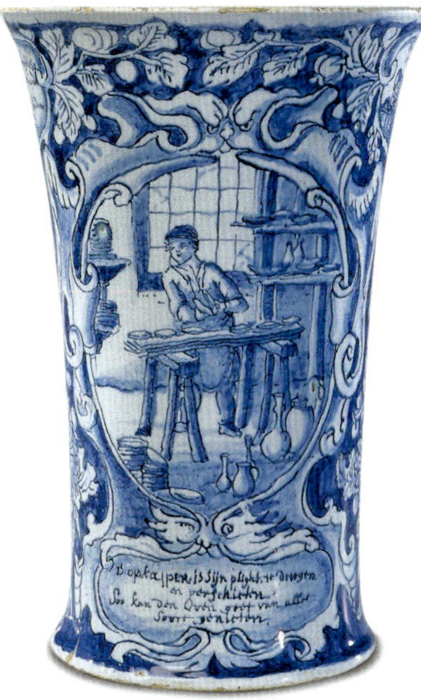

added dimension by nestling small-scale representational scenes amid the swirls and eddies of ornament. The contrast between the lively, delicately embossed scenes from Roman history and the fleshy ornamentation in which they are embedded emphasizes the virtuosity of the silversmith's achievement. The ewer may have belonged to the silver collection of the king-stadholder William III of Orange, as a similar object is described in his inventory, fitted with a cover and making a set with a matching basin.

Chinese porcelain had considerable influence on European taste in the first half of the 17th century and had a lasting effect on the decoration of earthenware. From the early 1600s, Dutch potters felt the challenge presented by VOC-imported porcelain, which stimulated technical and artistic improvements in their own products. Between 1625 and 1640 the potters of Haarlem and Delft enhanced their wares by using better clay to make pieces with thinner walls. They also adopted the blue and white palette, with blue painting on white tin glaze, ultimately borrowing or adapting the motifs and patterns of the Chinese porcelain. The resulting faience objects, referred to as *Hollants porceleyn* (Dutch porcelain) in the 17th century, are commonly known as Delftware today. The new and improved product competed successfully with Chinese porcelains. From the 1640s, when the supply of porcelain to Europe declined dramatically as a result of civil war in China (1644–1647), Delftware potters concentrated on the production of faience that was Chinese in both shape and decoration.

A spice pot made between 1660 and 1680 (no. 26) shows how Chinese scenes and decorative motifs were translated and applied in Delft faience. The elegant cranes and plants look distinctively Asian. Between 1680 and 1700 Delft became an important center for such deluxe ceramics, with over twenty independent potteries producing wares for customers throughout Europe. Not only were the Delft potters capable of producing luxury objects that looked like Chinese porcelain, they also made a wide variety of items featuring Western designs executed in blue and white.

A beaker vase (no. 27) is a remarkable Delft example. Unlike most vases of this type, which were generally made in sets to form a garniture, this is a unique piece. It is decorated with two large medallions within a cartouche in the auricular style (which is rarely used in ceramics). The medallion on one side shows a workman in a pottery, a so-called *opkapper*, who made sure the Delftware was properly packed and stored to dry before being fired in the kiln and finished. The medallion on the reverse shows a cobbler at work. Between the large medallions are two smaller ones, showing two boys packing Delftware. Below the figures are a few lines of verse about their occupations. Foliage motifs are painted in paired symmetry, a time-consuming and costly way of decorating used in many exclusive pieces after 1700. The cartouche is painted in varying shades of blue, bringing out the plasticity of the ornamentation. The beaker is dated inside "ANNO 1693–12/11" (December 11, 1693) and inscribed ". . . se pals-Graaf." The inscription can be identified as naming IJsaacq Dirckse Palsgraaf (1651–1712), who is documented as an employee of many years at the De Metaale Pot Delftware pottery. The precise dating and the unusual decoration suggest that Palsgraaf was probably the *opkapper* at the pottery, and this vase was made for him as a presentation piece on a special occasion.

The guilds that played such an important role in the organization of daily life in 17th-century Dutch cities were not limited to the trades. There were also guilds in each city of civic guards and militia companies, who were to support city authorities in emergencies. The members of these guilds were drawn from the burghers of the town. They held competitions, joined in processions, and participated in military campaigns. The guild halls of the militia companies, called *doelen* (target ranges), developed into gentlemen's clubs. The impressive group portrait *The Governors of the Kloveniersdoelen* (no. 28), painted in 1642 by Govert Flinck (1615–1660), was made for such a hall. It was commissioned to hang over the chimney of the Great Hall of the Kloveniersdoelen (House of the Arquebusiers Civic Guard) in Amsterdam. This vast room was filled with group portraits of Amsterdam's civic guard companies, including the famous *Nightwatch* by Rembrandt. Flinck, who had been Rembrandt's pupil from 1633 to 1636, was among Amsterdam's foremost painters of portraits and biblical scenes when he was asked to paint this work. It was the task of the four governors he immortalized to supervise the daily running of the Kloveniersdoelen, with its buildings and grounds. The coat of arms with a claw (*klauw* in Dutch), hanging on the right, alludes to a corruption of the guild's name, Klauweniers (*kloveniers* = *arquebusiers*). The official drinking horn of the guild (preserved in the Rijksmuseum today) is solemnly carried in by the warden of the Kloveniersdoelen, emphasizing the ceremonial aspect of the business meeting in Flinck's depiction.

Though he also painted the cityscapes of Amsterdam and The Hague, Gerrit Berckheyde (1638–1698) was particularly famous for his views of Haarlem. He based his compositions on drawings done on site and preferred to paint buildings set in open surroundings, such as canals or squares, which could serve as defining elements within the composition. In *The Town Hall on the Dam, Amsterdam* of 1693 (no. 29, p. 56), Berckheyde celebrated the central edifice of the largest and most important commercial hub in 17th-century Holland. Designed in 1648 by Jacob van Campen in a classical Italian style, the building became famous even before its construction was completed in 1655. By filling his canvas almost entirely with the new Amsterdam town hall, the artist echoed the general admiration of Van Campen's architecture—one of Berckheyde's contemporaries, the poet Constantijn Huygens, even called the building "the Eighth Wonder of

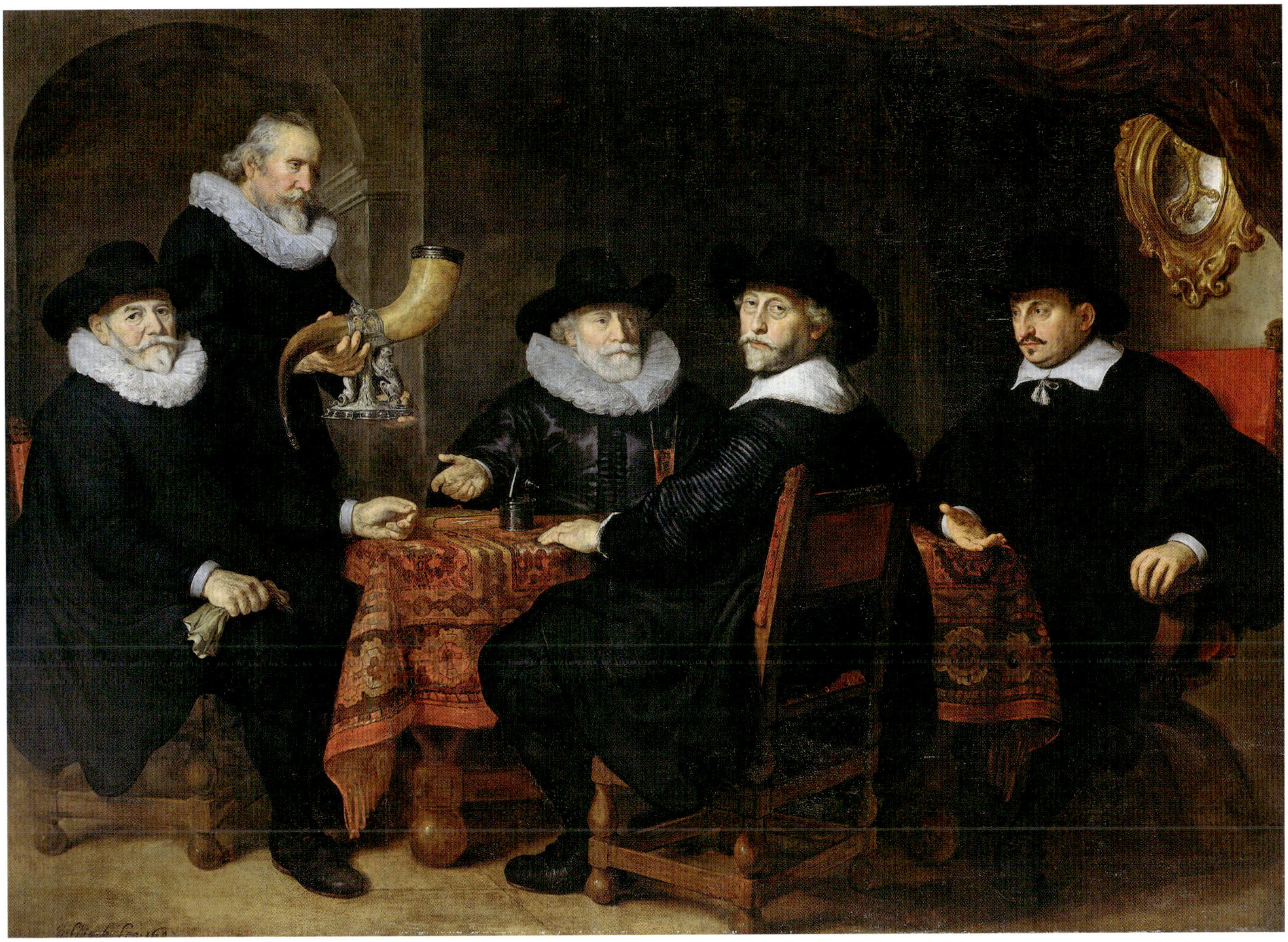

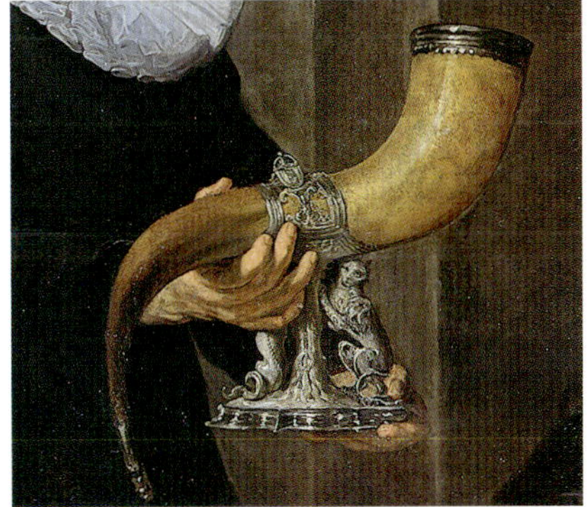

28 Govert Flinck (1615–1660) · *The Governors of the Kloveniersdoelen* (1642) · Oil on canvas · 80 × 110 inches

the World, with so many Stones on high, on so much Wood beneath," referring to its impressive size and the nearly fourteen thousand pilings that formed the foundation in the watery soil. By the activity in the foreground Berckheyde suggests the richness and diversity of life in this thriving urban center. A print shop, on the left side of the square, displays a globe above the second floor, referring to the interest in exploration and trade in the New World. City fathers, merchants, and town councilors congregate in the square. The cosmopolitan nature of Amsterdam and its role as the nucleus of international trade are signaled by several elegantly dressed businessmen, some of whom wear Eastern-style turbans and robes.

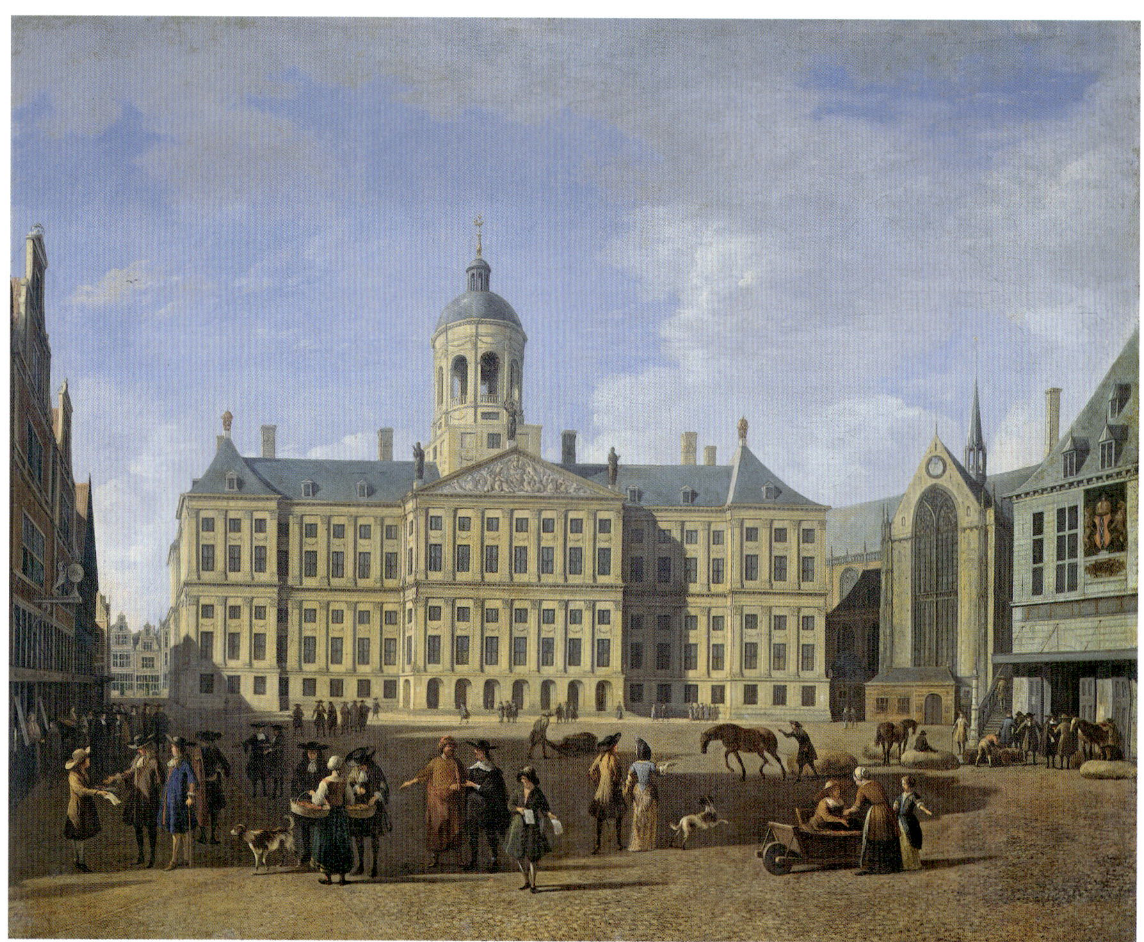

29 Gerrit Berckheyde (1638–1698) · *The Town Hall on the Dam, Amsterdam* (1693) · Oil on canvas · 20½ × 24¾ inches

30 Gerrit Berckheyde (1638–1698) · *The Waag (Weigh House) and Crane on the Spaarne, Haarlem* (c. 1670–1675) · Oil on panel · 12½ × 18 inches

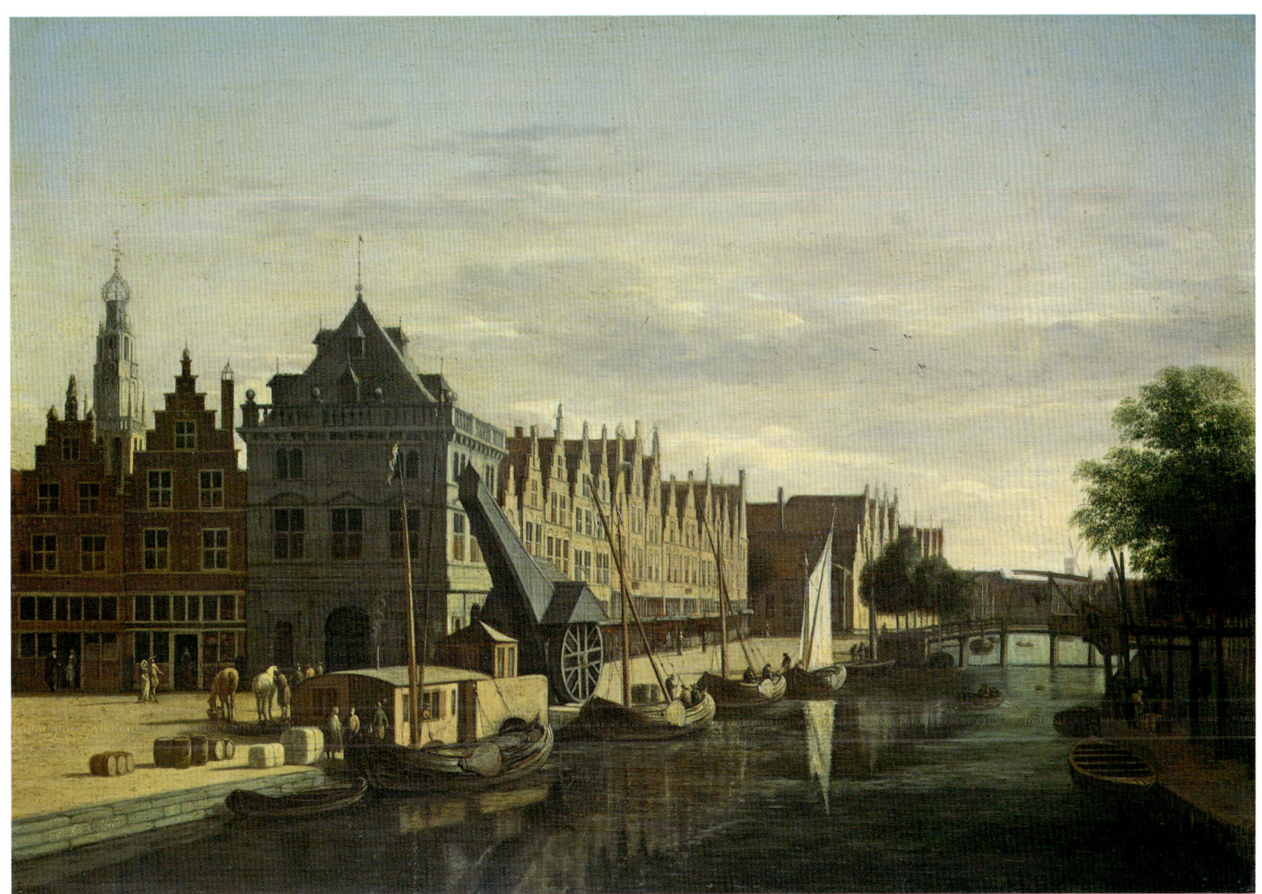

Berckheyde's *The Waag (Weigh House) and Crane on the Spaarne, Haarlem* (no. 30), dating c. 1670–1675, shows us one of Haarlem's most characteristic views. Except for the crane, which is gone today, and the buildings on the far side of the square, this area of Haarlem has changed very little over the centuries. The Weigh House and the Bakenessen church (whose spire is on the left) still dominate Haarlem. The river Spaarne was Haarlem's main artery in the 17th century, and most travelers on the inland waterways disembarked at the Dam, the small square with its great wheeled crane. Almost all cargo ships arrived there as well, as is evident from the loaded barges in Berckheyde's painting. The goods imported into the city had to be weighed or measured at the city's official public weigh house, where the appropriate duty was assessed. The Weigh House of Haarlem is the impressive 16th-century building on the corner of the Dam, erected in blue Namur stone. Heavy goods were hoisted from the barges by the wheeled crane beside the building. Berckheyde's view of the Weigh House as the center of trade, with the omnipresent water, cargo boats, and goods in transit, underscores Haarlem's many commercial links with the outside world.

*The Nieuwe Zijds Voorburgwal with the Oude Haarlemmersluis, Amsterdam (with Topographical Liberties)* (no. 31, p. 58) is typical of the work by the Amsterdam painter Jan van der Heyden (1637–1712). At first glance this would appear to be a true-to-life glimpse of Amsterdam, but Van der Heyden combined various existing buildings and elements from different parts of the city to

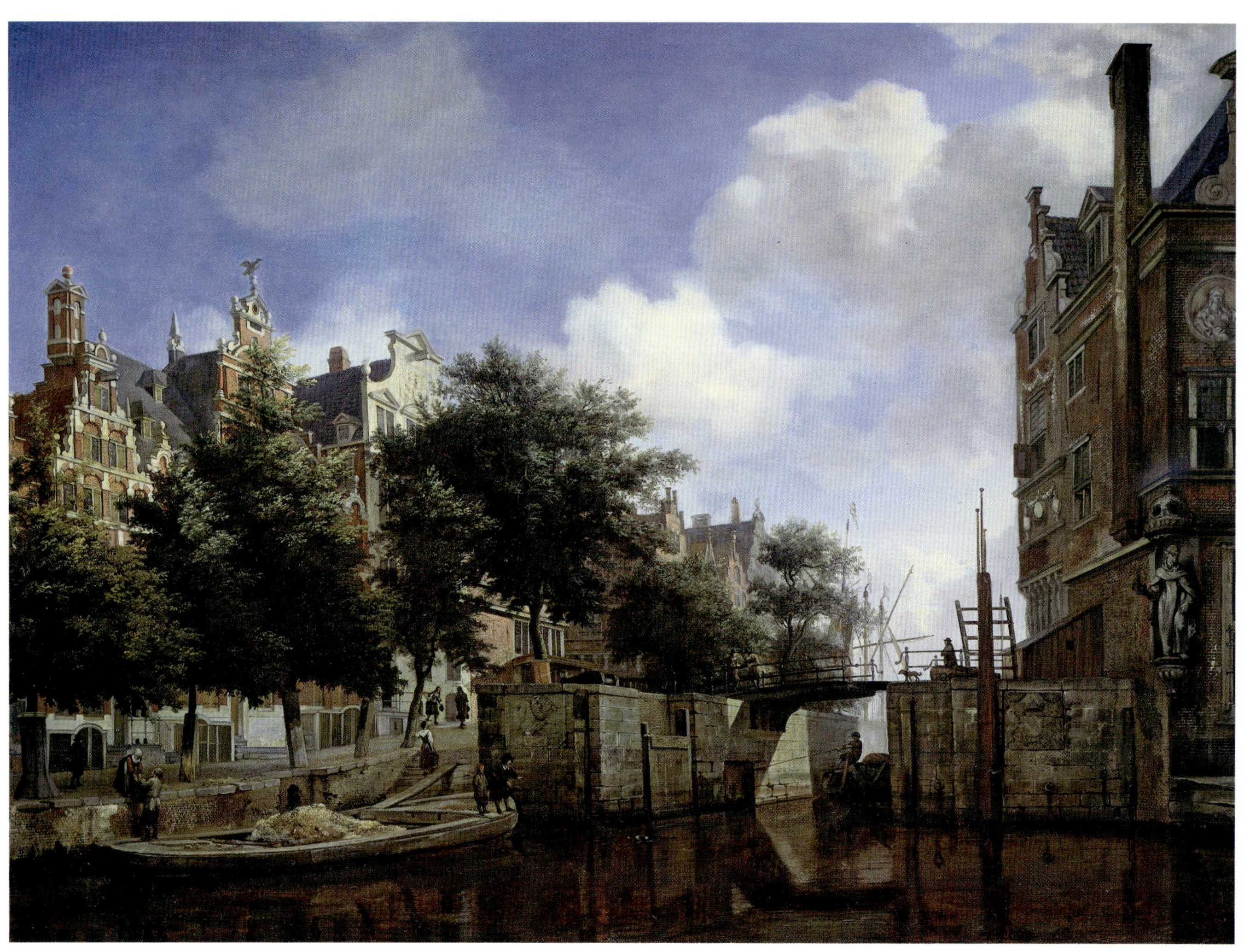

31 Jan van der Heyden (1637–1712) · *The Nieuwe Zijds Voorburgwal with the Oude Haarlemmersluis, Amsterdam (with Topographical Liberties)* (c. 1667–1672) · Oil on panel · 17¼ × 22¾ inches

32 Ludolf Backhuysen (1631–1708) · *The IJ in Amsterdam, with the Frigate "De Ploeg"* (c. 1680–1708) · Oil on canvas · 26¾ × 32 inches (overleaf)

form a new—imaginary—townscape. The main motif is the Oude Haarlemmersluis (Old Haarlem Locks) viewed from the Nieuwe Zijds Voorburgwal, a waterway in the north of Amsterdam that gave access to the harbor. The stately houses at the left were not in fact beside the lock gates but located more to the south, on the Herengracht, one of Amsterdam's four main canals. The house at the extreme left was the home of Martinus and Clara Alewijn, whose portraits by Dirck Dircksz van Santvoort are included in this volume (see p. 117).

Van der Heyden's ingenuity was not confined to the art of painting. In 1667 he invented a new form of street lighting that made Amsterdam the best illuminated city in the world. Some twenty-five hundred oil lamps were scattered across the city, lamps Van der Heyden made and maintained himself. Several years later he was granted a patent for an even more important invention: the fire engine equipped with hose and pump. Because the leather hose was flexible, it could be guided through alleyways and houses, enabling fire fighters to get closer to the seat of a fire. This innovation made it possible to fight fires far more effectively than by the old method of passing along buckets of water. Moreover, the pumps of the new system guaranteed a powerful, continuous jet of water. The income earned through his inventions made Jan van der Heyden a wealthy man, and soon there was no need for him to paint for a living. Nevertheless, he is known to have done some 120 townscapes and 90 other paintings, including landscapes and still lifes.

*The IJ in Amsterdam, with the Frigate "De Ploeg"* (no. 32, pp. 60–61) by Ludolf Backhuysen (1631–1708) depicts the rich trading city of Amsterdam on the horizon and, in the foreground, bustling shipping traffic with countless vessels of all sorts and sizes. Even though the emergence of the VOC had made Amsterdam the preeminent shipping center, it faced constant competition from Rotterdam, today one of the world's most important ports. The frigate *De Ploeg,* a vessel of the Amsterdam admiralty, is seen under full sail with its stern turned toward the viewer. In the shadow cast by passing clouds, the ship forms an impressive silhouette against the illuminated sky. Fishermen pull in their nets on the right; an elegantly dressed couple converses while walking toward a fisherman sitting on a barrel on the left. In an amusing detail, Backhuysen introduced two dogs whose pedigrees echo the differences in social status: a stray dog, addressed by the bearded fisherman, and a beautiful greyhound, accompanying the well-heeled couple.

Backhuysen had a long, successful career as a painter of highly detailed sea, river, and port scenes, which were much admired for their smooth technique and spectacular lighting effects. Around the age of eighteen he left the German town of Emden, where he was born and trained as an office clerk, and settled in Amsterdam. There he worked his way up from bookkeeper and calligrapher to draftsman and, ultimately, painter. Although he undoubtedly had a number of instructors, he appears to have been a self-taught painter who found his own way in art.

Market scenes occur in Dutch paintings as early as 1560. In the 17th century a number of artists had a preference for the subject: the Rotterdam painters Cornelis Saftleven (c. 1607–1681) and Hendrick Martensz Sorgh (p. 63), but also Adriaen van Ostade from Haarlem (p. 62), were particularly successful. Their paintings provide a vivid impression of markets in the 17th century. In Van Ostade's *Fishwife* of 1673 (no. 33), a fresh catch is simply laid out on wooden planks for customers. As is still the case today, the fish were filleted on the spot. In the background we can

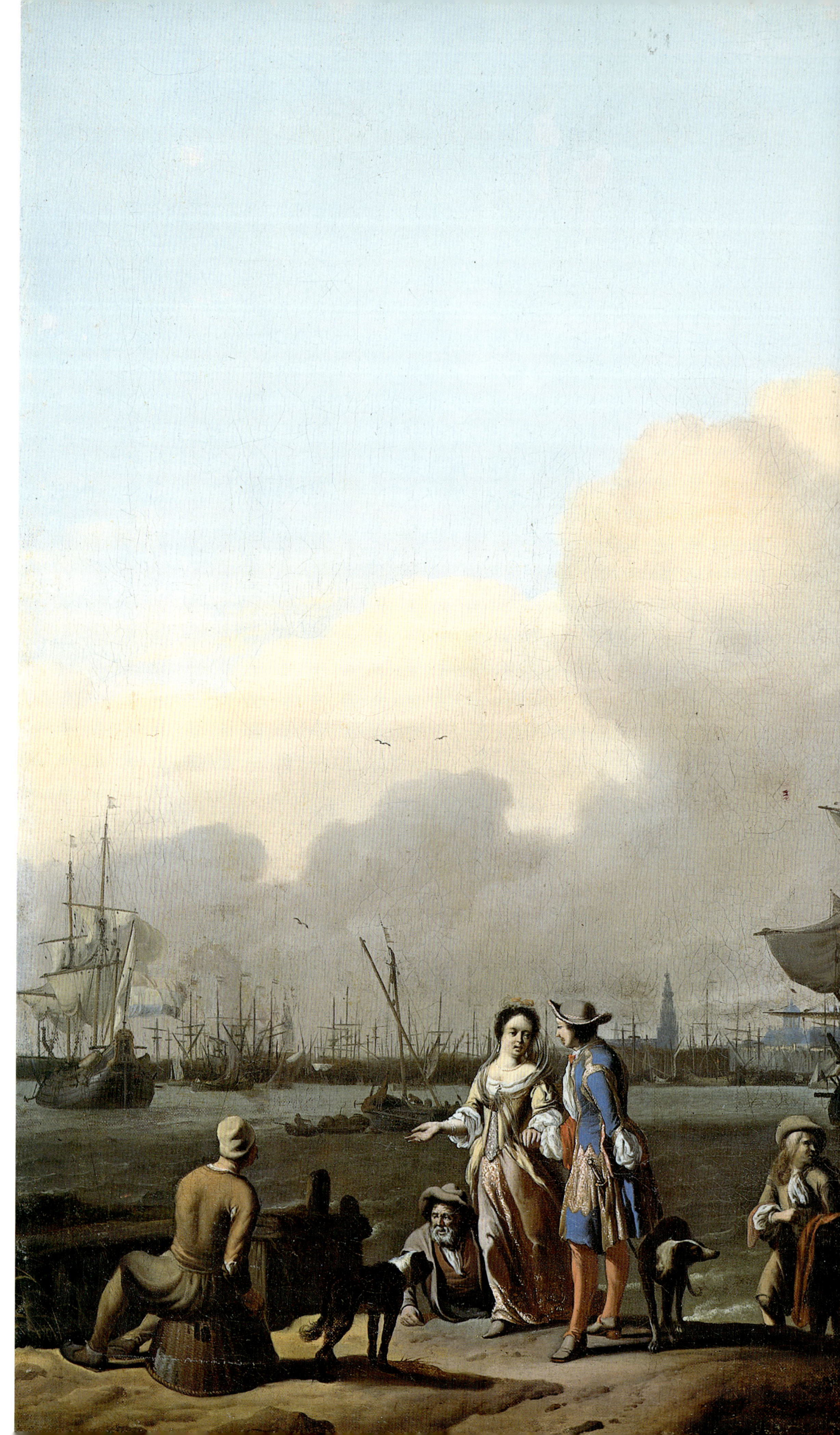

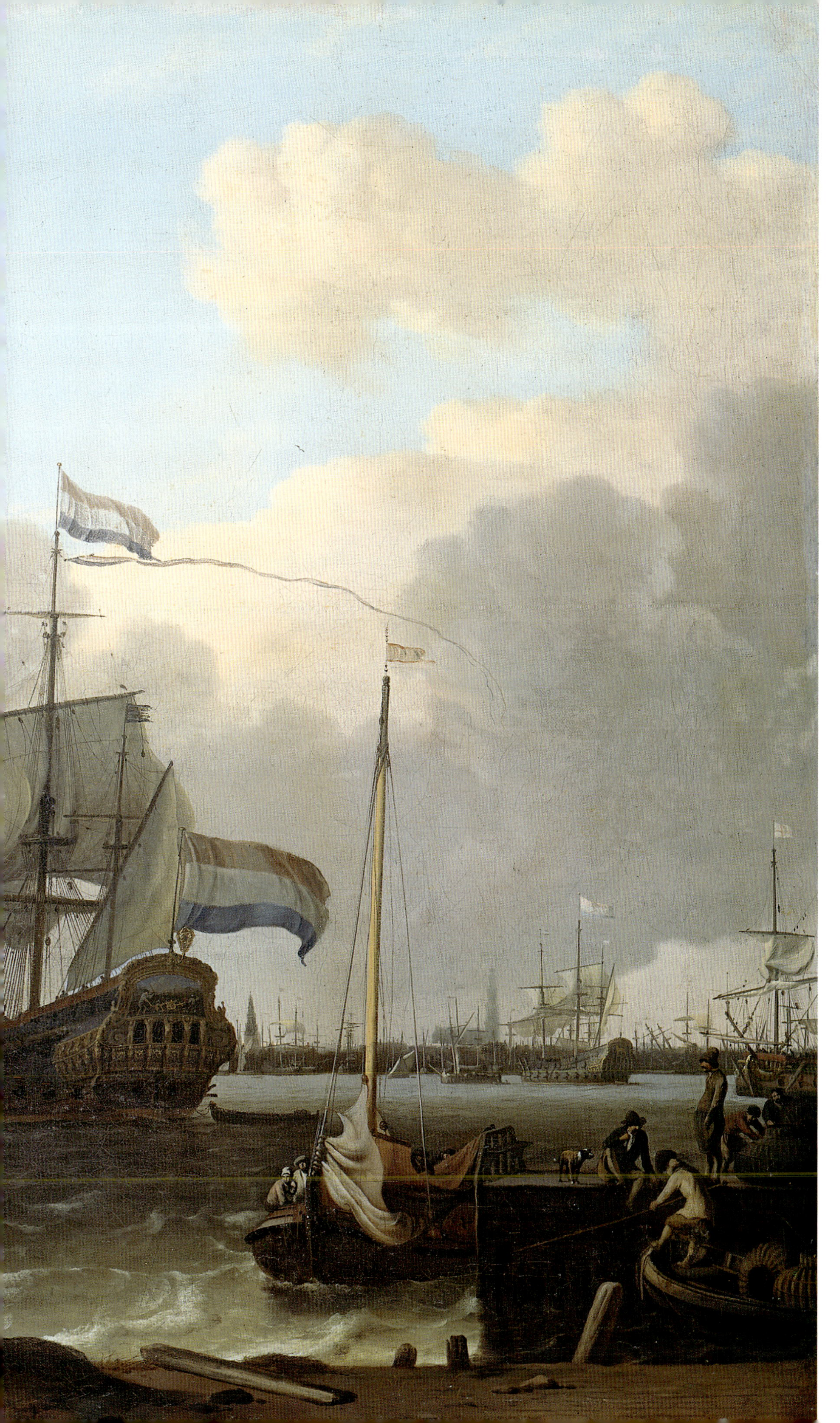

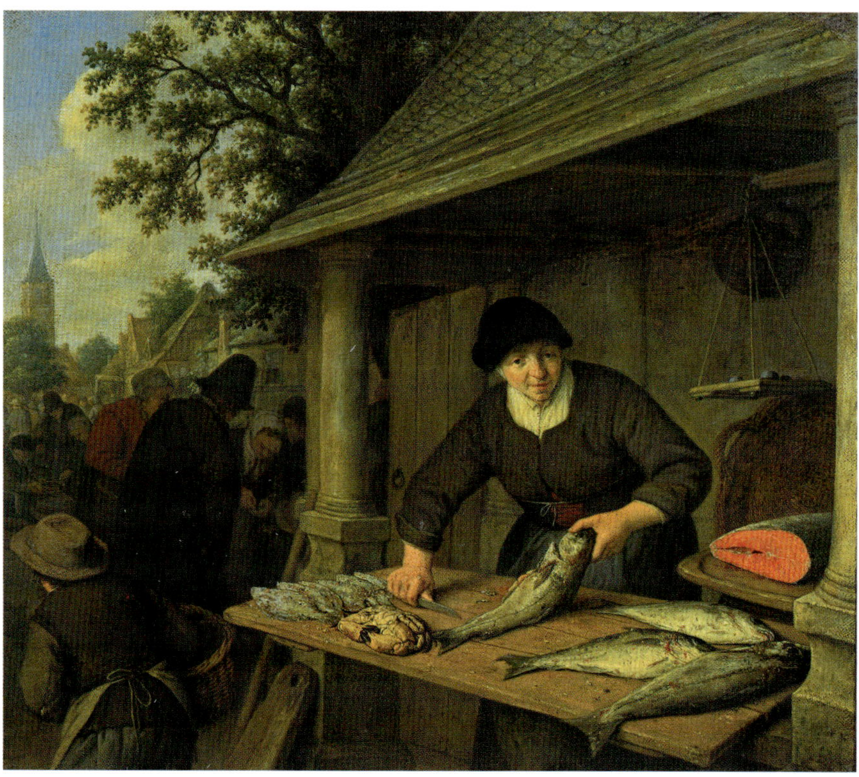

see reed baskets and part of an old-fashioned set of scales: two planks suspended by rope with a weight. It is a lively scene, not in the least because the fish seller looks out from the painting as if talking directly to the viewer. The cropping of the composition strengthens the impression that we are standing at the stall. Van Ostade modeled the stall on those in the fish market of his home town of Haarlem. Whereas fishwives—even in those days—are renowned for their loud, shrill shouting, this woman makes a quiet and friendly impression. The scene can in fact be interpreted as a tribute to honest work and an upright lifestyle: the fishwife carries out her tasks with great care and attention, and she is portrayed as an example of virtuous behavior. Van Ostade's work was extremely popular in his own time. Other Haarlem painters, Van Ostade's own pupil, Cornelis Dusart (1660–1704), among them, chose the same subjects for their paintings and imitated his work.

The commercial activities taking place in Van Ostade's painting are seen again at close range in *The Vegetable Market* (no. 34), painted around 1662 by Hendrick Martensz Sorgh (c. 1611–1670). Sorgh, whose father was a market-barge skipper in Rotterdam, was an influential

33 Adriaen van Ostade (1610–1685) · *The Fishwife* (1673) · Oil on canvas · 14½ × 15½ inches

34 Hendrick Martensz Sorgh (c. 1611–1670) · *The Vegetable Market* (c. 1662) · Oil on panel · 20 × 28 inches

specialist in this type of scene. In this composition the whole commercial enterprise of Dutch life is played out in the exchange of goods and money between the merchants and customers in the background, and men unloading vegetables from boats docked along the quay. Like Van Ostade's fishwife, a saleswoman in a straw hat in the foreground looks directly at the viewer, to whom she offers a muskmelon. She sits surrounded by baskets piled high with the produce she is selling. Like the still-life painters, Sorgh clearly enjoyed conveying the weight and specific textures of a variety of fruits and vegetables. Although the architecture depicted in market scenes can be imaginary, often it is a faithful rendering of a particular location—as with Van Ostade, who used elements of the Haarlem fish market. Here, the square, lined with sun-lit facades and the gabled roofs of houses, resembles the Grote Market in Sorgh's native Rotterdam.

Gabriel Metsu (1629–1667) was born in Leiden, the son of a Flemish painter who had settled in that city. He was probably taught by his father before becoming a pupil of Gerard Dou, the preeminent Leiden genre painter at that time. In *The Old Drinker* of 1657–1658 (no. 35, p. 64), Metsu's painting style reveals the influence of Dou, above all in the fine detail with which he shows the drinker's surroundings. The textures of the pewter jug, buttoned felt coat, fur trimmed cap, and German stoneware pitcher are all rendered masterfully. Even though the old man looks rather the worse for wear—he sags rather than sits on the chair as he peers through watery eyes—his smile and friendly face make his appearance sympathetic. There may be more to this scene

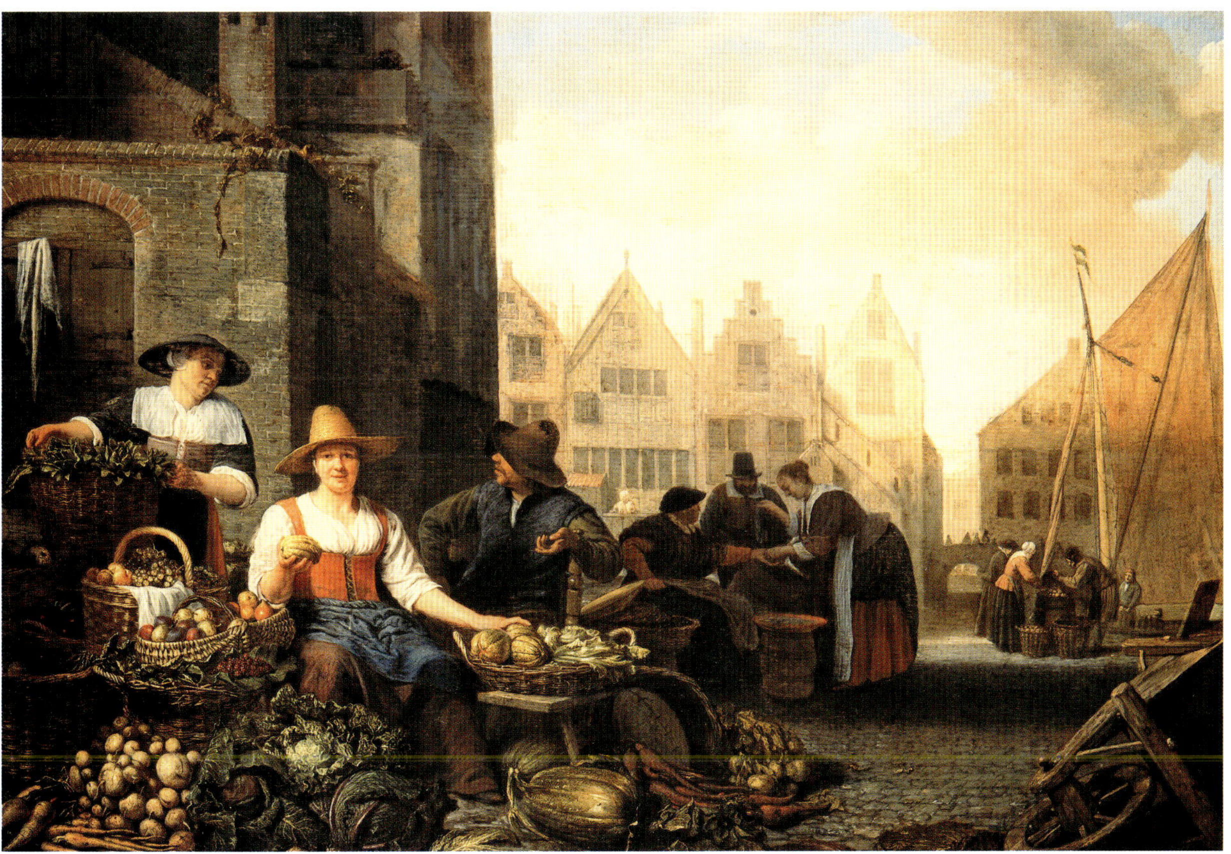

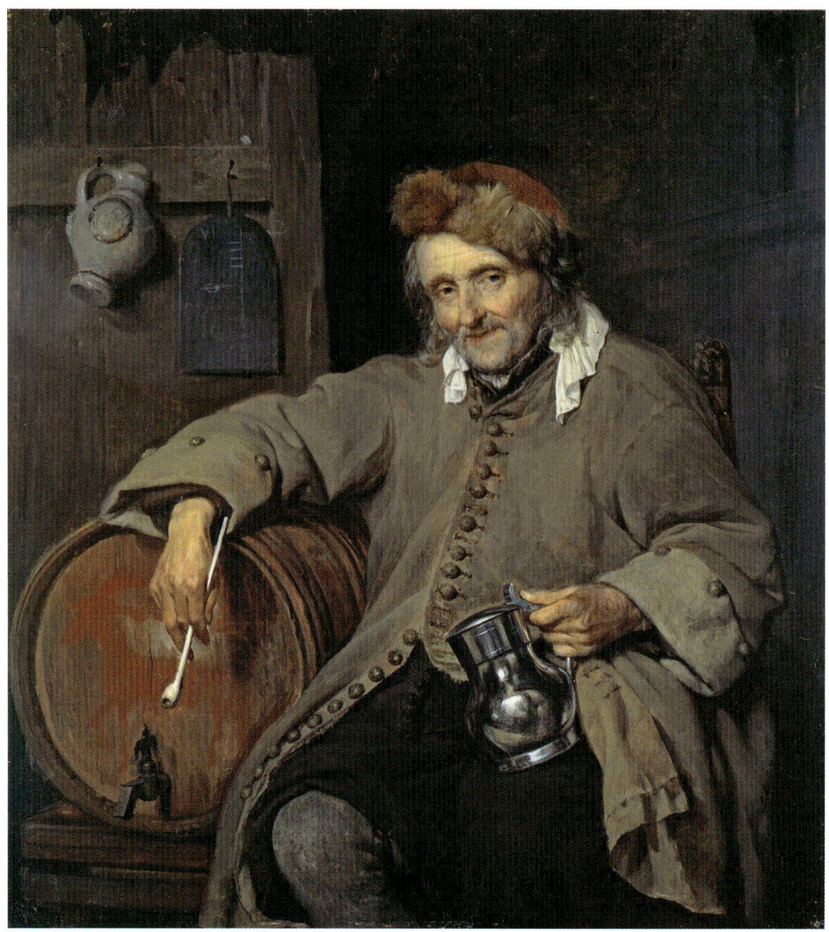

than meets the eye: perhaps the portrait of this old drinker can also be interpreted as a warning to avoid excessive indulgence in alcohol and tobacco, as many in the 17th century believed this accelerated the aging process. Beside the pitcher is a slate on which the number of beers consumed is chalked up. The sign of a red deer painted on the keg was the trademark of the Amsterdam brewery 't Roo Hart (Red Deer). Metsu lived on the Prinsengracht in Amsterdam near this very brewery when he painted this work, and the deer is a subtle aside in which the painter quietly advertised his neighbor's business.

The "physician" in Jan Steen's painting *The Quack* (no. 36) is engaged in advertising as well, but far less discreetly. Steen shows an audience gathered in a village square around a stage, where a man cries out in pain as the quack holds up the stone he has supposedly cut from his patient's head. In the 17th century quack doctors convinced people that stones blocking the

35 Gabriel Metsu (1629–1667) · *The Old Drinker* (c. 1657–1658) · Oil on panel · 8¾ × 7¾ inches

36 Jan Steen (1626–1679) · *The Quack* (c. 1650–1660) · Oil on panel · 14¾ × 20½ inches

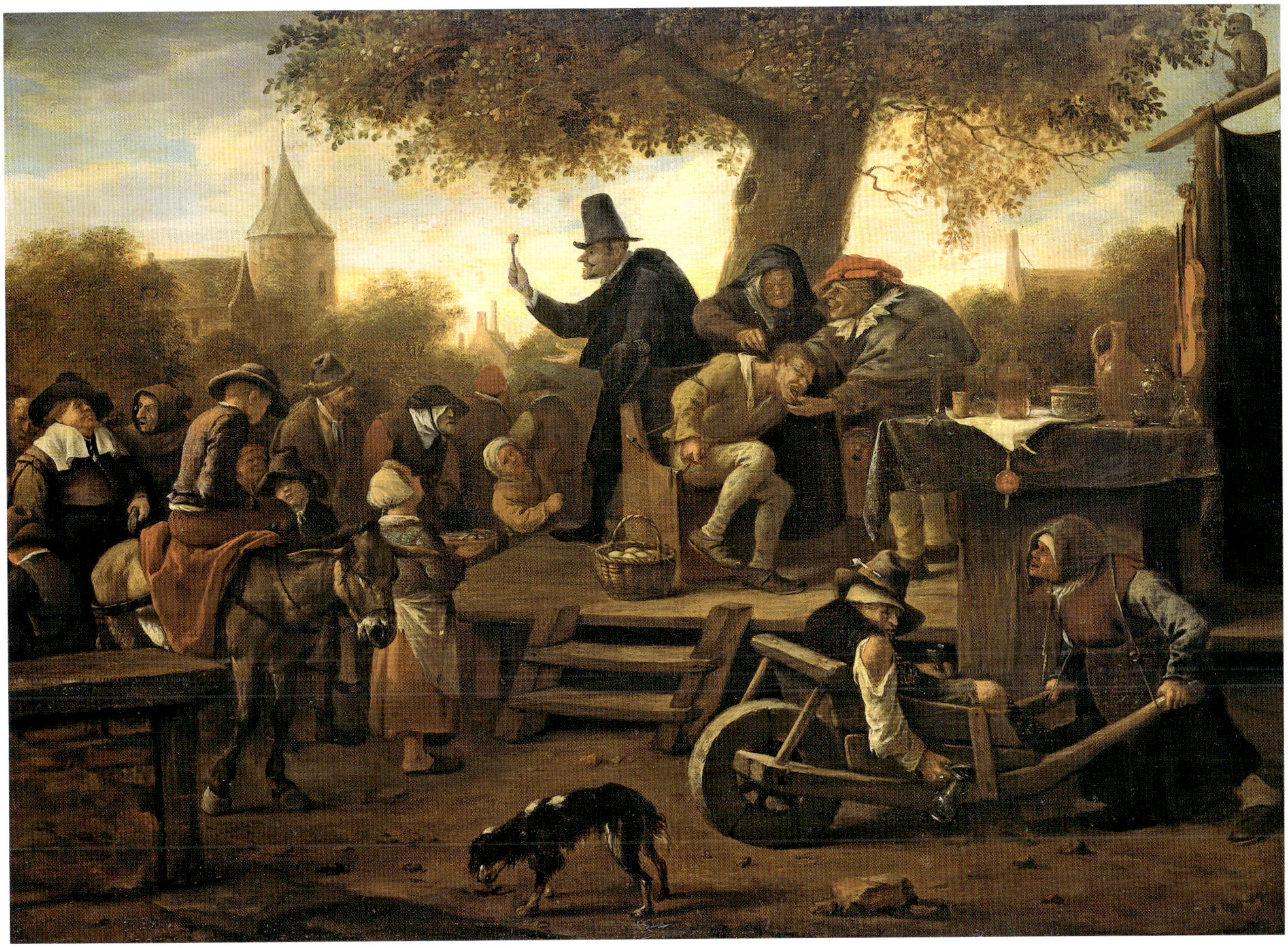

circulation of blood in the head could cause severe headaches. They often hired an actor to serve in a fake operation whereby the stone was removed, after which the patient's pain was miraculously cured by drinking the quack's special elixir. The quack offered the elixir for sale to the public but never stayed around long enough to learn whether his medicine had the desired effect. In Steen's painting the elixirs are seen on the table to the right. A monkey, symbol of foolishness, sits close by on the high wooden structure behind the table. The drunken peasant being trundled away in a wheelbarrow by his wife adds to Steen's satire on the dim-witted behavior of country bumpkins.

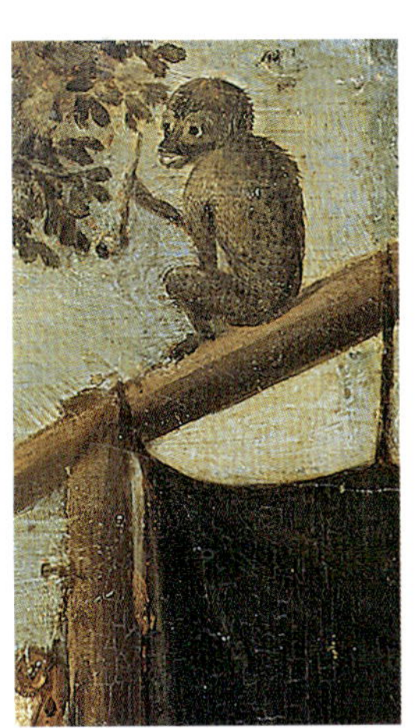

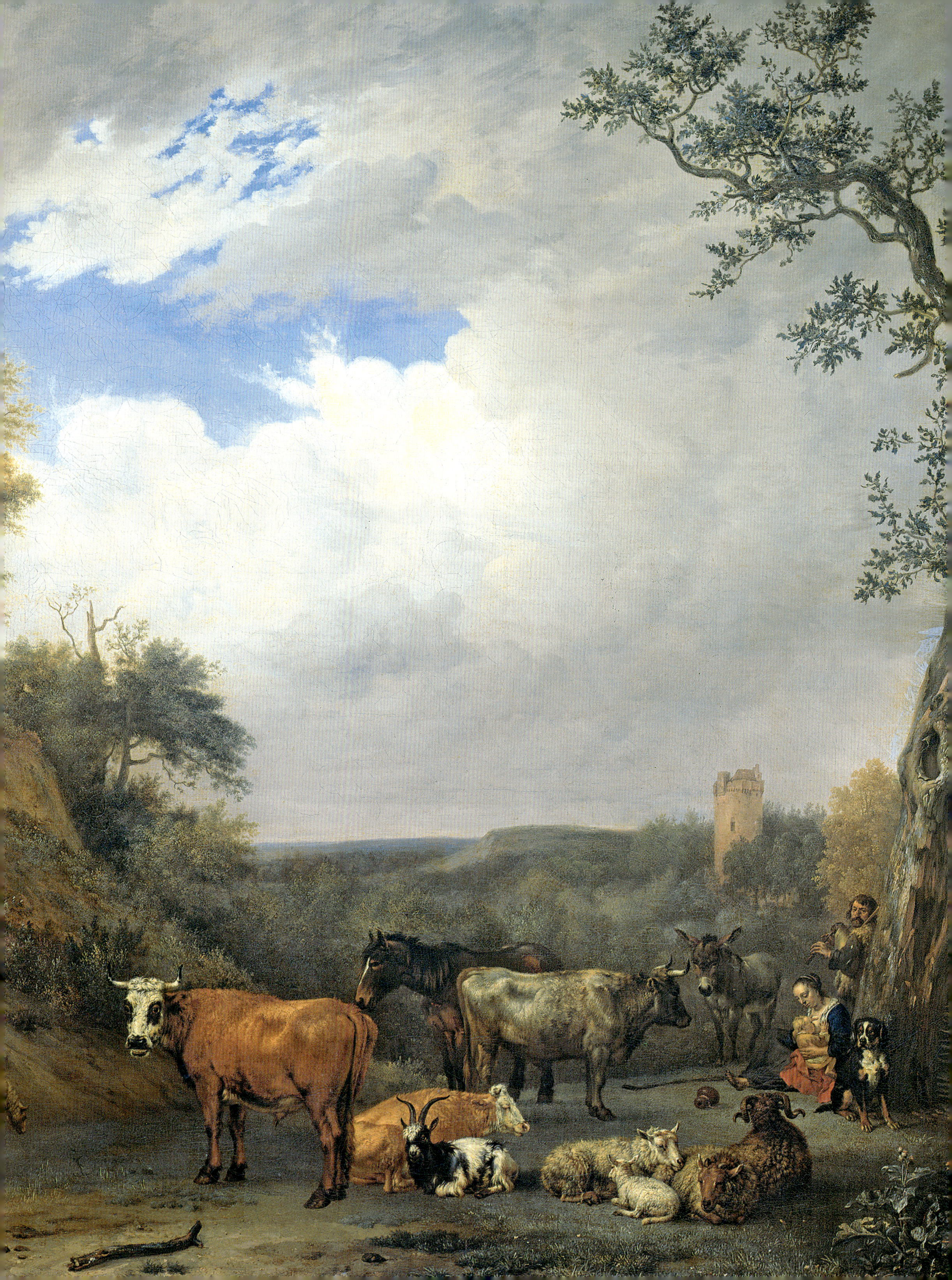

# 4
# THE COUNTRYSIDE

DUTCH PAINTERS OF THE 17TH CENTURY "DISCOVERED" for the first time their own surroundings: the vast panoramas of the flat Dutch countryside, crisscrossed by rivers. Before this time they had responded to the landscape mainly as a source of inspiration for imaginary backgrounds. Now their scenes became more recognizable and realistic, dominated by water and sky or, in the winter, by large expanses of ice filled with skaters. The artists gradually opted for a lower horizon and less contrast between the foreground and background.

Concurrently a number of Dutch artists who had traveled to Italy chose to depict the idealized landscape of Italy rather than their native surroundings. The trend began in the 1620s and intensified between 1640 and 1675. These painters, known as the Dutch Italianates or Italianate painters, devoted themselves to the portrayal of the sun-infused Italian landscape, with its mountains and ruins from classical antiquity, together with travelers, shepherds, or a few cows. Many of the artists came from Utrecht, a largely Catholic city which traditionally maintained strong ties with Rome.

The artistic attractions of the Eternal City drew painters from northern Europe who tried to find work there. Dutch and Flemish artists living in Rome founded a club known as the Bent. It not only served as a meeting place but also furthered the interests of its members, the Bentvueghels ("birds of a feather"). Various groups were represented in the Bent, including painters, sculptors, engravers, and goldsmiths, and amateur artists were also encouraged to join. The best known of the Bentvueghels were Jan Asselijn and Jan Both, both of whom specialized in Italianate landscape subjects. The Italianate painters influenced the work of Dutch colleagues who never visited Italy, such as Paulus Potter, Aelbert Cuyp, Frans Hals, and Rembrandt. These artists applied the warm Mediterranean light they saw in the landscapes of the Italianate painters to their own idealized views of the Dutch countryside.

From 1641, the Amsterdam artist Aert van der Neer (1603/04–1677) painted a number of Dutch winter landscapes. They often feature a low horizon and a number of figures depicted in a palette confined to earthy tints of ochre, brownish yellow, and gray, with accents in light blue and brilliant white highlights indicating thin layers of snow. In *River View in the Winter* (no. 37, below and pp. 70–71), the outskirts of the city taper off along the left bank, while the right opens to the countryside and, in the distance, a village. The effect of spatial depth is maximized by groups of figures receding along the diagonal line formed by the frozen river, which runs from the lower left of the canvas all the way to the horizon on the right. A number of fashionably dressed players of *kolf* (a cross between hockey and golf) have been given a prominent place in the foreground, but the activities of various other figures farther away draw the viewer into the composition. Van der Neer was a master in the use of such painterly devices as creating texture by scratching into the still-wet paint and pushing up sparkling ridges of paint to suggest the reflection of sunlight on snow or ice. All this contributed to Van der Neer's success in capturing the poetic beauty of the Dutch countryside.

It was a tradition among Dutch artists to set their ice scenes just outside the walls of a town. The Italianate painter Willem Schellinks (1627?–1678) kept to this practice in *City Wall in the Winter* (no. 38), painted around 1650, but his imposing town walls are clearly not Dutch, and the Dutch skaters and *kolf* players have been replaced by Italian peasants. Schellinks did not travel to Italy until the 1660s, when he served as a tutor for the son of an Amsterdam merchant on the Grand Tour, escorting him between 1661 and 1665 to France, England, Malta, and Germany as well as to Italy. But Schellinks had already found a source of inspiration in the Italianate paintings of the slightly older Jan Asselijn, from whom he borrowed architectural motifs and various details. The ruins of a stone arched bridge in the background here is roughly based on the famous

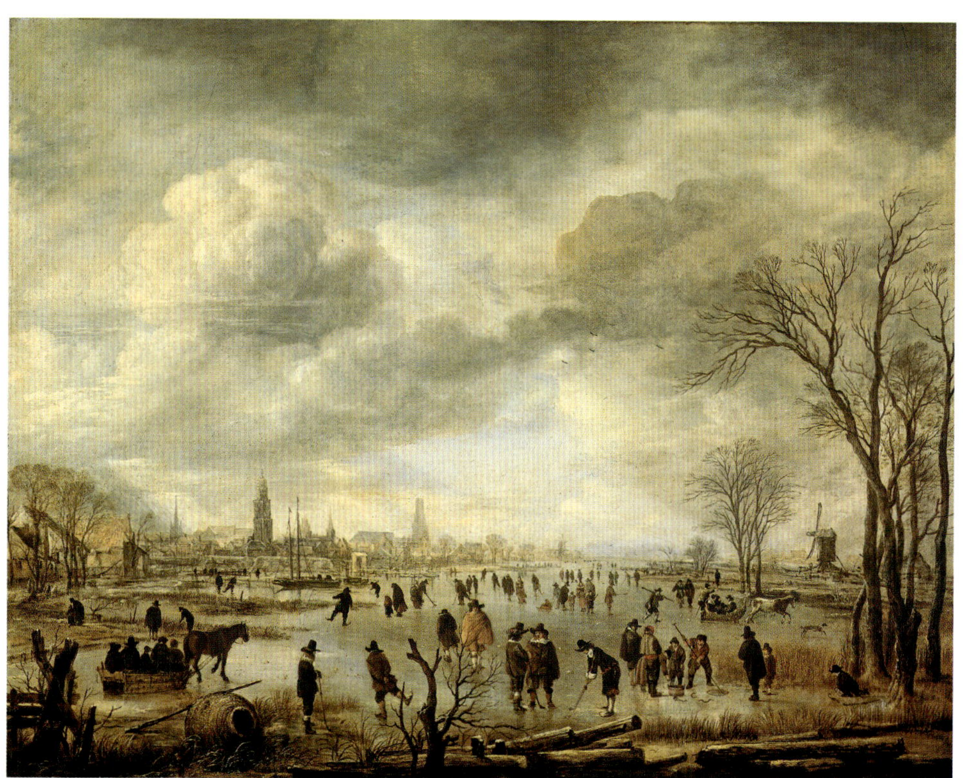

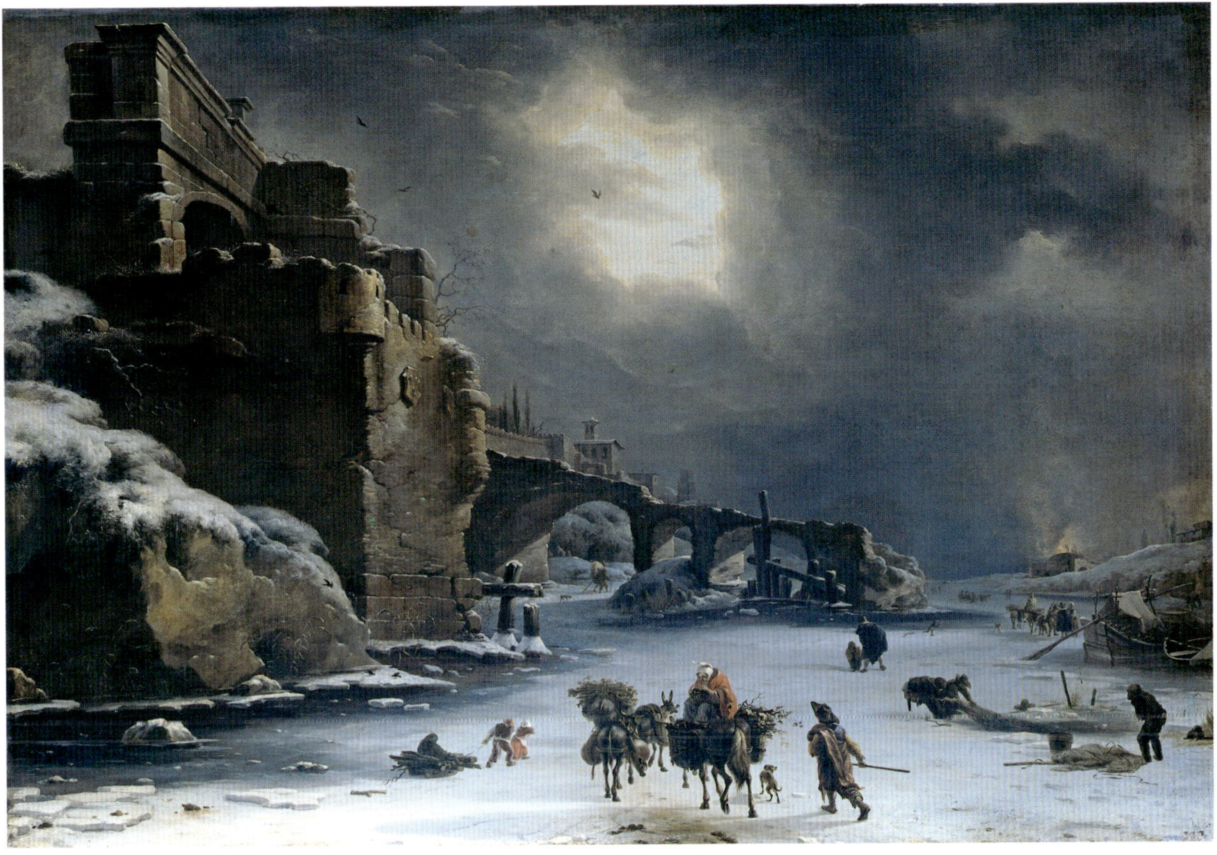

Roman Ponte Rotto, the ruin of the ancient Pons Aemilius. Schellinks's somewhat theatrical combination of a dark, cloudy sky with a pale, wintry sun can also be seen in the Italianate winter scenes of Asselijn and Nicolaes Berchem.

Jan van Goyen (1596–1656) was one of the most productive painters of the 17th century. His extant oeuvre comprises some twelve hundred paintings and eight hundred drawings, of which many were made on trips through the Netherlands and Germany. Van Goyen's rapid and efficient painting technique made this extraordinary productivity possible. His large *View of a Town on a River* of 1645 (no. 39, pp. 70–71) has only a few color accents; around 1627 he had replaced the variety of colors seen in his early works with monochrome tones. The limited color scheme functions to unify the composition. The figures, painted with delicate but rapid brushwork, are subordinated to the evocation of the atmosphere of the Dutch river landscape. Because he employed only a few colors, the artist could paint many areas wet-in-wet, thereby finishing the

37 Aert van der Neer (1603/04–1677) · *River View in the Winter* (c. 1655–1660) · Oil on canvas · 25¼ × 31 inches (overleaf)

38 Willem Schellinks (1627?–1678) · *City Wall in the Winter* (c. 1650) · Oil on canvas · 29¼ × 41¼ inches

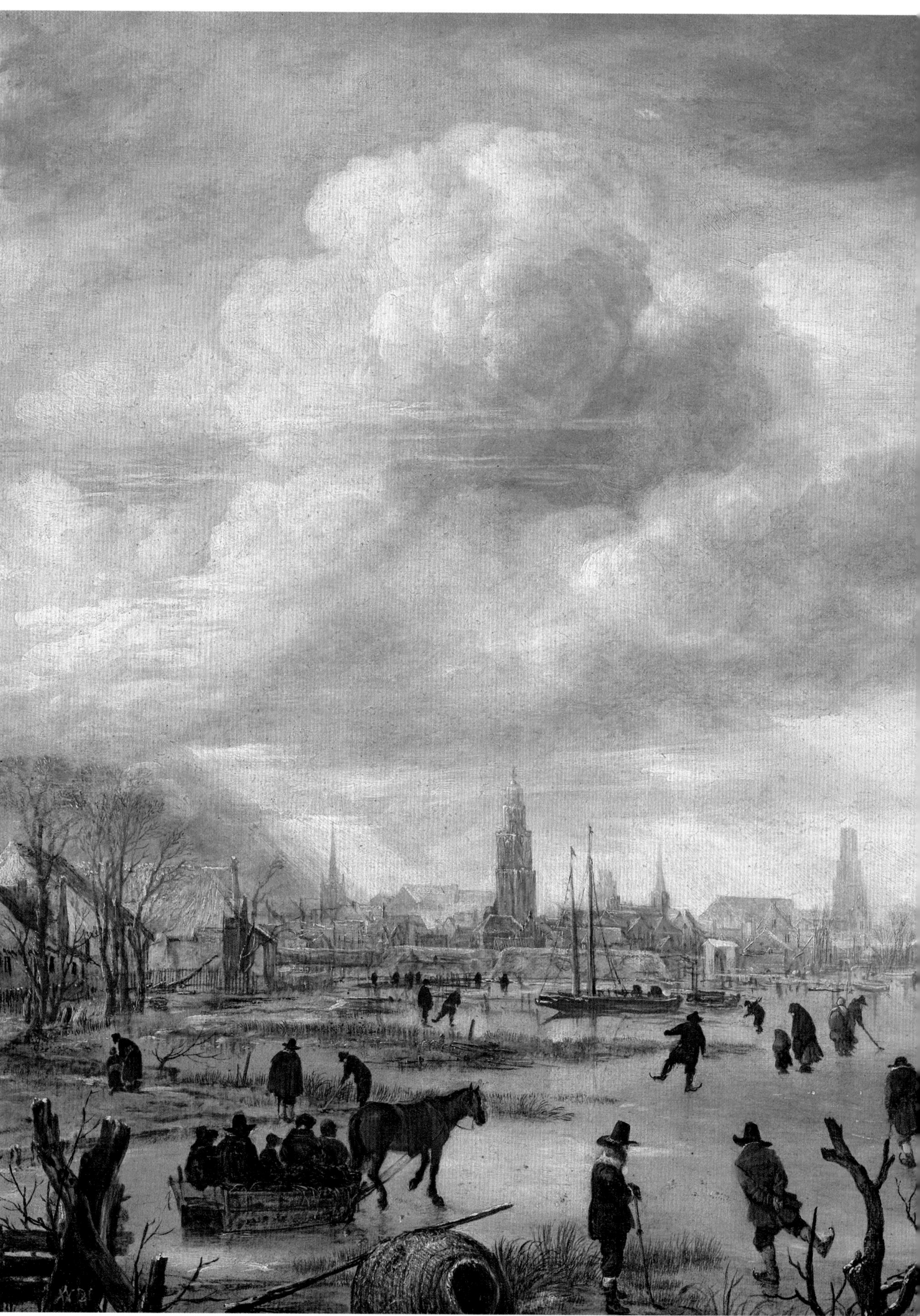

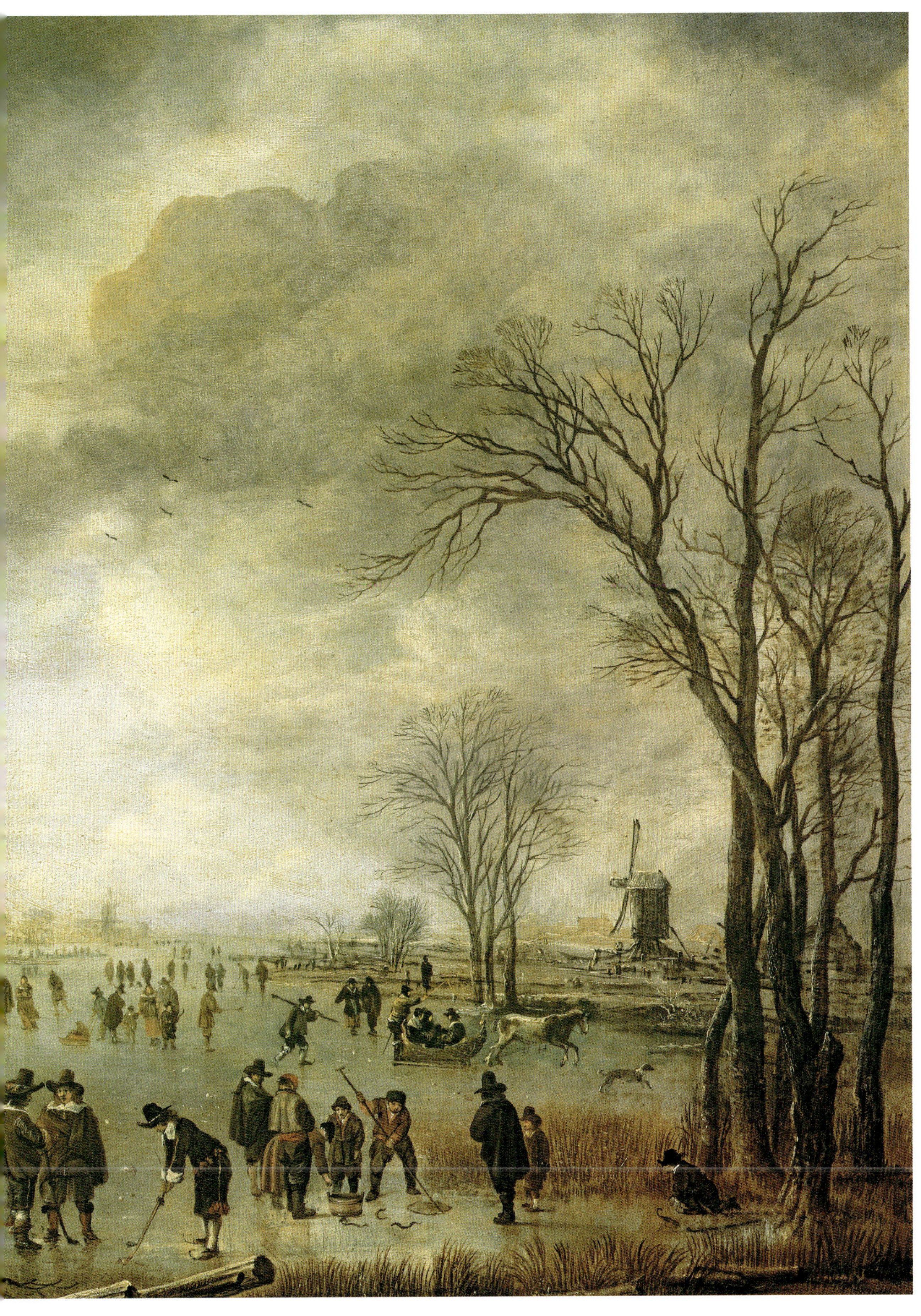

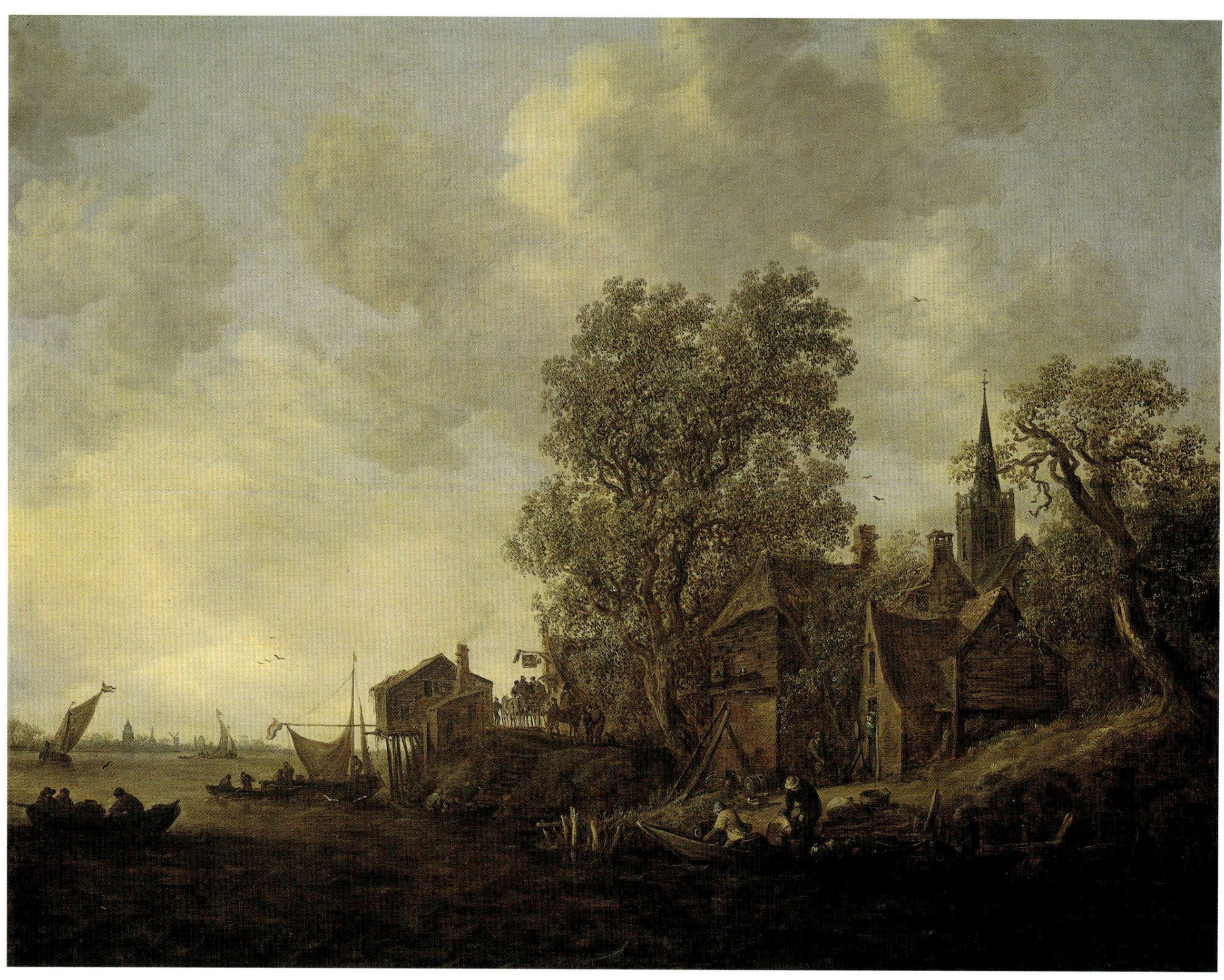

paintings much faster. The most frequently used pigments, such as ochres and other earth colors, were cheap, so the cost of materials was reduced as well. Together with Salomon van Ruysdael (c. 1600/1603–1670), Jan van Goyen is considered a founder of classic Dutch landscape painting. The monochromatic style they developed during the 1630s was imitated by many other painters.

In Leiden, where he lived and worked, Van Goyen began to pursue another source of income around 1625 by speculating in houses and gardens. He expanded into trading in tulip bulbs and other investments when he moved to The Hague in 1631/32. These business ventures ultimately proved unsuccessful, burdening his family with serious financial difficulties. Van Goyen's

39 Jan van Goyen (1596–1656) · *View of a Town on a River* (1645) · Oil on canvas · 51½ × 65¼ inches

40 Rembrandt van Rijn (1606–1669) · *Landscape with Three Gabled Cottages* (1650) · Etching and drypoint · 6¼ × 8 inches

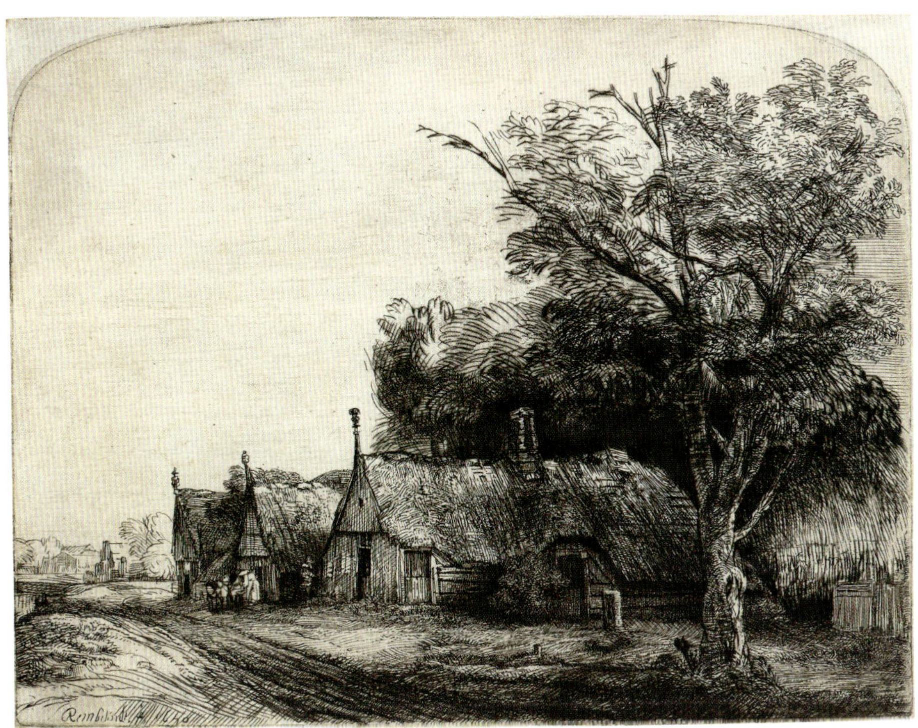

daughter Margaretha married Jan Steen, who was also from Leiden and studied with Van Goyen in The Hague.

*Landscape with Three Gabled Cottages* of 1650 (no. 40) is based on a drawing (now at the Kupferstichkabinett of the Staatliche Museen, Berlin) Rembrandt made, probably on the spot, of some cottages on the road called Schinkelweg, looking toward the hamlet known as the Overtoom, a few kilometers southwest of Amsterdam. The print is characterized by an extraordinarily subtle play of light and atmosphere: distant buildings are bathed in sunlight while the foreground remains partially shadowed. In the ten years after the death in 1642 of his first wife, Saskia (see p. 114), Rembrandt painted less and on smaller canvases. He focused instead on etching and drawing, and most of his landscape etchings date from this period. He employed a spontaneous drawing technique in these works and often appears to have taken prepared etching plates on his trips into the countryside to sketch directly from nature. This was a major departure from the usual practice of 17th-century artists. Like paintings, etchings were generally produced in the studio, based on preliminary sketches made on location. Although the latter working method was used for the landscape discussed here, the remarkable accuracy and realism of the representation is testimony to Rembrandt's unrivalled virtuosity as an etcher.

The name Meindert Hobbema (1638–1709) is inextricably linked to the subject of the watermill, which appears in more than thirty of his paintings. In some cases Hobbema made multiple views of the same subject, such as the structure seen in *A Watermill* (no. 41, p. 74), which recurs in a second painting in the Rijksmuseum. Hobbema saw the mill on his travels and recorded it in drawings from several different vantage points. His specific interest in watermills and his habit of collecting material for his paintings in the form of drawings made on his travels came from his master Jacob van Ruisdael. As far back as 1653, while traveling to Bentheim near the German border, Ruisdael had become convinced of the painterly possibilities of the motif, making several drawings of the watermills in the area around Denekamp, in the province of Gelderland. In the early 1660s Ruisdael again undertook a study trip, this time with his pupil Hobbema, which took them to Gelderland and Twente, where they both drew many watermills similar to this one. Back in Amsterdam, the sheets they had filled with watermill drawings could be used in the preparation of their paintings. The manner in which the two painters did so was different, and Hobbema's landscapes, being lighter in color and more lively, are not nearly as dramatic as those of Ruisdael. The present work was done around 1666, when Hobbema was at the peak of his career.

Landscapes with waterfalls, torrents, and rushing streams form the largest category in the extant oeuvre of Jacob van Ruisdael (1628/29–1682), with no less than 150 paintings of the subject. The waterfalls cascading over huge boulders and dead trees in northern landscapes with rugged mountains convince the viewer that the paintings are based on intense, firsthand study of the elements. In reality, Ruisdael never laid eyes on a waterfall in a mountainous northern landscape. He derived his *Rocky Landscape* (no. 42), and other paintings like it, from works by the Alkmaar artist Allart van Everdingen (1621–1675). Van Everdingen had introduced and popularized northern landscapes in the Netherlands following a trip in 1644 to the southeastern coast of Norway and the area around Göteborg in Sweden. On his return he settled in Haarlem with a stock of Scandinavian themes, which he incorporated into his paintings and graphic works from 1646

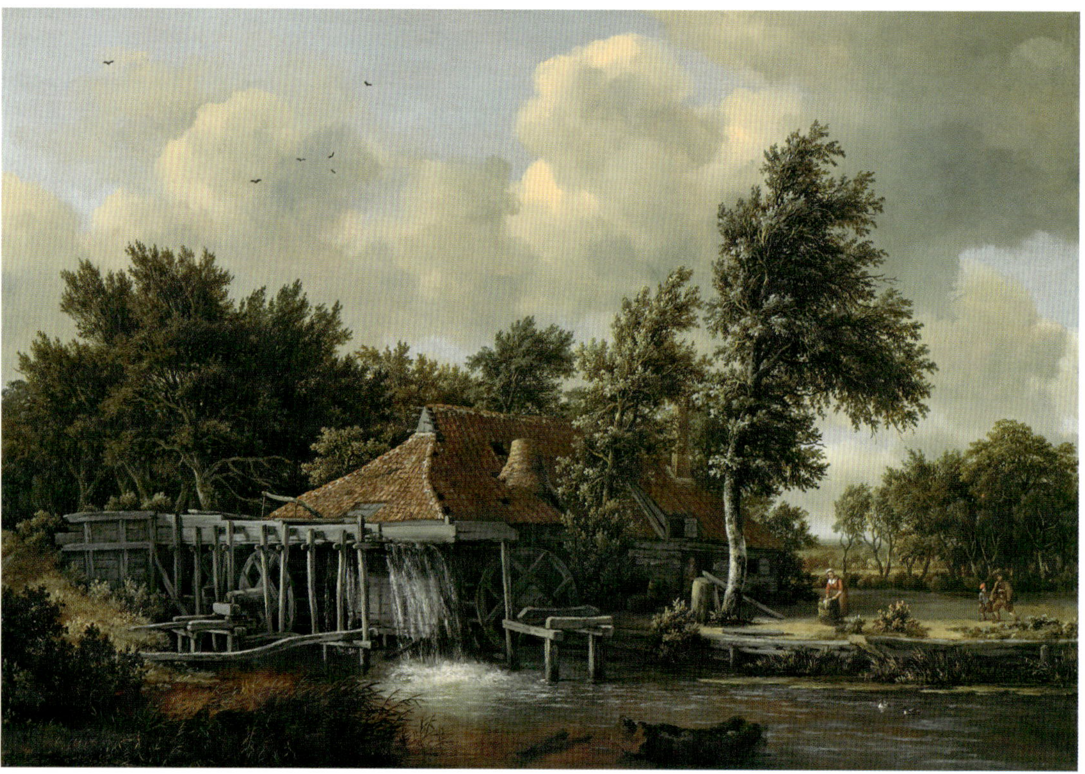

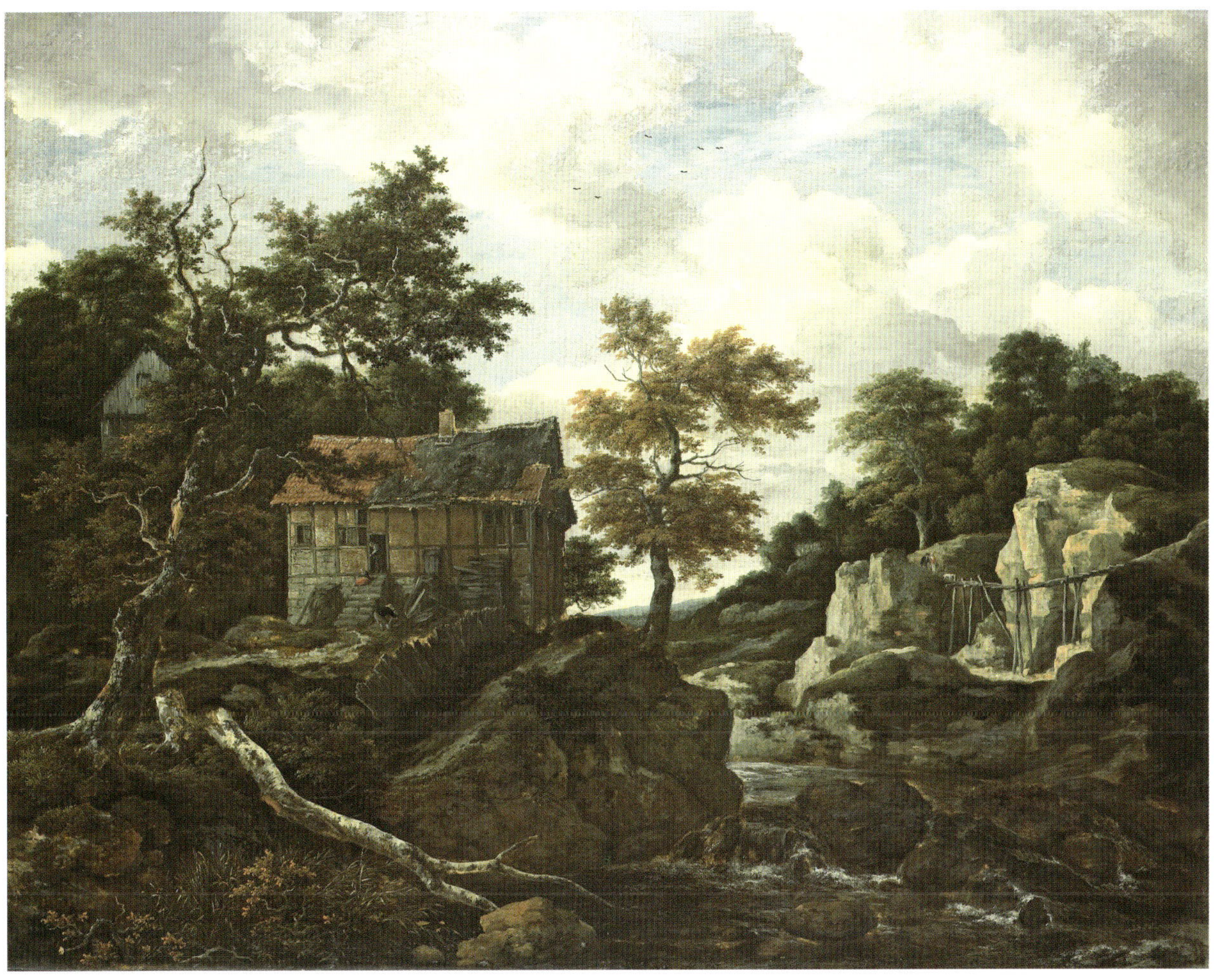

onward, about the time the young Ruisdael appeared on the scene in Haarlem as a fully accomplished artist. Ruisdael began to use Van Everdingen's cascading waterfalls in northern scenery in paintings datable to the late 1650s and early 1660s. *Rocky Landscape* is one of the earliest works in which Ruisdael closely followed Van Everdingen's example, employing an abundance of rocky clefts and fallen trees, painted in subtle tones of brown, red, gray, and green.

Around 1635 Jan Asselijn (before 1610–1652) traveled to Rome, where he drew inspiration from the warm southern light and ancient buildings and ruins. Until 1643/44 he lived in Rome, where he joined the Dutch artists' group the Bentvueghels. Traveling back to his native country through France, Asselijn married in Lyons and spent some time in Paris before settling in

41 Meindert Hobbema (1638–1709) · *A Watermill* (c. 1666) · Oil on panel · 24½ × 33¾ inches

42 Jacob van Ruisdael (1628/29–1682) · *Rocky Landscape* (c. 1655–1660) · Oil on canvas · 42¾ × 53¼ inches

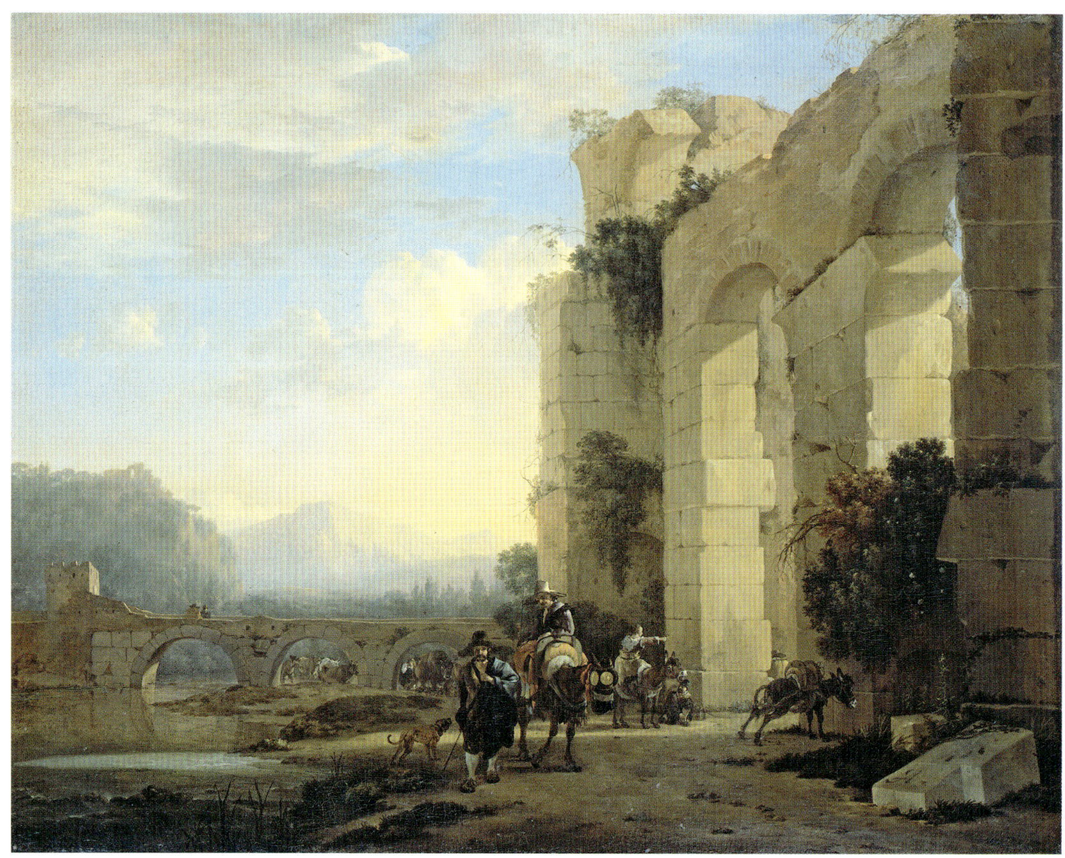

Amsterdam around 1645. There he became a highly influential Italianate landscape painter and produced his best work, on the basis of drawings he had made, often years before, in Italy. This holds true for *Donkey Drivers beside a Ruin in Italy,* painted around 1650 (no. 43). He must have sketched the picturesque old stone bridge in the background in Tivoli, near Rome. The arch too is based on his sketch (now in the Pierpont Morgan Library, New York) of the aqueduct at Frascati. In the painting, the arch has assumed monumental proportions due to the low viewpoint, dramatic lighting, and subdued colors of this extraordinary composition.

Nicolaes Berchem (1620–1683), the son and pupil of the still-life painter Pieter Claesz (who came from the village of Berchem, near Antwerp), is considered one of the most significant representatives of the second generation of Dutch Italianate painters. In *Italian Landscape* of about 1655–1665 (no. 44), the Haarlem painter presents an unmistakably Italian view painted in a light, clear palette that does full justice to the effect of the Mediterranean sunlight. Berchem

43 Jan Asselijn (before 1610–1652) · *Donkey Drivers beside a Ruin in Italy* (c. 1650) · Oil on canvas · 26¼ × 32¼ inches

44 Nicolaes Berchem (1620–1683) · *Italian Landscape* (c. 1655–1665) · Oil on canvas · 25½ × 32 inches

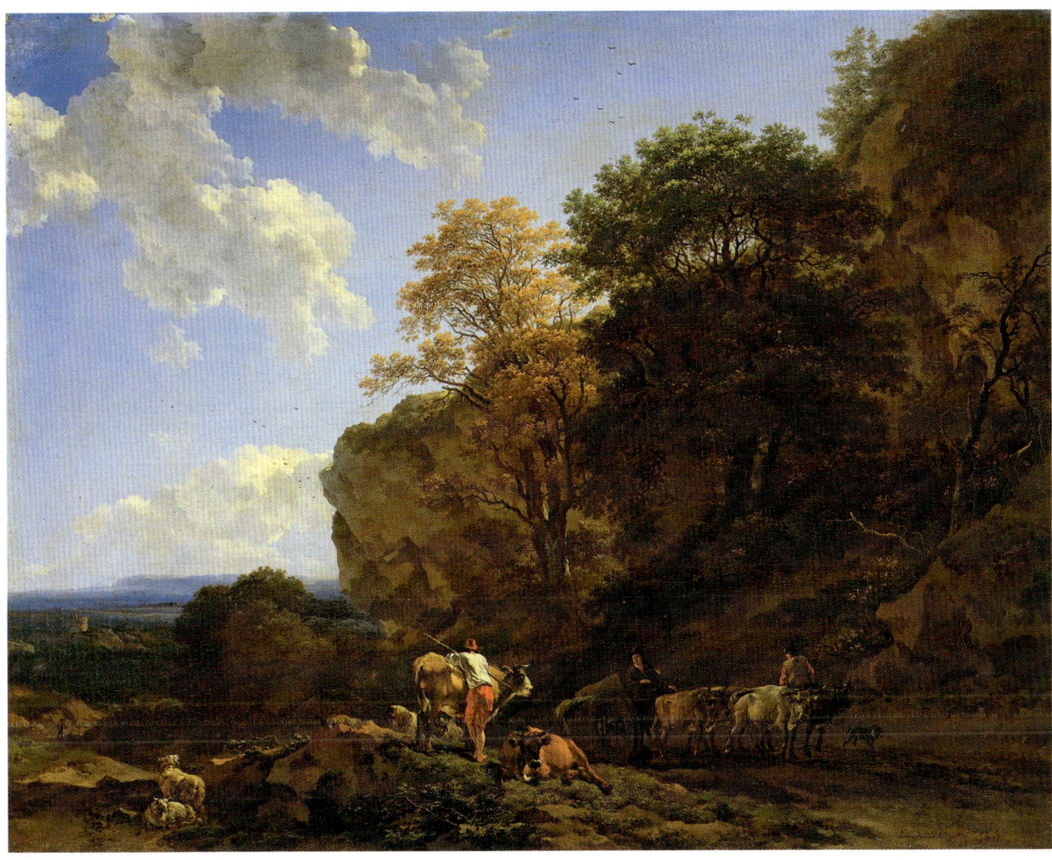

was a versatile master capable of quickly altering his style. His landscapes painted before 1653 display a greater similarity to the northern views of Jacob van Ruisdael, Berchem's friend, colleague, and fellow townsman, with whom the artist traveled to the German border country. After that time his style alters so suddenly that scholars suppose he must have traveled to Italy some time between 1653 and 1655. Berchem's later works are filled with warm sunlight and enlivened by herdsmen and travelers. They rarely depict a specific topography, but (as with the work of Jan Asselijn) rather are imaginative variations on a Mediterranean theme or combinations of various motifs borrowed from drawings he had presumably made in Italy.

Berchem was extremely productive: his oeuvre consists of more than six hundred paintings, five hundred drawings, and fifty etchings. His works were very popular, won praise from contemporaries, and fetched high prices. According to the artists' biographer Arnold Houbraken, "everything he made was usually sold before he'd finished it." Berchem collaborated with several colleagues, adding figures to paintings by Meindert Hobbema and Willem Schellinks, among others. He also had a profound influence on the work of his pupils, including Karel Dujardin and Pieter de Hooch.

Karel Dujardin (1626–1678) also won Houbraken's praise for many qualities, including his versatility. He was known not only for his Italianate landscapes and genre pieces but also for his portraits and a score of etchings. We may assume the artist was conscious of his status, as he boldly signed his name in capital letters (one of the first times Dujardin signed his work in

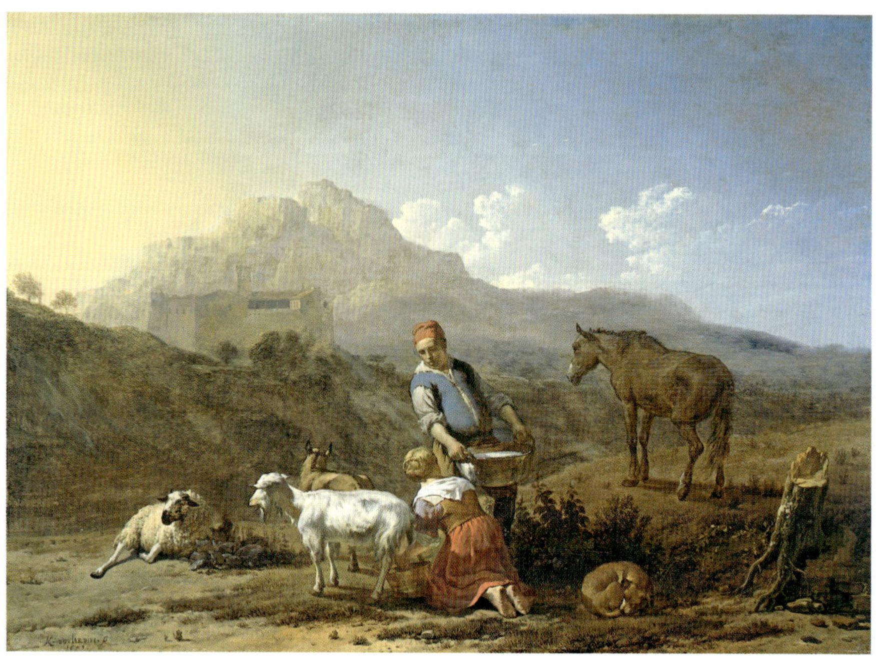

this manner) beside the date of 1652 in the lower left of *Italian Landscape with a Girl Milking a Goat* (no. 45). Dujardin was a master in the art of the Dutch *fijnschilders* (fine painters), a precisionist style introduced by Rembrandt's Leiden pupil Gerard Dou. From around the 1650s the exquisitely detailed and minutely executed paintings of the *fijnschilders* received a wide following in Amsterdam, where Dujardin is thought to have studied. Here, Dujardin's technical skill is found first and foremost in the detailed and finely outlined animals in the foreground, where two peasants are seen at work. A vast panorama of the Italian countryside with architecture and mountains opens up behind them. The milkmaid, her braids wrapped around her head, milks a beautifully painted white goat, while she talks with a man carrying a filled tub. The subtle gradations of color, from the dark tones in the foreground, enlivened by the man's bright blue vest and red hat and the milkmaid's vivid red skirt, to the pale silvery beige hues of the buildings and mountains in the background, are characteristic of the artist.

Paulus Potter (1625–1654) was among those artists who never visited Italy, but he applied the Mediterranean light he saw in the landscapes of the Dutch Italianate painters to his own idealized views of the northern European countryside. Especially from the mid-1640s, his paintings reflect the influence of artists such as Jan Both, whose use of natural light and atmospheric effects

45 Karel Dujardin (1626–1678) · *Italian Landscape with a Girl Milking a Goat* (1652) · Oil on panel · 14½ × 19¾ inches

46 Paulus Potter (1625–1654) · *Hilly Landscape with Herders and Animals* (1651) · Oil on canvas · 32 × 38½ inches

he greatly admired. Contrary to most of Potter's landscapes, his *Hilly Landscape with Herders and Animals* of 1651 (no. 46) does not recall so much the flat Dutch terrain, but the rolling German border area along the Rhine River. As is evident from this pastoral scene, Potter was above all a specialist in the portrayal of animals. In this work each and every creature is seen as an individual and characterized in great detail—sometimes quite literally to the bone. The atmosphere of a quiet, lazy summer afternoon has been beautifully captured.

Potter was born in Enkhuizen, son of the painter Pieter Potter (1597/1601–1653). His father, who not only made landscapes but also still lifes and history pieces, taught him the essentials of painting. He quickly grew into a respected specialist. His innovative and uncommonly realistic animal portraits found a great many imitators among contemporaries and in later centuries.

Landscapes were also depicted on ceramic pieces. Although most Dutch faience was decorated with motifs of Chinese inspiration until around 1680, the Rijksmuseum has a number of exceptional pieces painted with European landscapes. The following two examples are all the more exceptional because they are dated.

On the faience dish with a winter landscape dated 1650 (no. 47, p. 80), we see a realistic depiction of winter in the Dutch countryside. A frozen canal leads from the foreground into the far distance, and on either side several farmhouses stand among tall, finely branched trees.

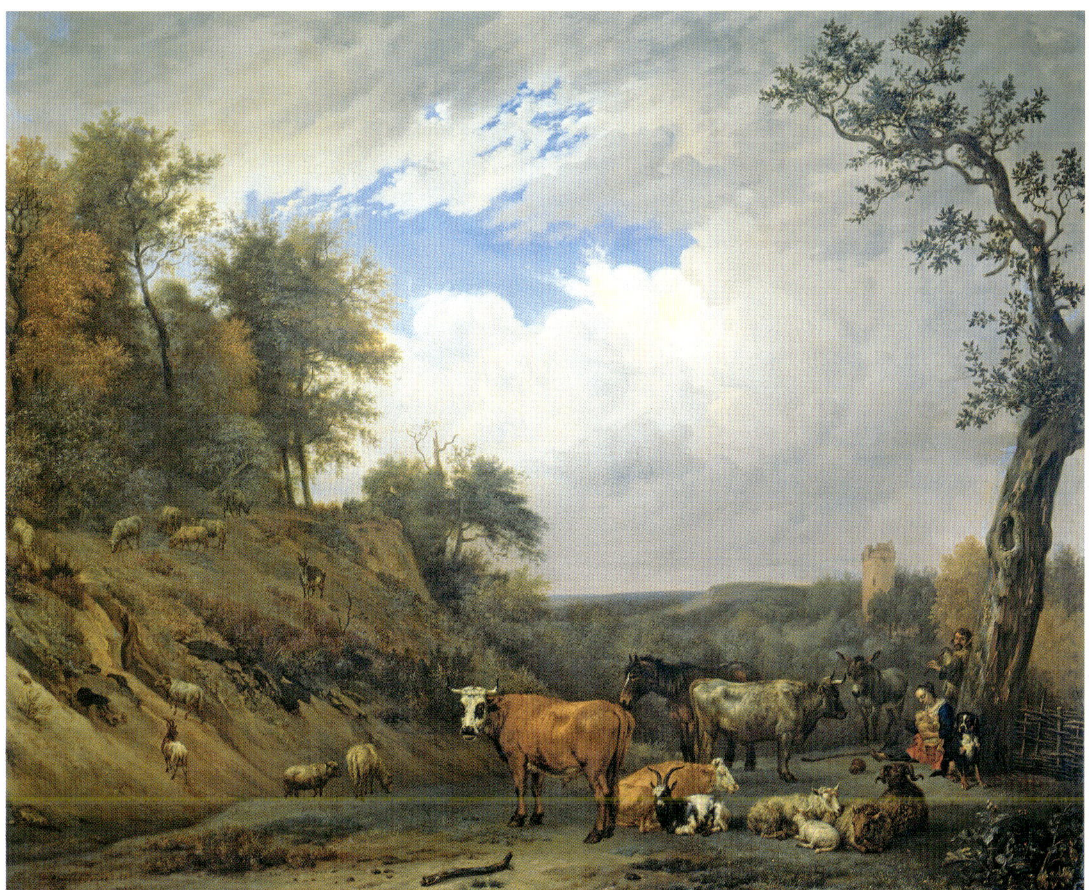

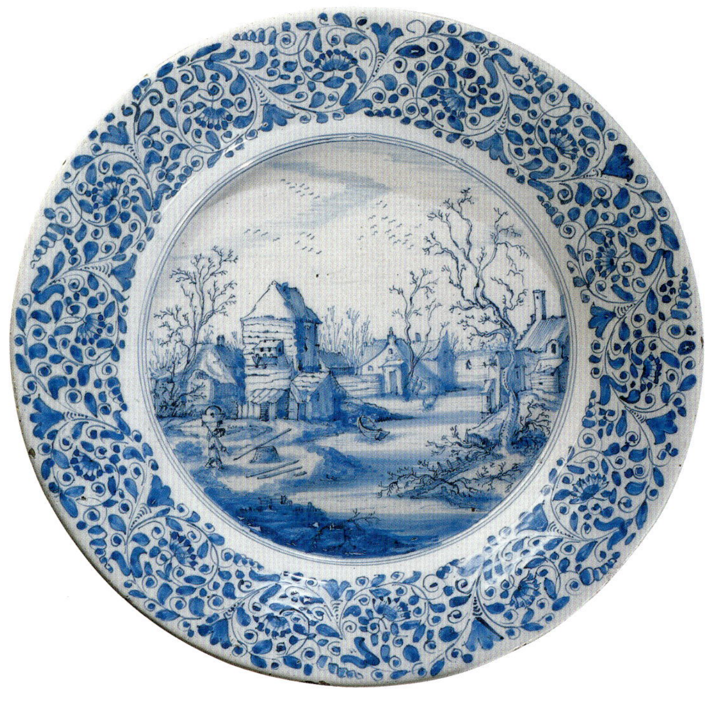

Migrating birds fill the sky, while a dense bank of clouds drifts by. The shape of this plate was derived from Chinese export porcelain that had been imported into Holland since about 1600. The dish was thrown on a potter's wheel, upside down over a form, and traces of the finger marks of the turner are still visible on the underside. The glaze is a lovely white but somewhat dull due to the sparse application of a flow-control agent, necessary to ensure that the fine blue lines of the decoration did not run. As was customary in faience production, the composition was transferred from a drawing by means of holes pricked in the paper and vigorously elaborated in fine dotted lines. The border is decorated with a continuous foliate scroll, and although the foliage is well painted, it looks a little stiff compared to the sketchlike winter landscape.

An anonymous plaque with a landscape dated 1660 (no. 48), like many other Delft faience plaques from the 1650s and 1660s, was probably meant to be framed and hung on a wall. In inventories of household effects these plaques are referred to as "porcelain paintings." Indeed, once framed, they looked like paintings. The Italianate landscape is in the style of Nicolaes Berchem, but the print on which it was undoubtedly based has not been identified. The elements of the landscape with hills and cows are well arranged over the surface and enough white has been left unpainted to give depth to the whole scene. After a first firing the clay body was covered with a glaze (a thin layer of glass that melts into and seals the surface of the piece when it is fired), to which a little tin was added, resulting in an opaque white. As a finishing touch, decoration was applied over the glaze with a paint containing cobalt oxides, which turn deep blue, and the piece was fired again. During this second glost firing, the melted white tin glaze filled in any irregularities, providing a fine, porcelain-like finish, and the blue decoration was fused to the surface. In this case the temperature was too high, and the painting ran slightly to the left (the plaque stood in the kiln with the left edge downward), producing a wonderful, slightly hazy effect.

A plaque with a landscape (no. 49) made between 1670 and 1700 is yet another fine example of an Italian-inspired scene. In this case, however, we know the artist who painted it: Frederik

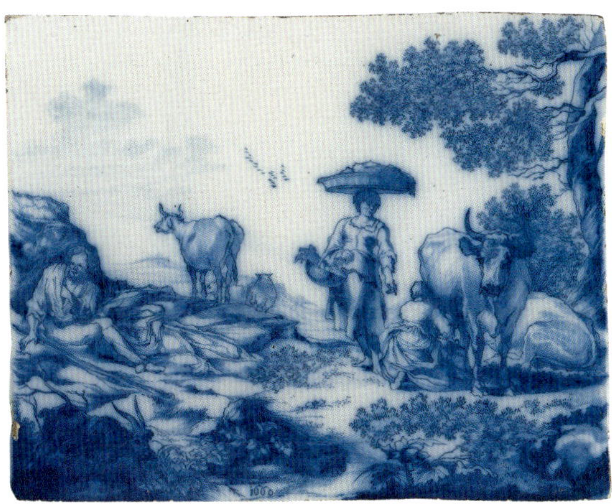

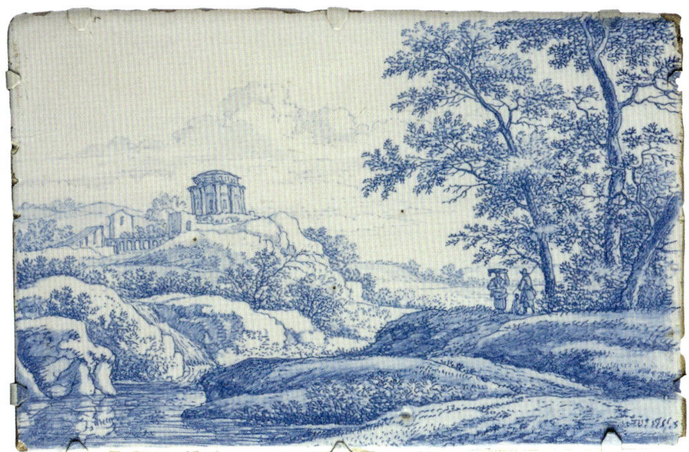

van Frytom (c. 1632–1702). Van Frytom was one of the very few independent decorators of Dutch faience, perhaps even the only one, active in Delft. He received many commissions from local factories but remained self-employed throughout his career. Because he did not labor as an anonymous decorator under a company name, he gained personal recognition within the profession. Van Frytom was famous above all for plates and plaques with draftsmanlike depictions of landscapes. In this piece, to suggest depth, he used a more vivid shade of blue for the foreground than for the background. There is little doubt this landscape, with its architectural elements of a round chapel near a Roman aqueduct and some houses on the banks of a river, is based on a print. The work recalls the idyllic landscapes painted in the area around Rome and Tivoli by the Frenchman Claude Lorrain (1600–1682), and also those of the Utrecht Italianate painter Jan Both (c. 1615–1652), who was active there at the same time.

47 Delft · *Dish with a Winter Landscape* (1650) · Faience · h. 2¼ inches, diam. 14⅝ inches

48 Delft · *Plaque with a Landscape* (1660) · Faience · h. 9¾ inches, w. 11¾ inches

49 Frederik van Frytom (c. 1632–1702) · *Plaque with a Landscape* (c. 1670–1700) · Faience · h. 6 inches, w. 9¼ inches

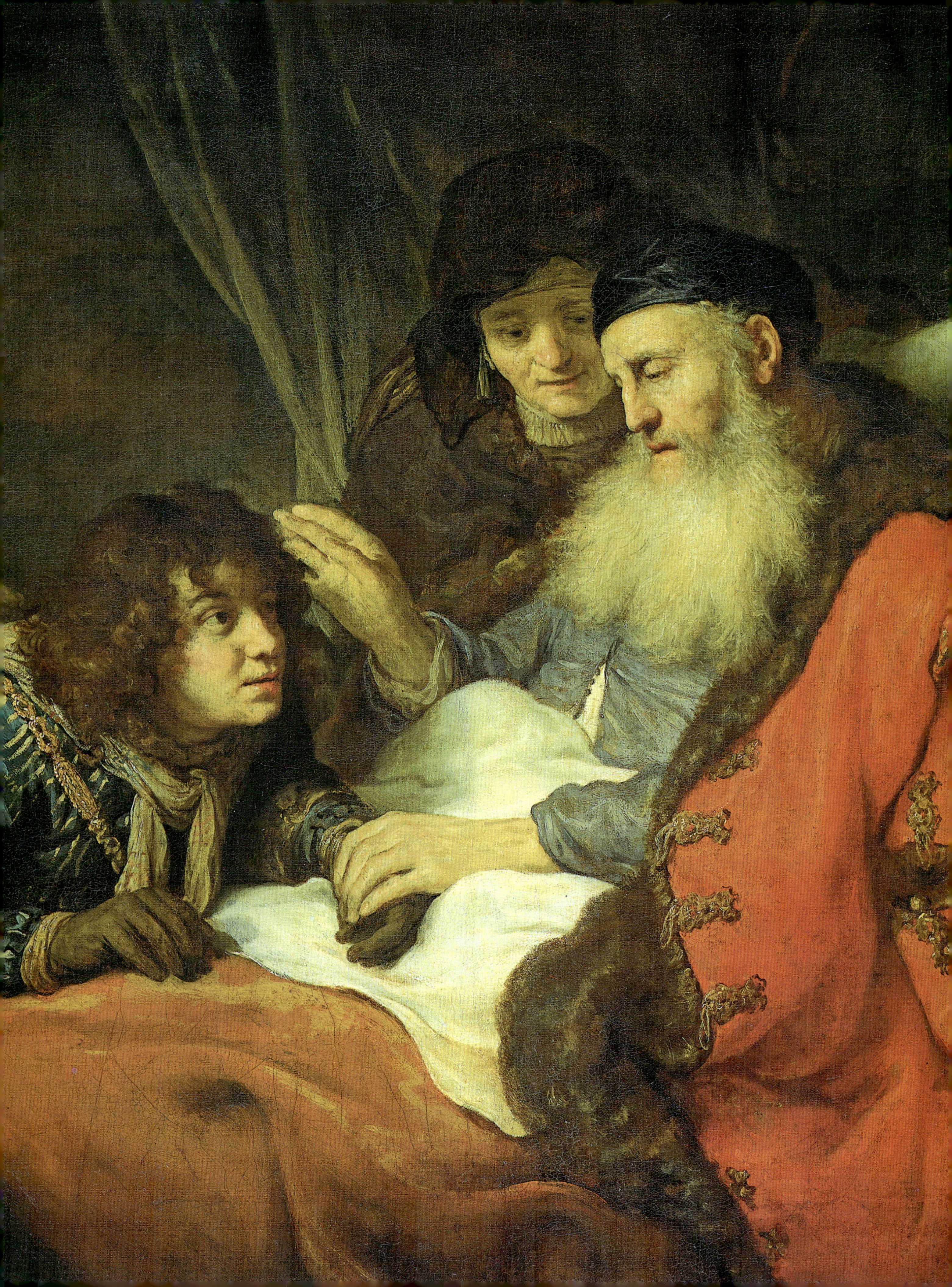

# 5

# RELIGIOUS IMAGES AND OBJECTS

PRACTICAL AND IDEOLOGICAL CONSIDERATIONS DICTATED a considerable degree of religious tolerance in the Dutch Republic in the Golden Age. Despite the fact that official documents referred to Calvinism as the only true Christian religion, attempts to accord it the status of a state church proved fruitless, since at least one out of three Dutchmen held other religious beliefs. Tolerance of religious dissent was not without friction. The war for independence from Spain was cast as a Protestant revolt against a Catholic empire. Even when the Republic and Spain ceased hostilities and a twelve-year armistice took effect (1609–1621), ongoing violent religious disputes brought the country to the brink of civil war. An influential champion of tolerance within the Protestant church was Johannes Wttenbogaert (1557–1644), preacher to the court of the princes of Orange. Rembrandt painted a portrait of Wttenbogaert, now in the Rijksmuseum, years after the preacher's banishment by Prince Maurice, whose religious views were more orthodox. Other works by Rembrandt, such as the intimate portrait of the Jewish physician and man of letters Ephraim Bueno (1599–1665), attest to the variety of religions, nationalities, and cultural backgrounds that coexisted within the Republic.

In 1631 the French philosopher René Descartes, who found a haven in the northern Netherlands, wrote to a friend abroad: "In what other country in the world can one find so many of the pleasures of life alongside all imaginable oddities? In what other country can one enjoy such total freedom?" Of course, Descartes's words are not entirely accurate: there was no question of total freedom in the Republic, but rather a policy of tolerance. Those who professed the Catholic faith were countenanced, but they were not eligible for public office. Catholics were not actively prevented from practicing their religion, but they had to do so in *schuilkerken* (hidden churches), places of prayer situated behind the facades of houses so that they were not recognizable from the street. In 1672, one-third of the population of the Republic was Catholic, one-third was Calvinist, and the rest consisted of Jews or members of one or another dissident Protestant movement.

Amsterdam, though in many respects typical of the northern Netherlands, was a special case. Between 1578 and 1675, the number of inhabitants rose from around 30,000 to 206,000, a seven-fold increase in less than a century. This was due in large measure to the huge influx of immigrants from other cities in the Republic and the countryside, as well as Protestants from the southern Netherlands and France, and Jews from Poland, Germany, and Portugal. The notarial archives of Amsterdam show that, between 1581 and 1811, on average 53.6 percent of the men and women who registered for marriage licenses actually came from outside the city; in the period 1606–1620, that rate reached almost 73 percent. From 1600 on, Amsterdam was the largest, wealthiest, and most powerful city in the Republic, and throughout the 17th century, the city council, which was in effect totally autonomous, acquired more and more influence over both domestic and foreign policy. This city of merchants was highly cosmopolitan, and in comparison with other parts of the Republic, there was a considerable degree of freedom—not only of action, but also of thought and religion. This religious benevolence was enjoyed by everyone except the Roman Catholics, who in Amsterdam were less free to worship as they pleased, even in their hidden churches.

Utrecht presented an exception to the religious demographics of the Republic. The majority of its population was Catholic, and this was reflected in the policies observed in the city throughout the 17th century. As Protestantism was less extreme in character there than elsewhere in the northern Netherlands, Catholicism remained a powerful force. The locations of many Catholic *schuilkerken,* often richly decorated inside and filled with altarpieces commissioned from local artists, were well known to the city authorities, but their existence was tolerated in the name of religious peace. Utrecht's Catholics were permitted to worship unhindered in private, and they maintained close ties with Rome. This was reflected in the artistic life of the city.

Today Hendrick ter Brugghen (1588–1629) is seen as the greatest of all the Utrecht Caravaggesque painters, and even in his time he was a celebrated artist. Rubens called him the only true painter among all the artists he met during his visit to the Republic in 1627. Although he was himself a Protestant, Ter Brugghen painted a great many biblical works and likenesses of saints for Roman Catholic patrons.

After studying in the workshop of the history painter Abraham Bloemaert in Utrecht, Ter Brugghen traveled to Italy at the age of fifteen. He lived and worked in Rome for about a decade, returning to Utrecht in 1614. Like his Utrecht colleagues Gerard van Honthorst (1590–1656) and Dirck van Baburen (c. 1595–1624), who both returned from Rome in the early 1620s, and Paulus Moreelse, who came back years before them, Ter Brugghen was filled with admiration for the work of Caravaggio (1573–1610). Caravaggio's chiaroscuro (dramatic contrasts of light and dark) and the natural portrayal of his models, often ordinary workmen whom he painted as such, made him the most talked-about Italian painter of the day. Ter Brugghen and his Utrecht colleagues were inspired by Caravaggio's paintings and imitated his style and subject matter. They became known as the Utrecht Caravaggisti.

50 Hendrick ter Brugghen (1588–1629) · *Doubting Thomas* (c. 1620–1622) · Oil on canvas · 42¾ × 53¾ inches (overleaf)

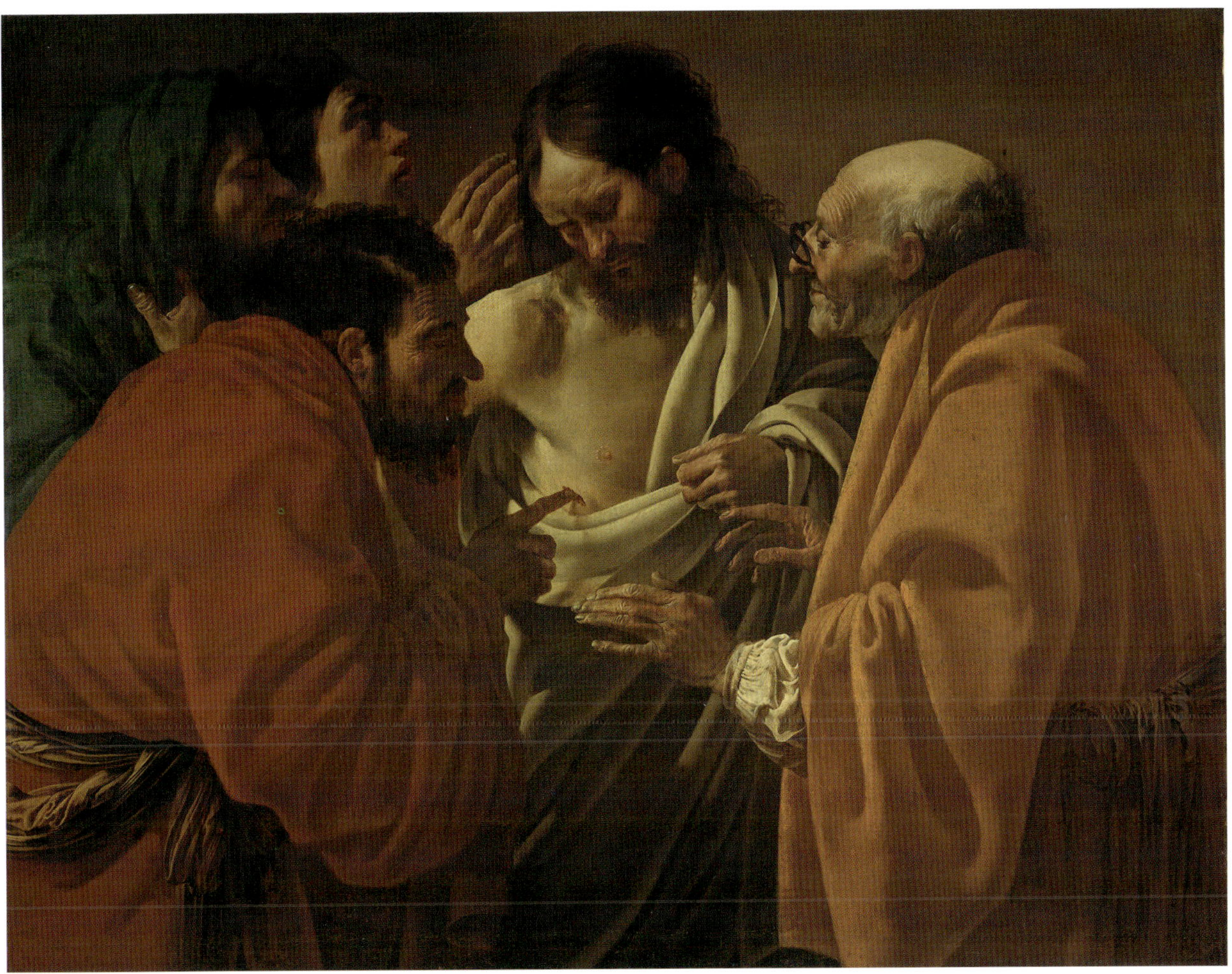

In Ter Brugghen's case it was not until about 1620–1622, well after his return from Rome, that the influence of Caravaggio became visible in his work. In *Doubting Thomas* (no. 50, above and pp. 86–87), a work datable to this period, Ter Brugghen depicted a New Testament story. When told by the other disciples that Christ had been resurrected, the apostle Thomas said he could not believe it, not even if he were to see Christ's wounds with his own eyes and feel them with his own hands. Jesus then appeared and let him see and feel for himself, curing Thomas of his incredulity. Following Caravaggio's realistic approach, Ter Brugghen chose working-class models and made no attempt to idealize their sunburnt, weather-beaten faces, or the pointed nose and small eyes of the model he chose for Jesus. To heighten the effect of reality, he portrayed the balding man seen in profile peering through pince-nez, the better to see Thomas touching the wound in Christ's side. Employing Caravaggio's dramatic formula, Ter Brugghen illuminated the act with a single ray of light, cutting through the surrounding darkness that envelops the barely visible figures of Mary and John.

There could be no more Catholic work of art than *Relief from a Tabernacle Door, with the Virgin as Our Lady of Sorrows* (no. 51). Made in 1616, it expresses the adoration of the Virgin that Protestants opposed. Holes along the outer edges of the embossed and chased copper plate, which

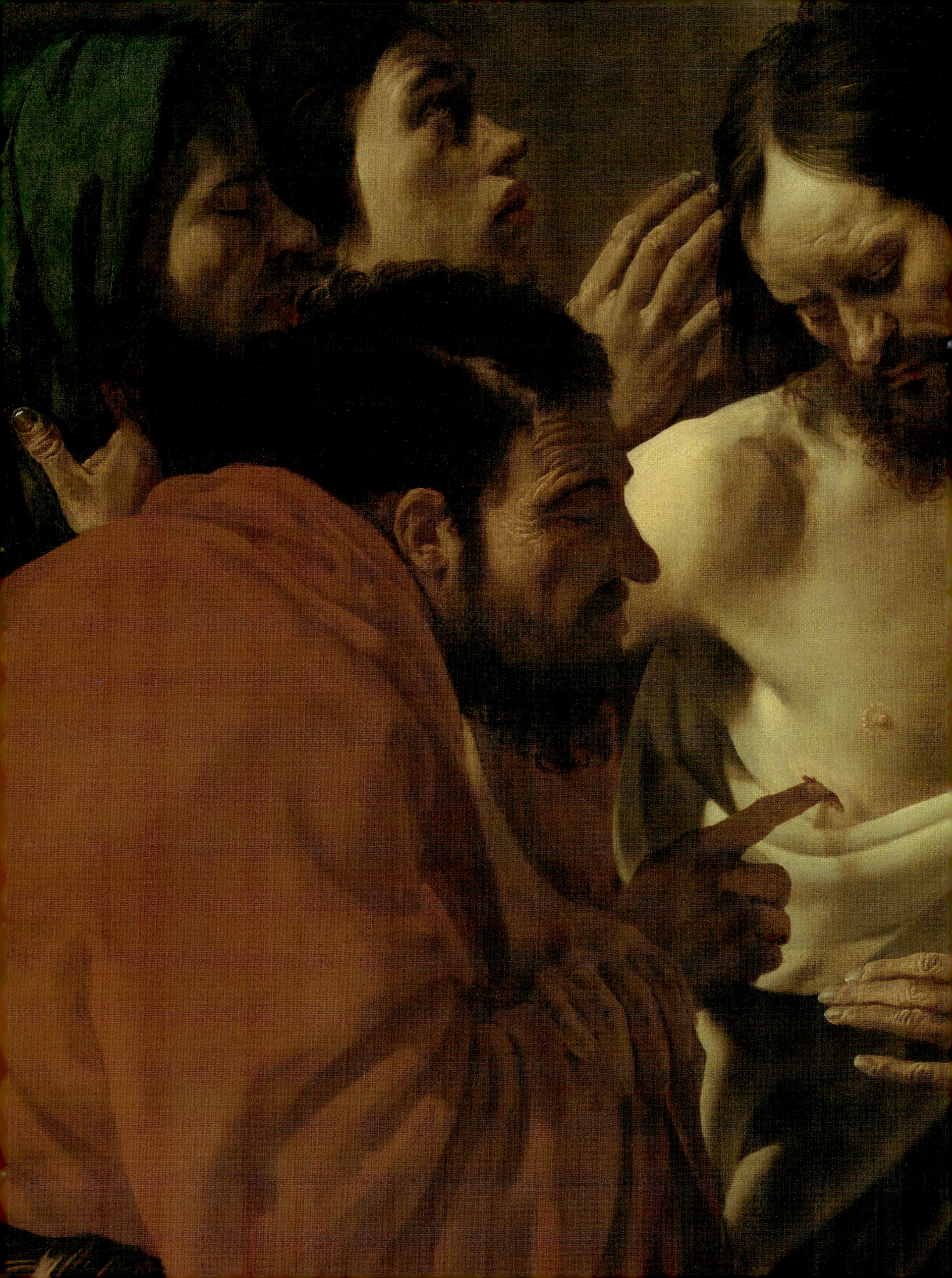

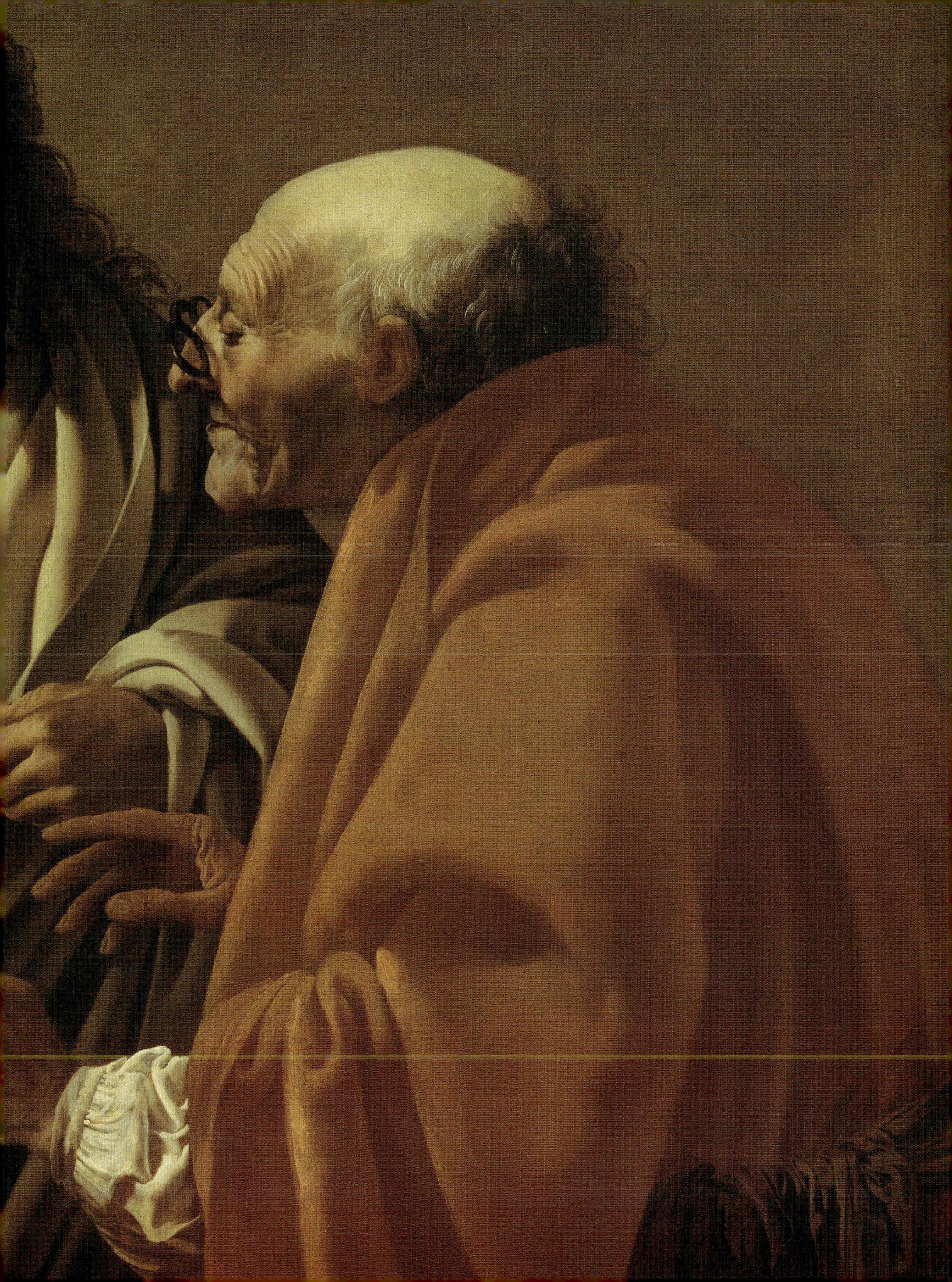

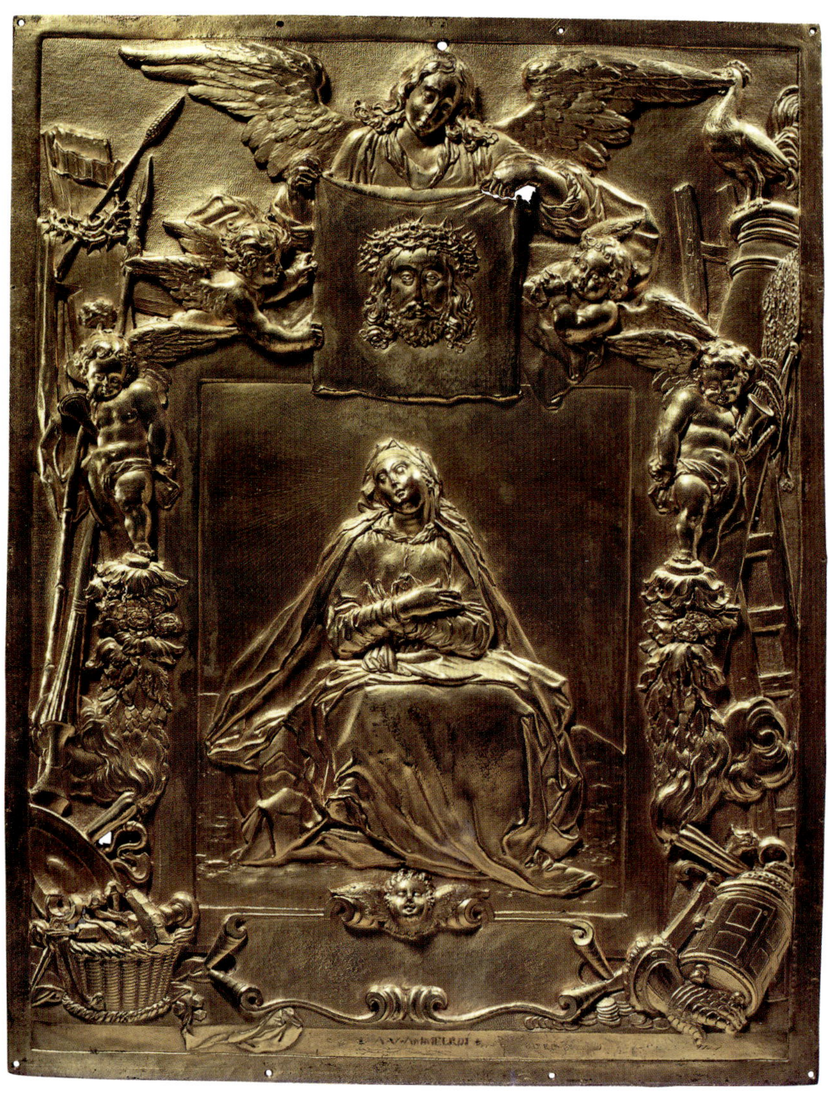

is gilded on the front, served for its attachment to the door of a tabernacle, the sanctuary behind the main church altar in which the Eucharist (consecrated host) and chalices were kept. The relief shows Mary in a rectangular frame as the Mater Dolorosa (Our Lady of Sorrows), seated with her arms folded over her breast, her face tilted upward. Above, an angel holds up the Vernicle, or Cloth of Saint Veronica, which bears the imprint of Christ's head crowned with thorns; on either side are putti with the instruments of Christ's Passion. Below Mary is an empty cartouche still awaiting inscription. Beneath the cartouche is the engraved signature of the Utrecht silversmith Adriaen van Ammelroi (active 1614–c. 1640?). His father, Cornelis van Ammelroi, was a well-known bell and ordnance founder who worked in Utrecht and Amsterdam.

The demand for ecclesiastical silver from Roman Catholic churches in Holland was met in Amsterdam by several silversmiths, either born in the capital or from elsewhere, notably Utrecht and Haarlem. Among these was Johannes Lutma II (1624–1689, a son of the silversmith

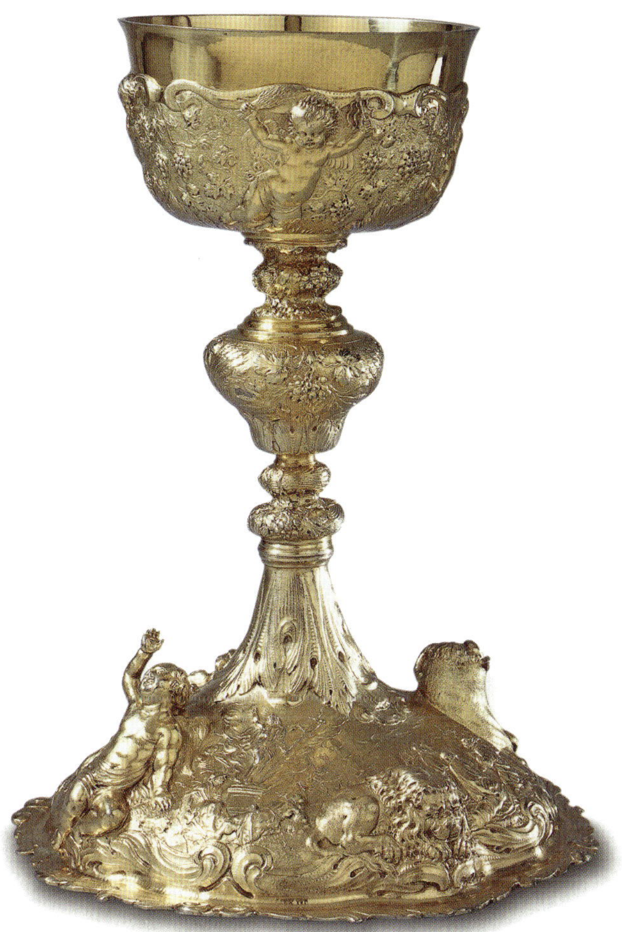

Johannes Lutma; see nos. 7 and 8, pp. 28–29). Like his father, Lutma worked as a silversmith in Amsterdam, where he was registered as a master in 1643. It is not certain exactly which works can be attributed to him, because he appears to have used the silver mark of his famous father (or a very similar mark of his own) on the pieces he produced. The magnificent silver chalice date-marked 1663 (no. 52) bears that mark, a heart in a shield, and is almost certainly by the younger Lutma. The foot of the chalice is decorated in sculptural form with the symbols of the Four Evangelists (an ox for Saint Luke, an eagle for Saint John, an angel for Saint Matthew,

51 Adriaen van Ammelroi (active 1614–c. 1640?) · *Relief from a Tabernacle Door, with the Virgin as Our Lady of Sorrows* (1616) · Gilt copper · h. 16½ inches, w. 12½ inches

52 Johannes Lutma II (1624–1689) · *Chalice* (1663) · Silver, partly gilded silver · h. 11¼ inches, diam. (foot) 8¼ inches, (cup) 4¾ inches

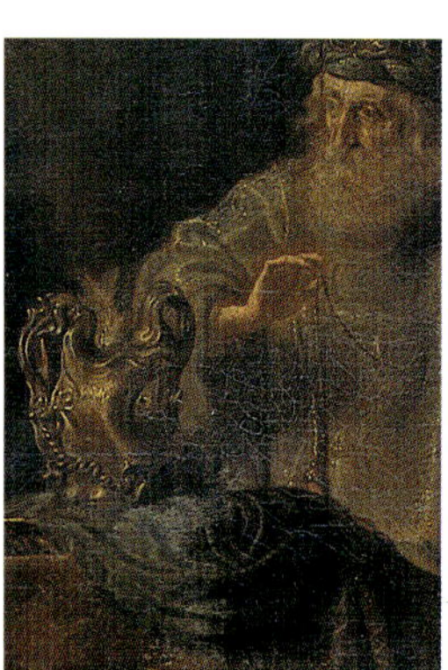

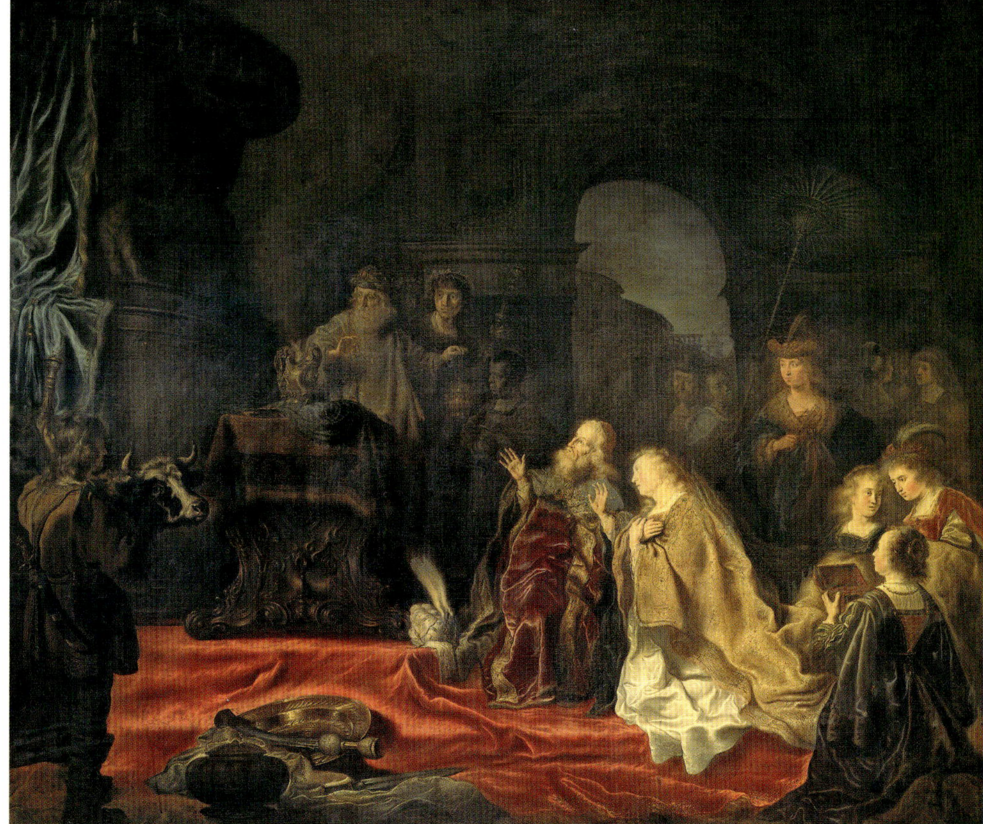

and a lion for Saint Mark). Between them are four scenes from the life of Christ: the Nativity, the Crucifixion, the Resurrection, and the Ascension. Grapes and sheaves of wheat representing the bread and wine of the sacrament ornament the stem. Three cherubs on the bowl bear the instruments of the Passion, while a fourth holds the Cloth of Saint Veronica. The upper edge is decorated with ornaments in the auricular style, for which Lutma's father had become so famous years earlier.

The outstanding achievements of Dutch silversmiths of this age are exemplified by the famous jug depicted in the 1644 painting *The Idolatry of King Solomon* (no. 53) by Salomon Koninck. This commemorative piece in the auricular style, executed in 1614 by Adam van Vianen, enjoyed great fame in the 17th century and was repeatedly depicted in paintings, particularly by artists of the Rembrandt school. Salomon Koninck, himself the son of a goldsmith, included Van Vianen's masterpiece in at least six of his compositions. He introduced it here in a subject taken from an Old Testament account of King Solomon, who, under the influence of his many foreign wives, in his old age angered God by turning to the worship of idols. Religious reformers and Protestants used this popular story as a warning against the veneration of effigies in the Catholic Church.

Koninck enjoyed the patronage of Amsterdam patricians and Christian IV, king of Denmark. He was deeply influenced by Rembrandt, as is evident in his paintings of mythological and biblical stories—especially in the costumes, figural types, and use of chiaroscuro. *The Idolatry of King Solomon* is a clear case in point.

Protestant clients favored images of Old Testament scenes, and the story of Isaac and Jacob was particularly preferred among artists in Rembrandt's circle. Several versions were painted by Govert Flinck, who worked in Rembrandt's studio for three years before setting up on his own in 1636. Painted in 1638, *Isaac Blessing Jacob* (no. 54) was Flinck's first large-scale history painting and created high expectations for the young master, then twenty-three. It portrays Jacob, his hands covered with goat skin to imitate the hairy physique of his older brother, hoping to trick his blind father Isaac into giving him the blessing that was actually the birthright of Esau, the eldest son. Jacob's mother, Rebecca, is his accomplice and has cooked Isaac's favorite dish (the goat meat on the plate in the left background). Just as Rembrandt would do, Flinck focused all attention on one key moment of the story: will Isaac be persuaded to lower his hand to his son's head, so Jacob can steal his blessing?

In Flinck's canvas the influence of Rembrandt is easily recognized in the somewhat woolly style of painting, the exotic costumes of the protagonists, and the dramatic contrasts of light and

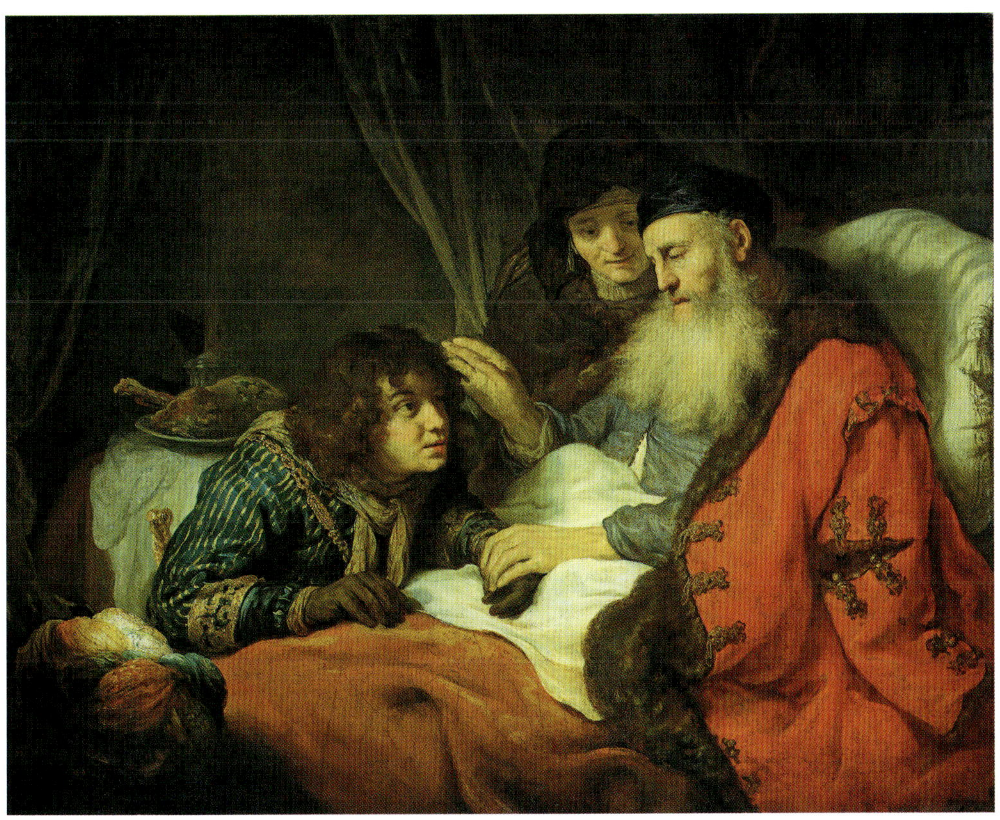

53 Salomon Koninck (1609–1656) · *The Idolatry of King Solomon* (1644) · Oil on canvas · 61 × 67½ inches

54 Govert Flinck (1615–1660) · *Isaac Blessing Jacob* (1638) · Oil on canvas · 46 × 55½ inches

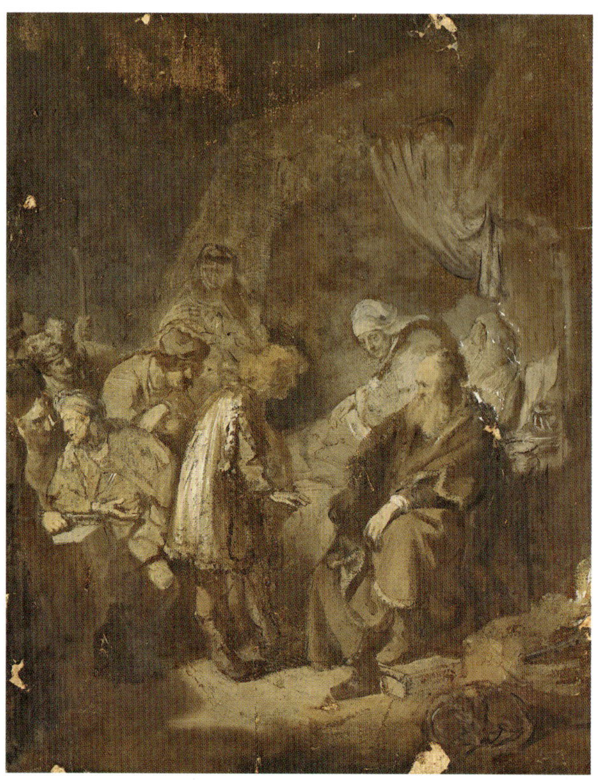

dark. The contemporary biographer Arnold Houbraken observed that Flinck's works were often mistaken for Rembrandt's because his style remained so close to that of the master.

Among the Old Testament stories that Rembrandt himself depicted is that of the seventeen-year-old Joseph, the son of Jacob and Rachel, in *Joseph Telling His Dreams to His Parents and Brothers* (no. 55). Joseph had related a dream to his brothers in which their sheaves of corn bow down to his. When Joseph later dreams that the sun and moon and eleven stars made obeisance to him (the dream being interpreted here), his brothers decide to do away with him.

Rembrandt made this oil sketch in the early 1630s, just after he had moved from Leiden, where he was born, to the more cosmopolitan city of Amsterdam. He employed preparatory oil sketches for a number of his history subjects, and several have been preserved. Most, if not all, appear to be studies for specific etchings. This sketch has been identified as a large-scale preparation for his print of 1638 of the same subject, in which Joseph is placed in the center of a circle of figures, his face toward the beholder. Even in the artist's day, Rembrandt's preparatory sketches were regarded as works of art in their own right and avidly collected. This fine monochromatic oil sketch, executed on paper and painted in a palette of gray-browns and ochres, was no exception. It was already documented, along with several other oil sketches by the master, in an inventory drawn up in 1669 of the belongings of his former pupil Ferdinand Bol.

In 1660, the date of *The Denial of Saint Peter* (no. 56), and in the following year, Rembrandt painted a number of apostles and evangelists, perhaps as part of a series. The *Denial of Saint Peter* resembles those works in atmosphere but differs in its size and narrative character. It is especially striking for its portrayal of the inner struggle of Saint Peter, who tries to reconcile his

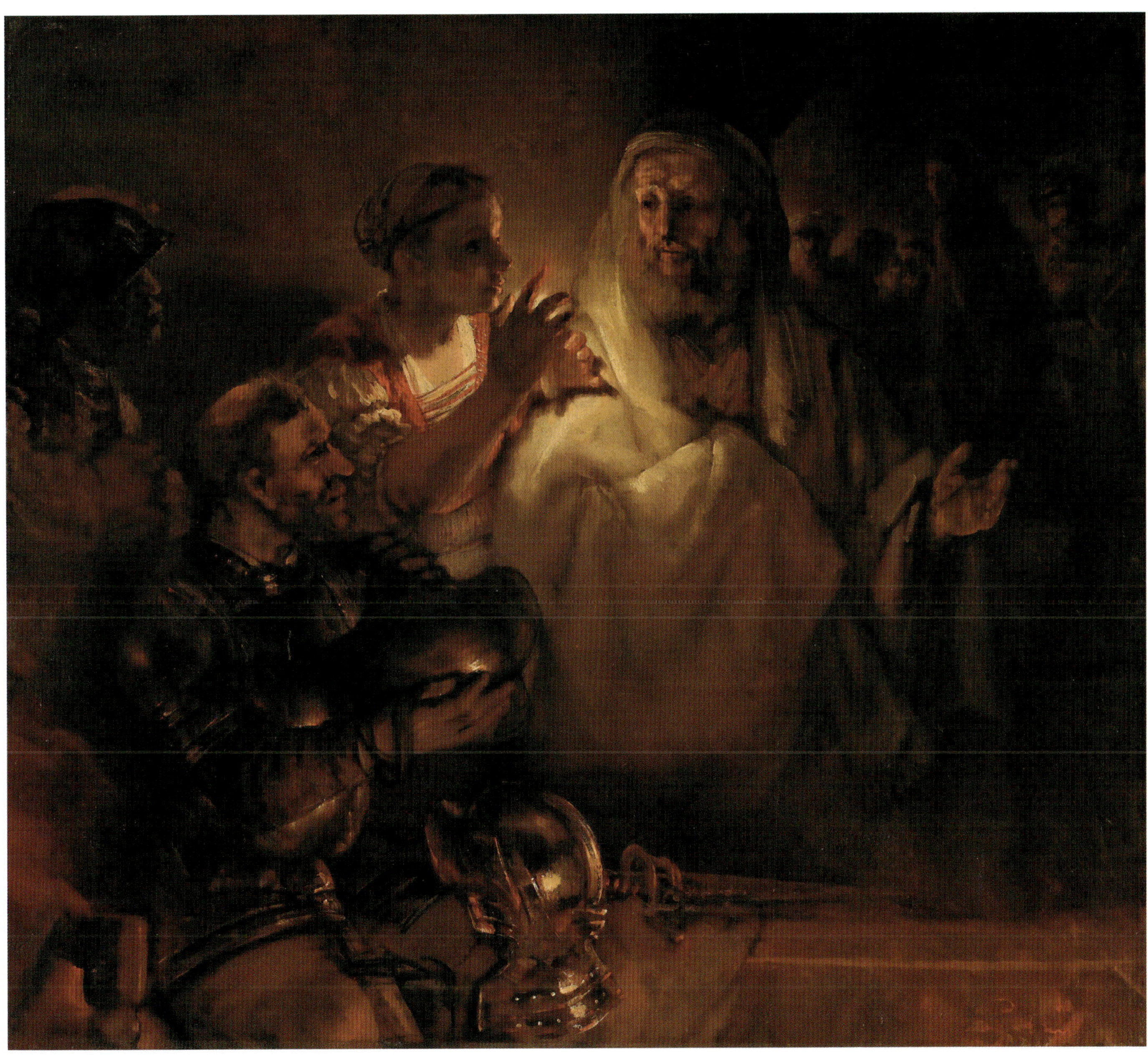

55 Rembrandt van Rijn (1606–1669) · *Joseph Telling His Dreams to His Parents and Brothers* (1633) · Oil on paper laid on cardboard · 20 × 15¼ inches

56 Rembrandt van Rijn (1606–1669) · *The Denial of Saint Peter* (1660) · Oil on canvas · 60½ × 66½ inches

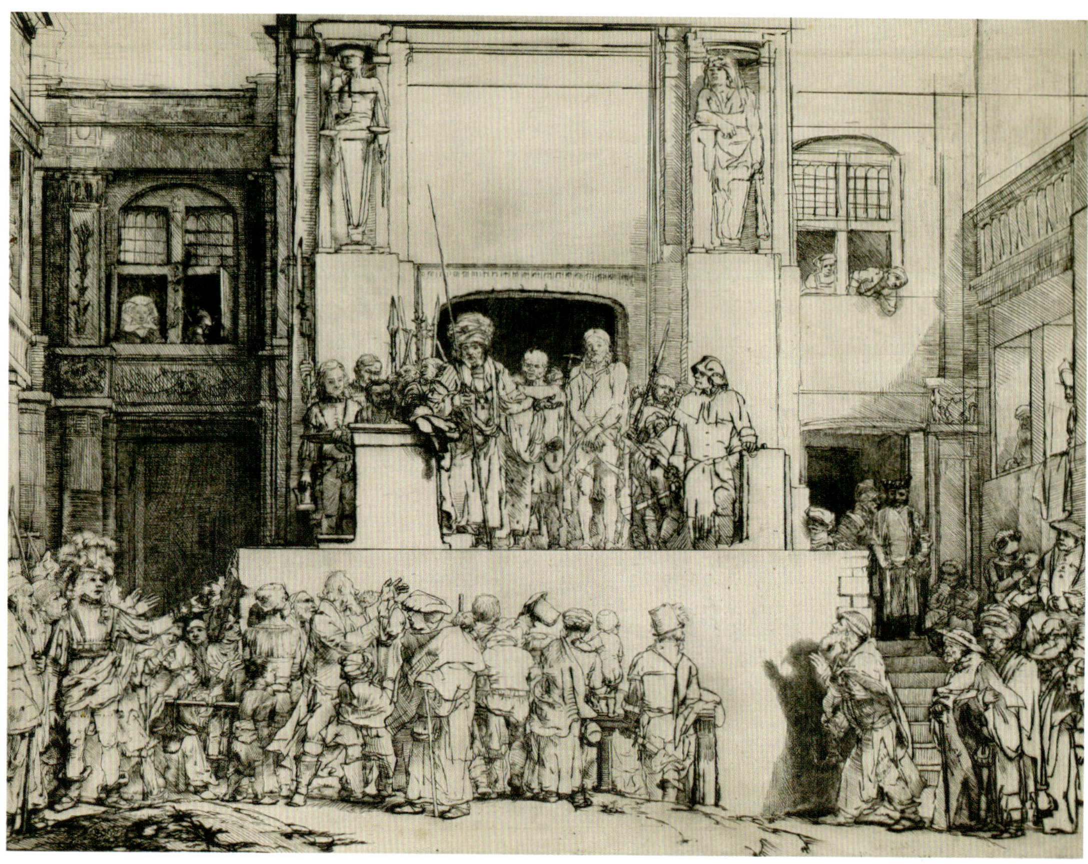

faith with human doubt. In the dark, two soldiers anxiously await his answer to their question: does he know Jesus? To the right, in the background, Christ and some bystanders turn and listen. Rembrandt focused attention on the confused face of Saint Peter by illuminating it from a hidden source—the light of a candle blocked from our view by the hand of the girl next to Peter. With a radically new technique, Rembrandt employed his palette knife as well as his brush to manipulate the paint. He also left several parts of the painting unfinished, as he often did in his later history paintings.

Rembrandt's acclaim as a printmaker has always been equal to his reputation as a painter. His prints were much sought after in his day, and collectors would often buy different versions of the same print. Prints are generally produced in a series of states, the first impression being known as the first state. If the illustration or text on the copperplate is changed, subsequent impressions are referred to as the second state, and so on. The subsequent states of Rembrandt's 1655 print *Christ Presented to the People,* of which the fifth and the eighth are included here (nos. 57 and 58), are particularly illustrative of Rembrandt's working method.

In this impressive print, we see Christ half-naked with his wrists tied. Surrounded by soldiers, he is presented to the people from high on a balcony of the palace of the Roman governor Pontius Pilate. Pilate, recognizable by his turban and scepter, is asking the crowd whether he should release the infamous murderer Barabbas or Christ. Pilate utters the words "Ecce homo" (Behold the man), while pointing to Christ beside him. On the far left of the platform stands a

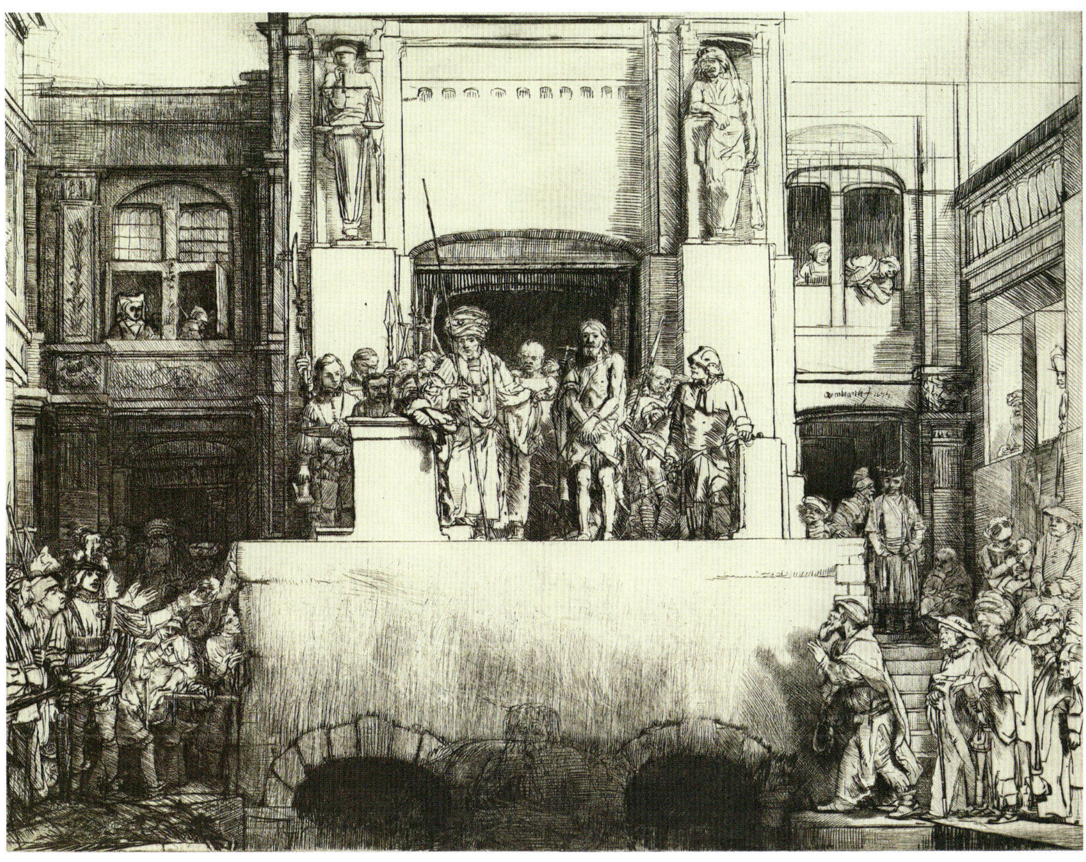

boy holding a jug of water and a large bowl in which Pilate, quite literally, will wash his hands of the affair. Influenced by the high priests standing below, the people decide to set Barabbas free and have Jesus crucified.

Rembrandt effectively summarized the story from the gospel of John in a broad tableau. The central characters on the balcony stand out against the dark entrance to the palace and are slightly larger than the people in the crowd. A large engraving of the same subject by the 16th-century Dutch printmaker Lucas van Leyden inspired the overall composition. Rembrandt greatly admired Van Leyden and owned several of his prints. It is thought Rembrandt tried to surpass his famous predecessor by executing his Ecce Homo entirely in drypoint. In this technique, a design is first scratched onto a polished copper plate with a sharp, hard needle. This throws up a rough ridge of metal, or burr, along the incised line. When the plate is inked, the printing ink collects in

57 Rembrandt van Rijn (1606–1669) · *Christ Presented to the People* (1655) · Drypoint (fifth state) · 15 × 18 inches

58 Rembrandt van Rijn (1606–1669) · *Christ Presented to the People* (1655) · Drypoint (eighth state) · 15 × 18 inches

the grooves and on the burrs. On transferring the print to paper, the typical fuzzy drypoint lines are left behind, and the print is given a texture rather like a drawing. Here Rembrandt presented the figures in velvety, unbroken lines and created shadows with closely drawn hatching.

There are only small differences among the first three states of the print. Rembrandt gradually made the left part of the composition darker to put more emphasis on the main group. In the fourth state, he cut a large piece from the top of the plate, removing the upper edge of the central building and bringing the top margin down to just above the two statues. The reasons for this were both practical and artistic: the plate was slightly too large for the Japanese paper he had in stock, and he did not want the architecture to overwhelm the human drama below. After he had made impressions of the fifth state (no. 57, p. 94), Rembrandt must have noticed the plate's generally worn appearance. Much of the burr had disappeared, depriving the plate of its rich accents of black. It was then that Rembrandt decided to drastically change the composition. In the sixth state he burnished away the entire crowd in front of the platform from the lower half of the plate. In the seventh state, he replaced this passage with two large cellar vaults, flanking a bearded figure reminiscent of a river god. In the rest of the composition he camouflaged the wear by strengthening the existing lines in drypoint and rehatching various areas. Finally, he signed and dated the plate 1655, indicating that he was then pleased with the work. After making only a few impressions of the (subsequently rare) seventh state, Rembrandt appears to have had second thoughts about the river god in the foreground. In the eighth and final state (no. 58, p. 95) this figure is largely concealed under an area of dark shadow.

In the revisions from the first state of the print, where Christ is protected from the crowd by a high balcony, to the final image in which the foreground is empty of figures, Rembrandt increasingly brought out the desertion and desolation of Christ as he focused the attention of the viewer more directly on the events taking place on the platform. Rembrandt printed most impressions of the early states with surface tone on exclusive Japanese paper. The later states (including the present impressions of the fifth and eighth states) were printed on Western paper, which was less expensive and more absorbent.

There is only one known state of *The Descent from the Cross by Torchlight* of 1654 (no. 59, p. 97), possibly because Rembrandt completed the etching in a single urgent and spontaneous operation. This is one of the fine early impressions of the print, for which the artist used thin Japanese paper from the early 1650s. The print is one of Rembrandt's most dramatic works. The composition is ingenious: just a small section of the cross is visible, and the main action takes place not in the center of the picture but in the upper left. The large dark areas, achieved by deeply bitten, cross-hatched, etched lines, are contrasted with a white shroud, draped over a bier in the foreground, and the lifeless body of Christ, lit by torchlight. This is the only source of light, and because of its position, the gruesome detail of the nail driven through Christ's right foot immediately catches

59 Rembrandt van Rijn (1606–1669) · *The Descent from the Cross by Torchlight* (1654) ·
Etching and drypoint · 8¼ × 6¼ inches

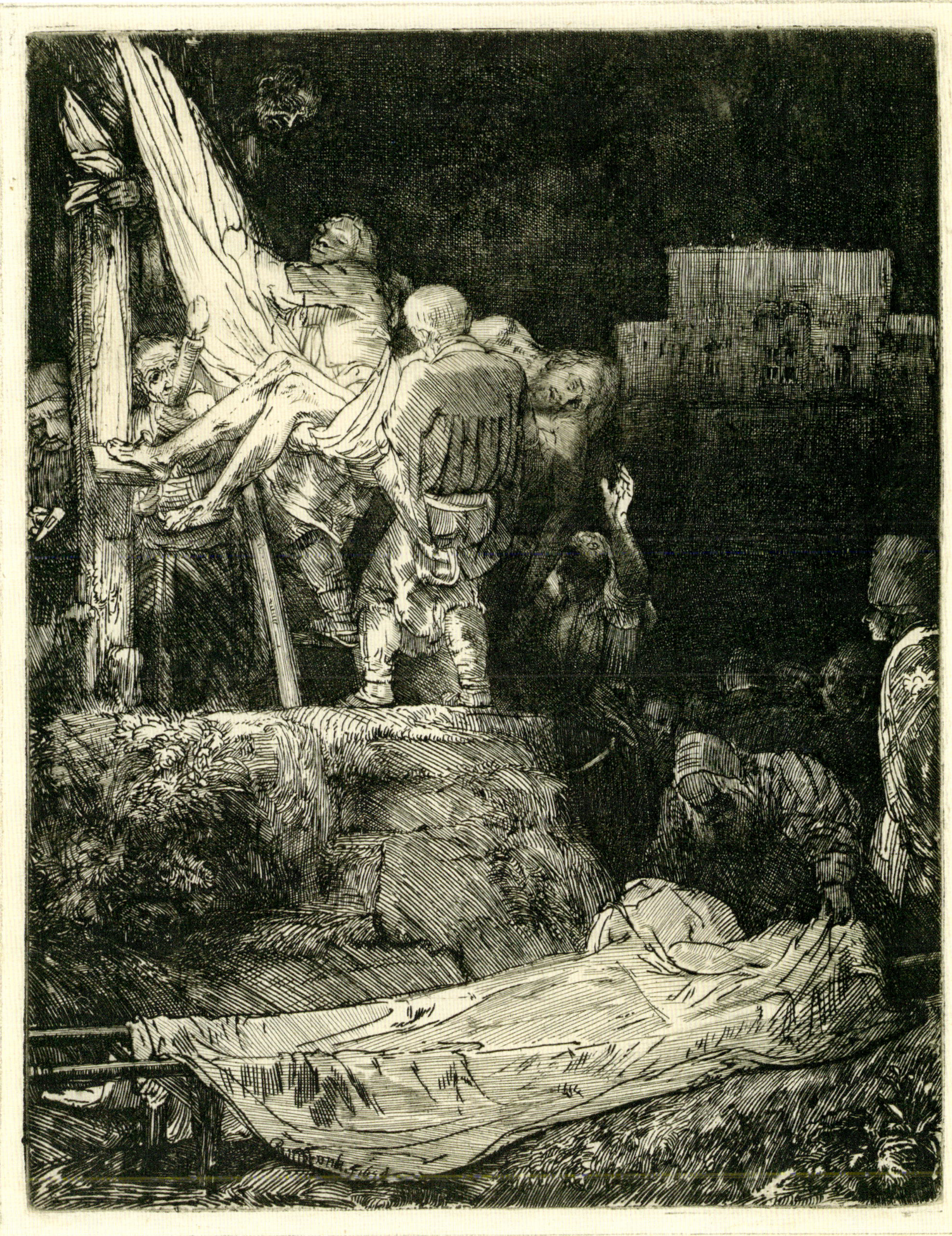

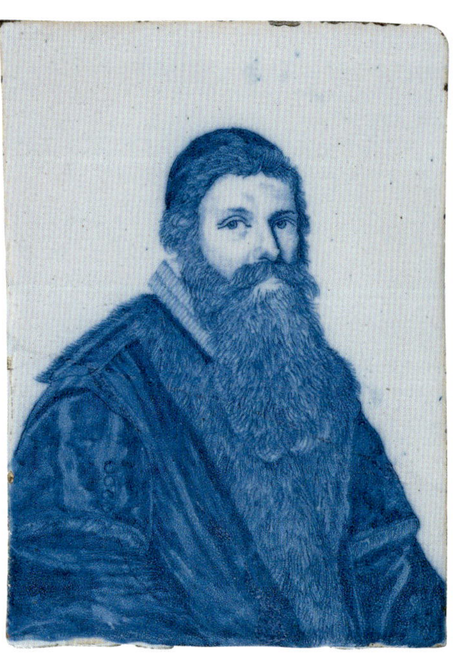

the eye. In the shadow below, Joseph of Arimathaea kneels at the bier to straighten the cloth that will be wrapped around the body of Christ.

Engravings often served as models for the decoration of Delft pottery. *Plaque with a Portrait of Dionysius Sprankhuyzen, Minister in Delft,* dated 1660 (no. 60), is part of a series of Delftware plaques with portraits of local Reformed ministers. The portraits were based on a series of engravings from about 1645 by Chrispijn van Queborn (1604–1652). These engravings were used to transfer the design to the plaque surface and were closely followed by the Delft painter, but, surprisingly, the latter's skill and the properties of Delftware have produced portraits that are better drawn, and artistically more appealing, than Van Queborn's prints. The contrast of the blue of the minister's gown against the white of the glaze creates a sense of depth. The sitter, Dionysius Spranckhuyzen, had been a minister at Delft since 1625. He was appointed the guardian of Isaack Junius (1616–after 1657), whose parents had died in 1636. Later the same Isaack Junius became a painter in Delft specializing in battle scenes. He is also known to have decorated a few Delftware plaques in 1657, although he probably never painted Delftware professionally. Junius remained active in Delft throughout the 1640s and 1650s, after which he was appointed to the post of sheriff of two nearby villages. The artist who painted the portrait plaque of Spranckhuyzen may well have been his protégé Junius.

Like most churches in the Republic, the Mariakerk in Utrecht was originally built for Catholic worship. When the subject of *The Westernmost Bays of the South Aisle of the Mariakerk in Utrecht* (no. 61), painted around 1640 by Pieter Saenredam (1597–1665), was adapted to the requirements of Protestants in the late 16th century, almost all the decoration was removed from the interior, and the walls were whitewashed. The fact that the space alone makes a lively impression is, above all, to Saenredam's credit. He was the first artist to devote himself to painting existing architecture, and from 1628 on he depicted mainly church interiors. He had a gift for evoking the calm

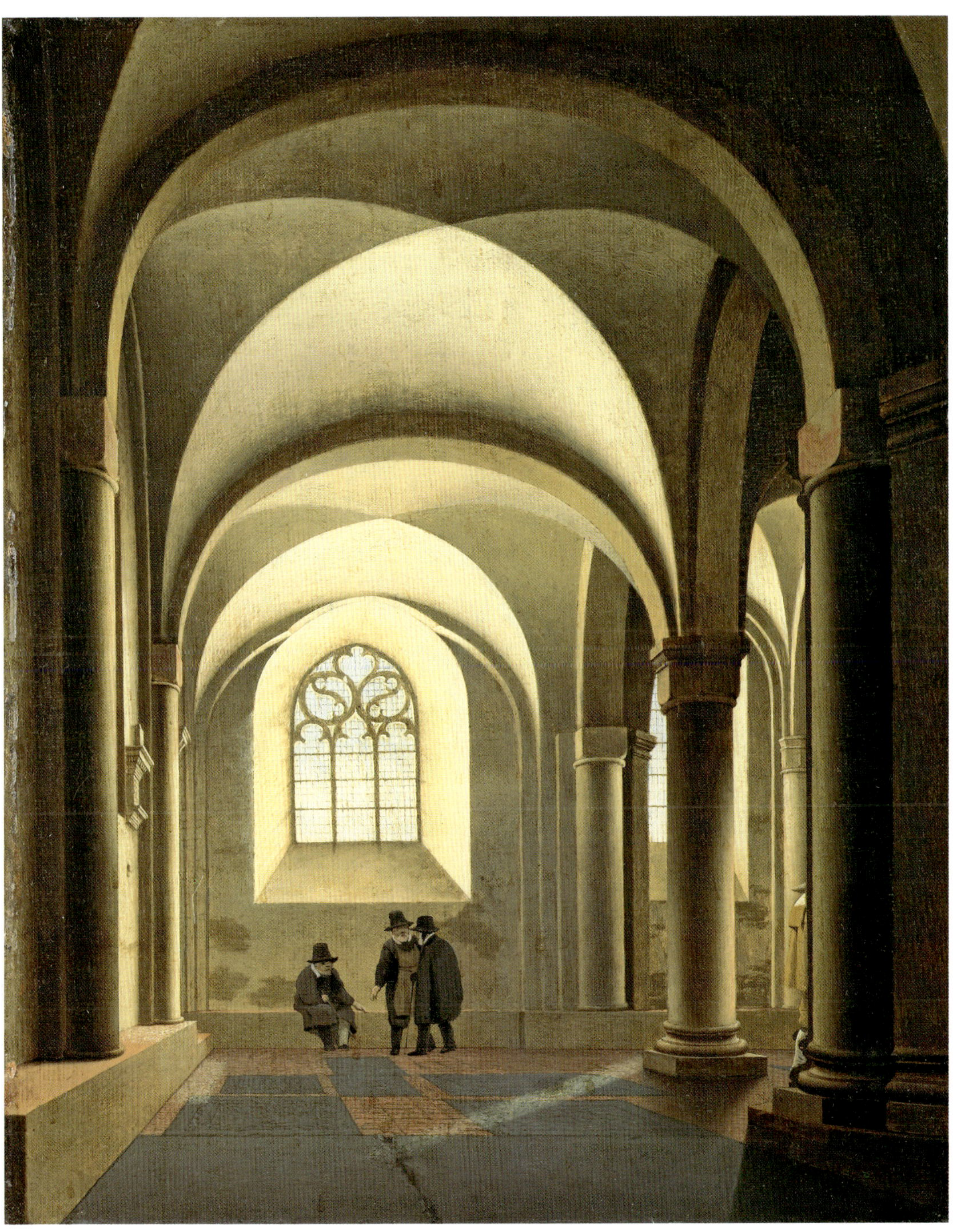

60 Delft · *Plaque with a Portrait of Dionysius Spranckhuyzen, Minister in Delft* (1660) · Faience · h. 7¾ inches, w. 5½ inches

61 Pieter Saenredam (1597–1665) · *The Westernmost Bays of the South Aisle of the Mariakerk in Utrecht* (c. 1640) · Oil on panel · 15¼ × 11¾ inches

devotional atmosphere of these houses of prayer in a style all his own, employing a restrained palette ranging from bright yellow to soft ochre-brown. He worked in a uniquely painstaking manner: he sketched, noted dimensions, and made construction drawings, with the aid of perspective. Only then did he take up his brush. Saenredam painted only sixty works. He had inherited VOC shares that his father, the engraver Jan Saenredam (1565–1607), had purchased when the company was founded. Thanks to the VOC's enormous success, the dividend Saenredam received each year enabled him to live comfortably. The fact that he was not dependent on the sale of his work meant he could afford to indulge in such a time-consuming, highly precise manner of painting.

Like Saenredam before him, Gerrit (or Gerard) Houckgeest (c. 1600–1661) developed church interiors as a specialty, notably in Delft, where he worked from 1635 to 1653 and became a prominent architectural painter. Houckgeest painted imaginary churches and palaces in the 1640s before focusing on interiors of the Oude Kerk and the Nieuwe Kerk in Delft in the early 1650s. Although these interiors appear to be accurately represented, Houckgeest made slight alterations. Sometimes he applied artistic tricks, as for example, in the *Interior of the Oude Kerk in Delft* (no. 62), probably dated 1651 (the last digit of the date is too obscure to read definitely as a "1" or a "4"), where a green curtain and a wooden frame behind it enhance the illusion of reality. (The same trick was used by Gerard Dou in his self-portrait, no. 5, p. 26). The complicated perspective is typical of Houckgeest. A plunging diagonal defines the vast depth of the building which opens up behind an enormous pillar at the center. The casual encounter of a man and woman in the foreground, the colors of the brightly lit stained glass windows, gleaming with a soft transparency, and the sunlight streaming through the whitewashed space are but a few of the elements Houckgeest employed to turn a depiction of a house of worship into an image of charm and beauty.

62 Gerrit (or Gerard) Houckgeest (c. 1600–1661) · *Interior of the Oude Kerk in Delft* (1651?) · Oil on panel · 19¼ × 16¼ inches

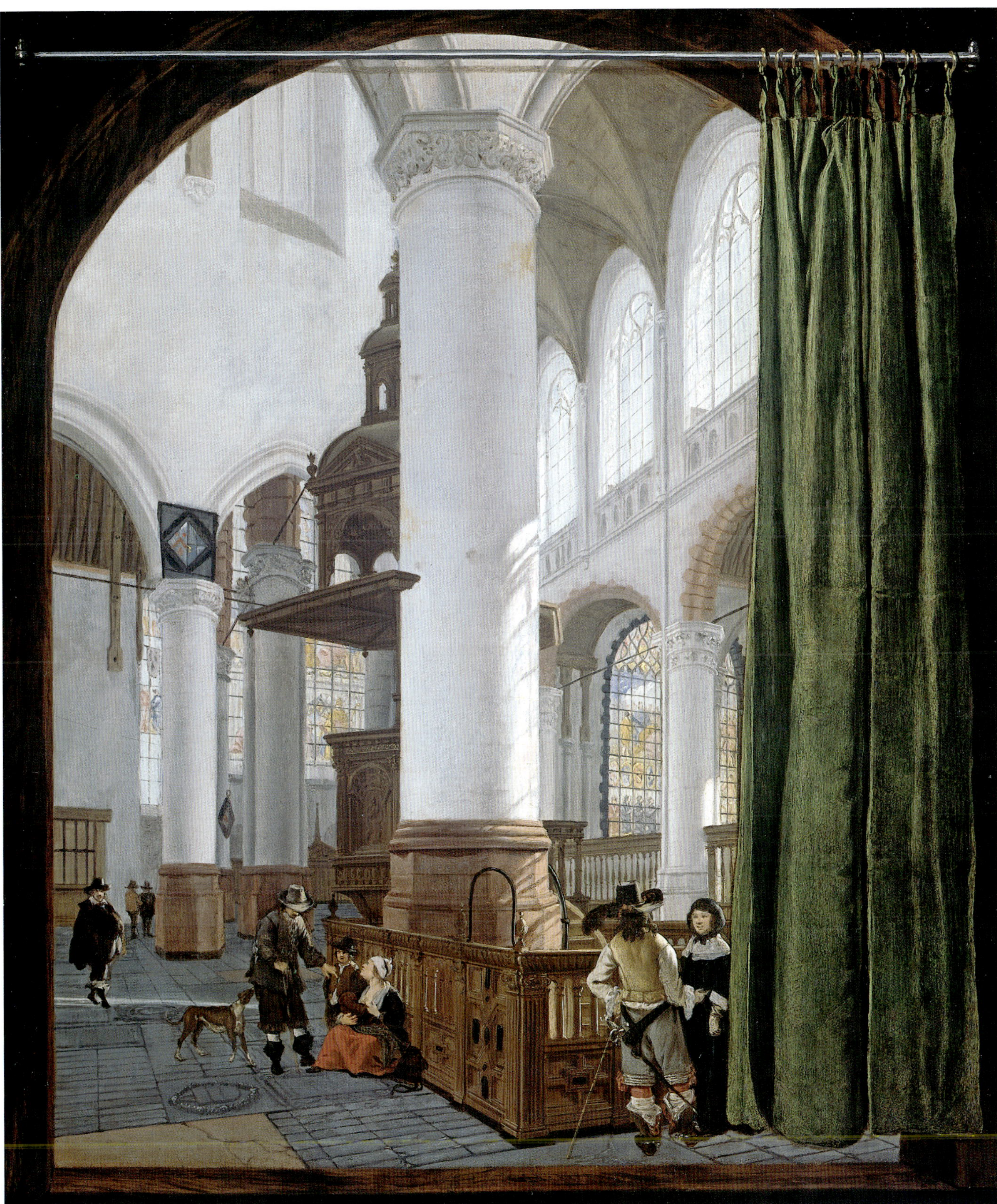

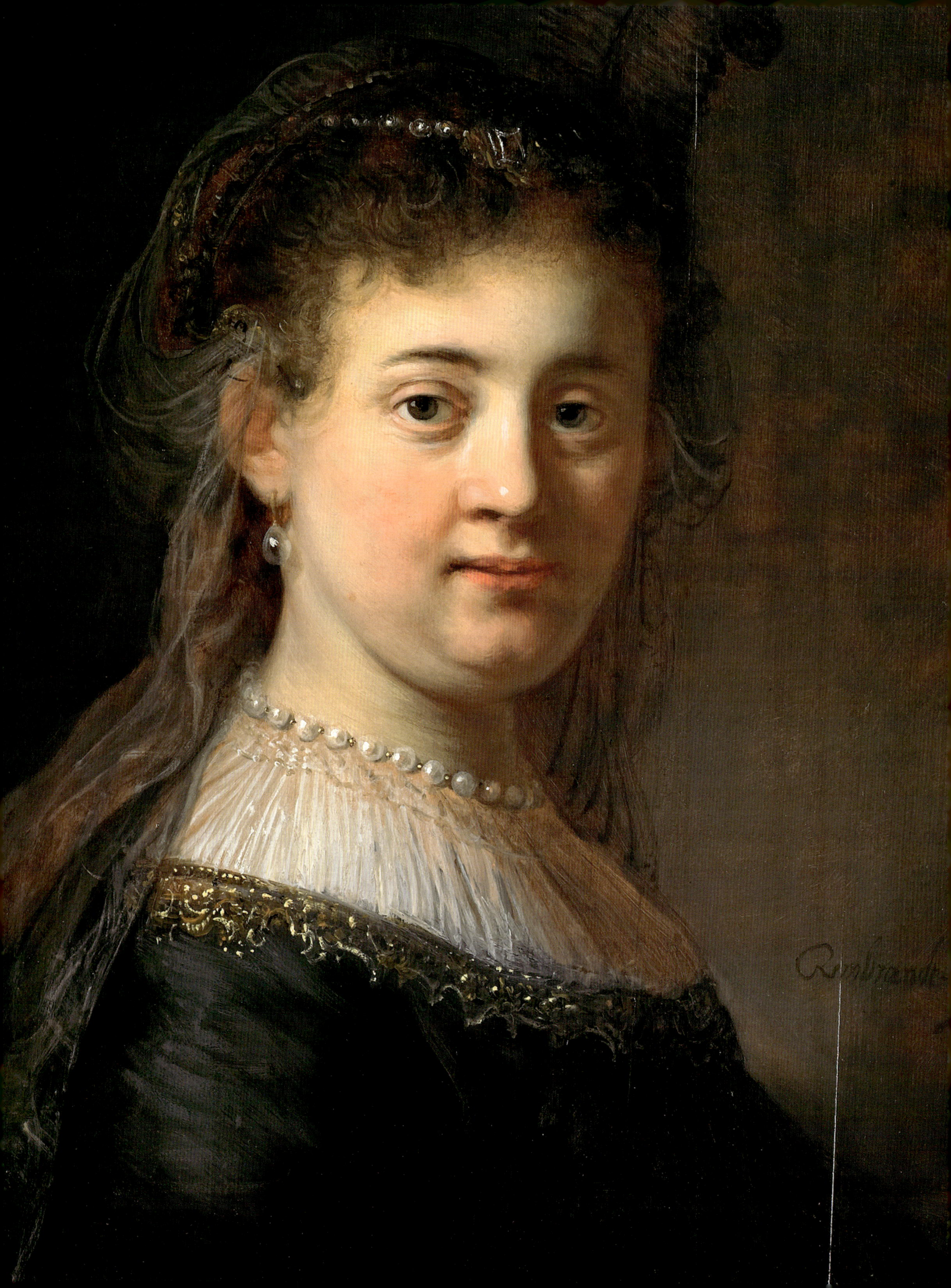
Rembrandt

# 6

# BURGHERS, REGENTS, AND ARISTOCRATS IN THE REPUBLIC

THE PROSPEROUS BURGHERS AND REGENTS of the Dutch Republic enjoyed a way of life in the second half of the 17th century that previously had been reserved for the nobility. Important to that life were country estates or manor houses outside the city, places where the newly rich could revel in rural pleasures. This was a favorable time for the arts, as patrons justly proud of their success or their family's standing were eager to have themselves immortalized in paint and stone. Many artists found a living by painting portraits of upper-class Dutchmen and their families.

A relatively small group of aristocratic families set their stamp on the quality of art produced during this period. Foremost among them were members of the court of the stadholders of the House of Orange, who increasingly competed with their peers in foreign courts. The stadholder William III and Mary Stuart, who became king and queen of England in 1689, were art lovers who built and decorated a number of palaces in England and the Netherlands.

Family portraits were prominently displayed in the richly furnished reception rooms of upper-class homes, often with images of members of the House of Orange, well-known clergymen, or other much-admired public figures. This custom underscored the strong economic and social identity of the household while broadcasting its reliability and solvency. The family portrait remained so popular throughout the first four decades of the 17th century that it evolved into an independent genre, with its own formal language and traditions.

The convention of portraying families in a single row made it easier to add children as they were born, but it created discrepancies in age and fashion. To overcome this problem, and in keeping with an increasing taste for historicizing portraits, after 1650 families were often depicted in timeless antique or pastoral costumes. Interaction between the various figures was muted so that the composition would be flexible enough to accept later additions. Around 1600 a family would most likely be painted indoors, gathered around a table groaning with delicacies, but in the second half of the century more specific motifs might be inserted, such as a country home in the background or attributes referring to a profession or great wealth.

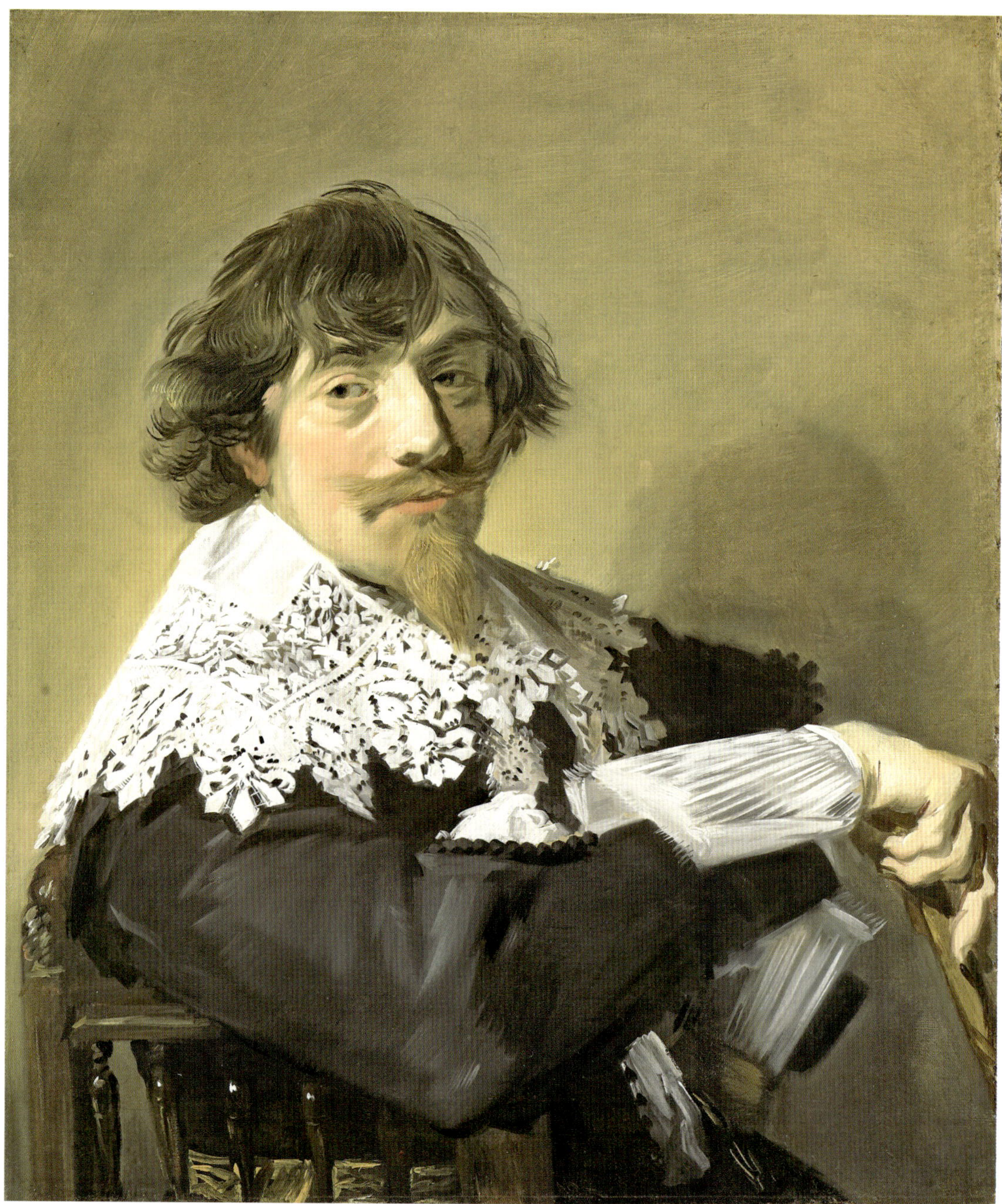

63 Frans Hals (1581/85–1666) · *Portrait of a Man, Possibly Nicolaes Hasselaer (1593–1653), Brewer and Captain-Major of the Civic Guard in Amsterdam* (c. 1633–1635) · Oil on canvas · 31¼ × 26¼ inches

64 Gerard ter Borch (1617–1681) · *François de Vicq (1646–1707), Burgomaster of Amsterdam for Several Terms from 1697* (1670) · Oil on canvas · 15¼ × 12¼ inches

65 Gerard ter Borch (1617–1681) · *Aletta Pancras (1649–1707), Wife of François de Vicq* (1670) · Oil on canvas · 15¼ × 12¼ inches

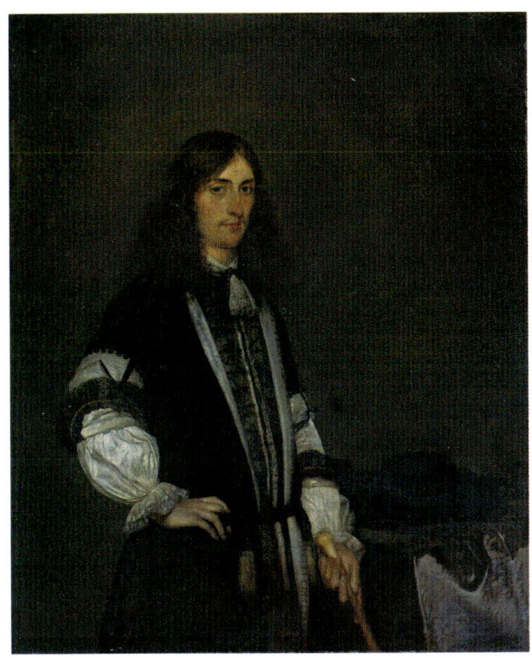

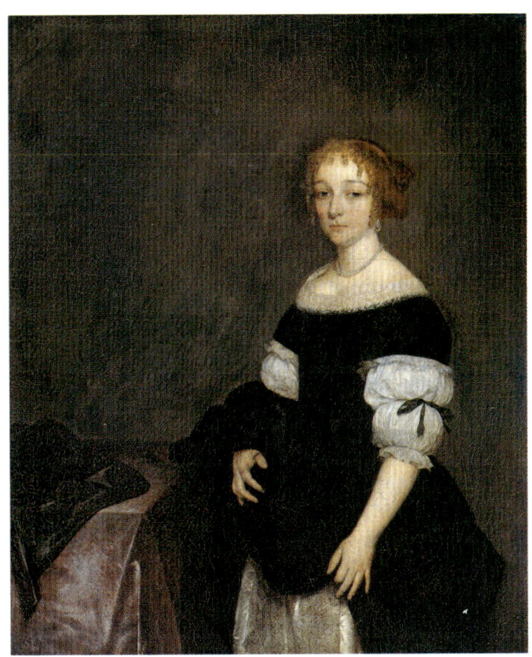

Frans Hals (1581/85–1666) found a clientele for his exceptional, dynamic portraiture among the burghers of the Netherlands. In *Portrait of a Man, Possibly Nicolaes Hasselaer (1593–1653), Brewer and Captain-Major of the Civic Guard in Amsterdam* (no. 63), painted around 1633–1635, the artist captured his sitter with great immediacy and directness, relying on the pose, the fall of light, and energetic brushstrokes to convey personality. The subject is thought to be the middle-class Dutch burgher Nicolaes Hasselaer, who made his fortune as a beer brewer and served in various public offices, including diplomat in Russia, regent of Amsterdam's municipal orphanage, and officer of the local military body.

Hals imbued this portrait with a sense of vitality and immediacy by painting directly onto the canvas, without any preparatory underpainting. The spatial arrangement is also quite daring. Instead of being seen in a frontal pose, the torso and left arm push diagonally into the picture plane; the right arm crosses in front of the chair, and the man's hand rests on a staff. The face is animated by the clear daylight falling presumably from a window on the left. Distinct from the theatrical light of Caravaggio, or the spiritual "inner" light of Rembrandt's late works, Hals's use of light looks forward to the Impressionists: it is the mobile, shimmering, animating light of day. The bravura brushwork, with which Hals captured the strength and life of the right hand in just a few strokes, is typical of the artist's bold, confident manner.

Around 1645 Gerard ter Borch (1617–1681) developed a relatively small-scale portrait type in which the subject is seen from the knees up against a neutral background. Many other painters adopted his innovation. Ter Borch painted *François de Vicq (1646–1707), Burgomaster of Amsterdam for Several Terms from 1697* and *Aletta Pancras (1649–1707), Wife of François de Vicq* (nos. 64 and 65) in 1670, when the sitters were twenty-four and twenty-one years of age, respectively. The couple belonged to a small group of immensely rich Amsterdam families who for generations had filled the most important public offices in the city. These regents aspired to nobility: they bought

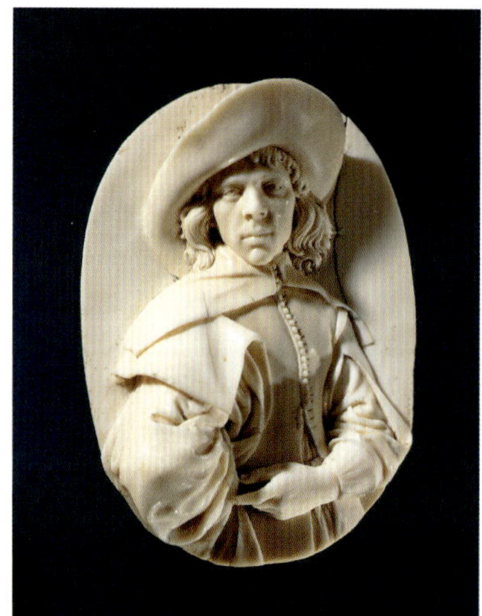

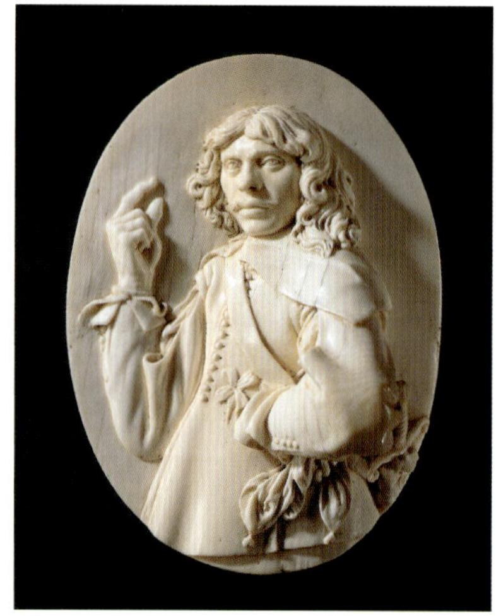

castles and land with titles and rights, had impressive family trees drawn up, built country houses, and extended their power by intermarrying.

Ter Borch's skill in rendering not only people but also a wide range of fabrics and surfaces was legendary among his contemporaries and during the 1670s led to portrait commissions from many of Amsterdam's dignitaries. In the case of the De Vicq portraits, Ter Borch probably landed the commission with the help of his brother-in-law, Sybrant Schellinger, an Amsterdam merchant and a relation of François de Vicq. The subdued richness favored by regents such as De Vicq and his wife is beautifully illustrated by their clothing in Ter Borch's portraits. De Vicq's brilliant white linen shirt, the gleaming satin lining of his overcoat, the silver brocade vest just visible underneath it, and the lace jabot at his neck, combined with the customary stately black of the trousers, lend him an aristocratic élan. Somewhat coquettish, Aletta Pancras subtly lifts her black overskirt with her fingers to show off a costly petticoat of wonderfully embroidered, gleaming satin. Her large pearl eardrop sparkles against the dark background.

Two ivory portrait medallions of young gentlemen (nos. 66 a, b) were undoubtedly carved as a pair. The degree of accomplishment suggests that their author was Rombout Verhulst (1624–1698), a Fleming who emigrated north, attracted by the favorable climate for sculpture in Holland during the second half of the 17th century. Verhulst became the most prominent sculptor in the Netherlands, renowned for his phenomenal technique and the naturalism of his sculptures, many of which were portraits. The subjects of these portrait medallions have not been identified, but the remarkable resemblance between the two men suggests that they are either

**66 A, B** Rombout Verhulst (1624–1698), attributed · *Portrait Medallions of Young Gentlemen* (c. 1660) · Ivory · h. 4¾ inches; depth: 1¼ inches (each)

**67** Abraham van den Tempel (1622/23–1672) · *David Leeuw (1631/32–1703), Amsterdam Merchant with His Family* (1671) · Oil on canvas · 74¾ × 78¾ inches

brothers or the same person at different ages. The bare-headed figure with the bushy moustache is attired in the military or paramilitary costume of a civic guard guild. His pose, with an arm held proudly akimbo, jutting out at the viewer, is often found in depictions of military officers. Both men, though one more obviously than the other, make a strange gesture. It may be symbolic of resolve, as it corresponds to the illustration of this virtue in Cesare Ripa's *Iconologia* (1593), a key source of symbolic images for Dutch 17th-century artists. Alternatively, it might be an indication of the measure between the thumb and forefinger, and the young men may thus be urging the viewer to practice moderation.

Virtue is also the subtle subtext in *David Leeuw (1631/32–1703), Amsterdam Merchant with His Family* (no. 67). The subject's Mennonite coreligionist Abraham van den Tempel (1622/23–1672) painted the Leeuw family in 1671 gathered on a terrace with a view of a garden, with all the children making music in one form or another. To the left, David Leeuw stands behind his wife, Cornelia Hooft, with their dog at her feet. On her lap their youngest daughter, Suzanna (age two), brandishes a flute. Next to them, Cornelia (age eight) holds a songbook, while Weyntje (age twelve) plays a harpsichord. To the right, their only son, Pieter (age fourteen),

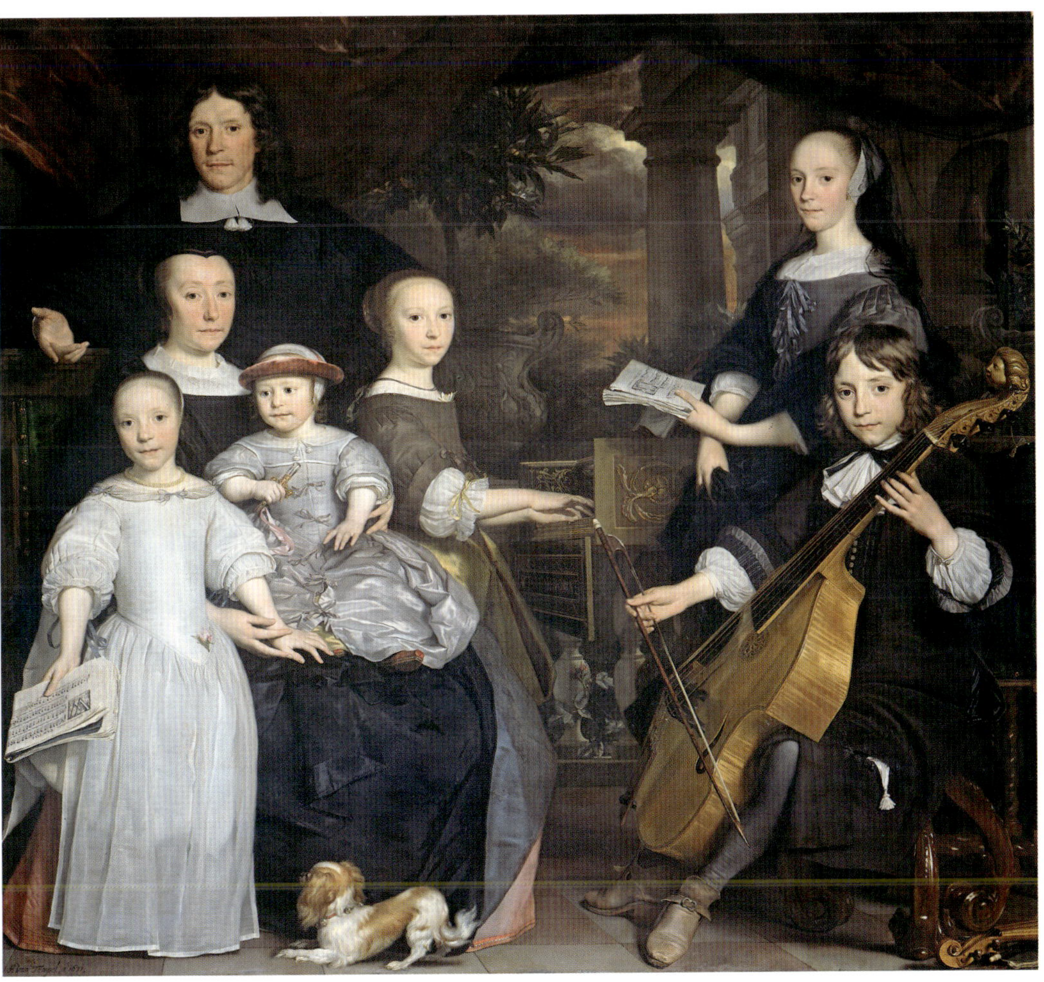

plays a viola da gamba, and their eldest child, Maria (age eighteen), stands behind him with a songbook. It appears that the four eldest children are about to sing a religious song. The emphasis in this portrait is on the accomplishments of the group. The sitters make music together, indicating that this is a good and harmonious family whose individual members are in tune with one another.

Other portrait types extolled an individual's social status. Depicting a man on horseback, for example, automatically cast him in the noble tradition of leadership. The Amsterdam portrait painter Thomas de Keyser (1596/97–1667), son of the famous architect and sculptor Hendrick de Keyser (1565–1621), made his first equestrian portraits in the 1660s. They are very elegant renderings of riders on horseback set against vast, broad landscapes. His masterpiece in the genre, and one the most famous Dutch equestrian portraits, is the monumental *Pieter Schout (1640–1669), High Bailiff of Hagestein,* dated 1660 (no. 68). It is painted on an unusually large copper plate, whose smooth surface was particularly suited to De Keyser's delicate execution and the high degree of finish in the rendering of textures. Both the horse, a black Andalusian, and its rider are lavishly outfitted. Schout wears a satin jacket with slit sleeves, high boots with shiny spurs, and a hat with a thin metallic braid at the edge of the brim. A striking feature is the sword with a lion's head, which hangs in an embroidered holder. De Keyser selected a low viewpoint to subordinate the river landscape, and placed the high bailiff on horseback against an open sky, thus enhancing the dignity of the portrait and recalling the equestrian portraits of monarchs. A print by Abraham Blooteling (1640–1690), possibly made in conjunction with the painting, reproduces De Keyser's work with a long laudatory poem commending Schout as an excellent horseman and loyal supporter of the House of Orange. The lion of the sword, a symbol for the House of Orange, clearly refers to this connection; the art of horse riding was associated with the ability to govern.

The attributes that surround the wealthy merchant Jan Six (1618–1700) in an etched portrait (no. 69, p. 110) by Rembrandt make it clear that here is a man of letters. Six was a major patron of Rembrandt, and contacts between him and the artist can be securely documented from 1647, when this print was made. Their relationship was one of friendship rather than simply that of patron and artist: Rembrandt etched the title page for Six's tragedy *Medea* (1648) and made two drawings for his Album Amicorum in 1652, and in 1653 Six lent the artist the considerable sum of one thousand guilders when Rembrandt found himself in financial difficulties.

In the print, Rembrandt has portrayed his friend as the poet and intellectual he was, reading as he leans casually on the windowsill of his Amsterdam home. Six's erudition and status are implied by the book he is reading and those piled on the chair before him, the ceremonial sword on the table, and the painting on the wall to the left. The painting, an Old Testament subject by the look of it, is largely covered by a curtain (just as in the paintings by Gerard Dou

**68** Thomas de Keyser (1596/97–1667) · *Pieter Schout (1640–1669), High Bailiff of Hagestein* (1660) · Oil on copper · 33¾ × 27¼ inches

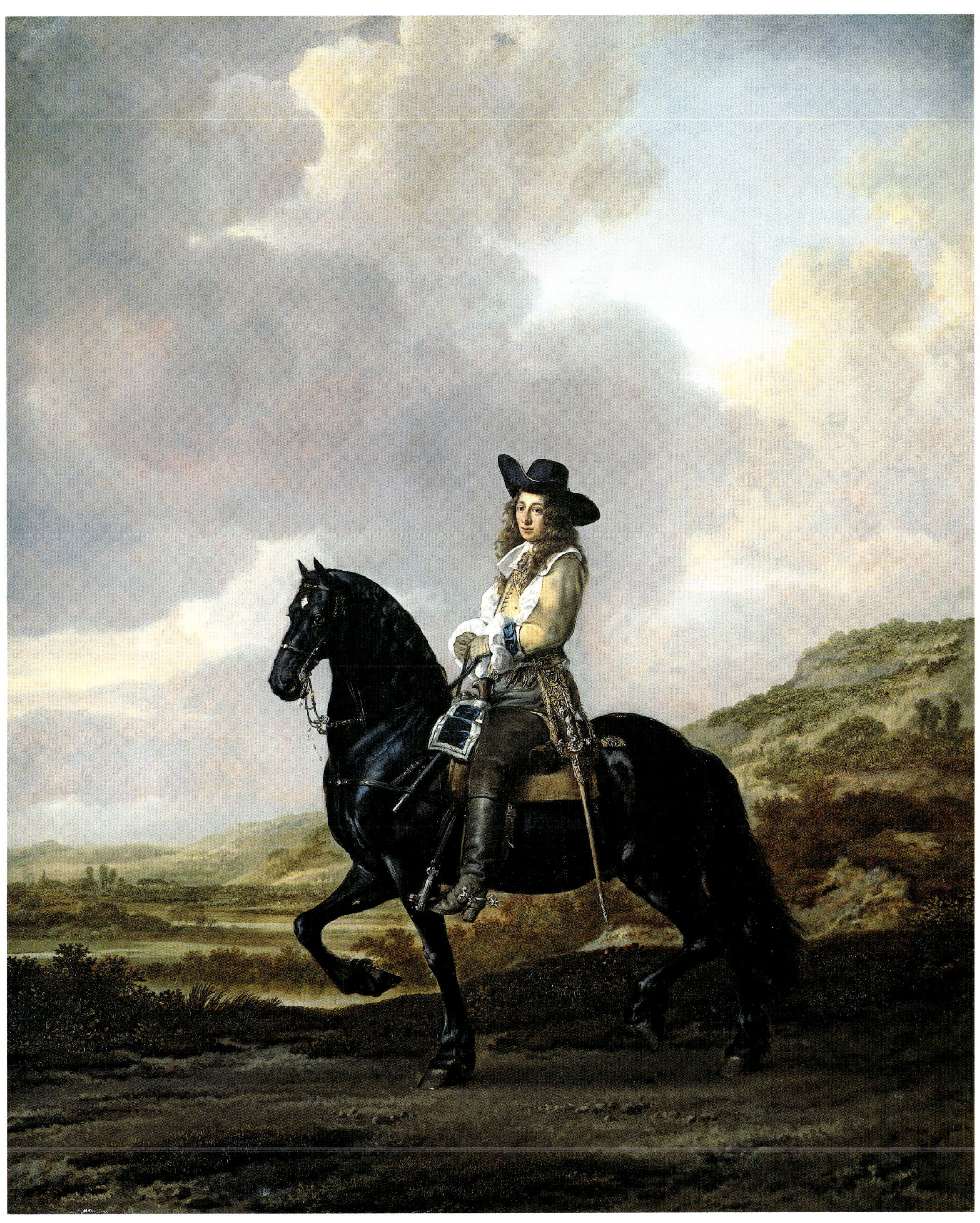

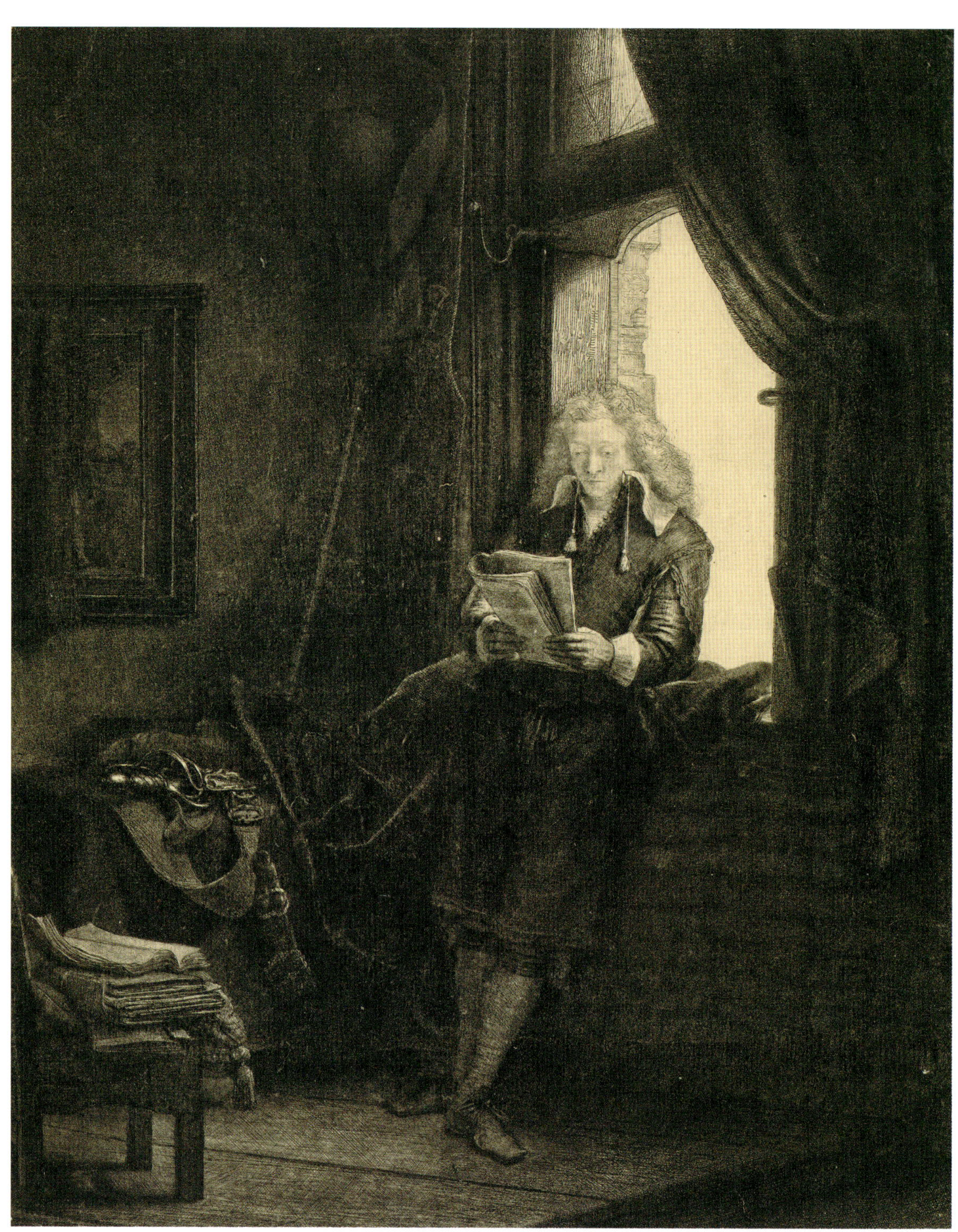

and Gerrit Houckgeest, pp. 26 and 101). Rembrandt obviously devoted considerable attention to this print and worked it out to the smallest detail. He achieved a remarkable refinement in the production of a rich, velvety background tone, etching and scratching layer upon layer, cross-hatching on the plate. The effects and softness of tone are particularly beautiful in impressions on Japanese paper, as in this example. In a sophisticated trick of lighting, Rembrandt placed Six with his back to the open window but illuminated his face only indirectly, by the light refracting off the white page of his book. Over the past centuries, an impression of Rembrandt's etched portrait of Jan Six has been the *non plus ultra* for a print connoisseur. The rarity of the print, of which only a small number of impressions were made in four states, Rembrandt's connection with the sitter, and above all the pictorial finish of the print help to explain why it attained such legendary status.

A man of many talents, the painter Paulus Moreelse (1571–1638) came in contact with a prestigious circle of potential patrons in Utrecht through his work as an architect; he also held a number of important public offices. Members of the stadholder's court commissioned him to create portraits, genre pieces, and paintings based on mythological or pastoral themes, such as *The Beautiful Shepherdess* of 1630 (no. 70, p. 112). Moreelse is believed to have introduced these pastoral half-length figures about 1617. The type gained great popularity with Utrecht's artists in the 1620s and subsequently with artists in other Dutch cities. In the 1630s depictions of a life-size half-figure in a diagonal composition modeled on the paintings of Caravaggio were part of the repertoire of several Utrecht artists. Moreelse had seen and been strongly influenced by Caravaggio's works when he visited Italy around 1596.

The pastoral idiom had developed in both literature and the visual arts in the early 17th century. Shepherds and shepherdesses figure in such plays as *Granida* (1605) by Pieter Cornelisz Hooft, inspired in part by Battista Guarini's popular *Il Pastor Fido* (1589). The upsurge of pastoral subjects, to a degree, was a response to urban growth and its attendant overcrowding and social ills. In contrast the country seemed a haven, and the depiction of the shepherd's life became a favorite expression of the yearning for an idealized retreat. Although most of Moreelse's provocative shepherdesses were conceived as independent paintings, some of them had a male pendant. Sometimes these were commissioned from the artist as official gifts, which is another indication of the enormous popularity of pastoral images in this period.

Moreelse's example was followed by the young Govert Flinck, among others, who painted *Rembrandt as Shepherd with Staff and Flute* around 1636 (no. 71, p. 113). It is Flinck's first known painting, from the time when he had just completed three years of training in Rembrandt's studio and established himself as an independent master in Amsterdam. Rembrandt's influence can be seen in the white sleeve and the gold decoration on the shepherd's tunic, where paint has been applied very thickly to suggest structure. Tradition has it that Flinck portrayed his former master dressed as a shepherd with a flute, shepherd's staff, and bag, although some experts now doubt

69 Rembrandt van Rijn (1606–1669) · *Jan Six (1618–1700), Amsterdam Merchant, Writer, and Art Collector* (1647) · Etching, drypoint, and burin on Japanese paper · 9½ × 7½ inches

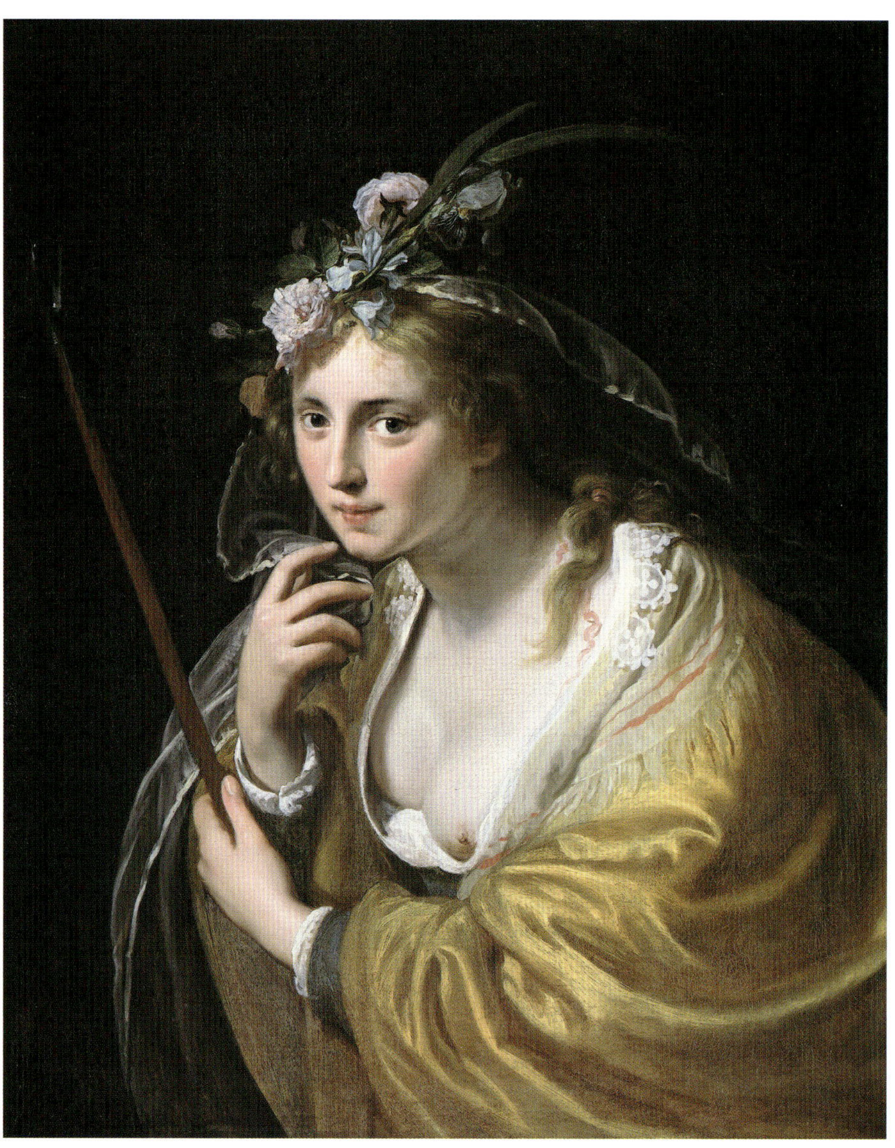

70 Paulus Moreelse (1571–1638) · *The Beautiful Shepherdess* (1630) · Oil on canvas · 32¼ × 26 inches

71 Govert Flinck (1615–1660) · *Rembrandt as Shepherd with Staff and Flute* (c. 1636) · Oil on canvas · 29¼ × 25¼ inches

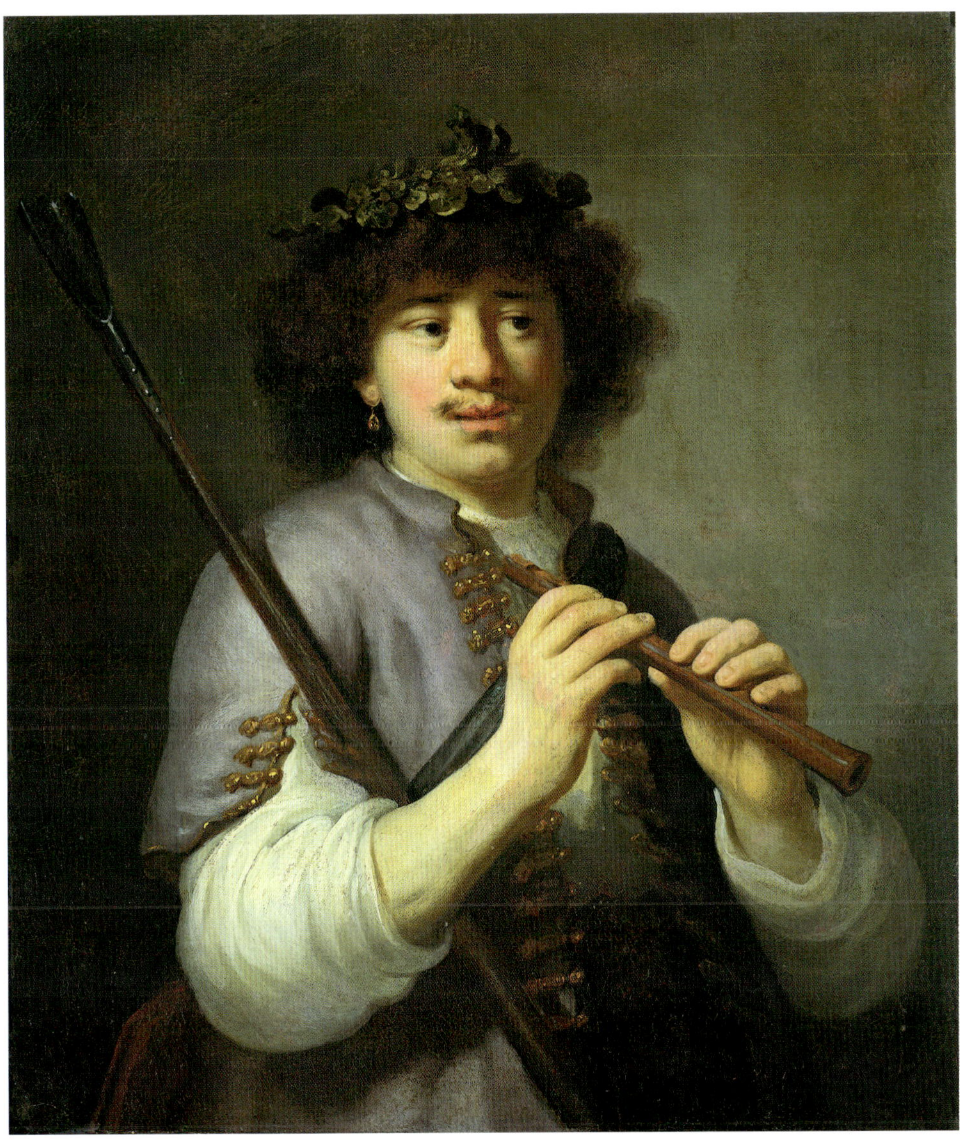

this identification. Because it corresponds in size and subject, Flinck's painting of a shepherdess now in the German Herzog Anton-Ulrich Museum in Brunswick is believed to be the pendant of the present work. This shepherdess has been tentatively identified as Saskia van Uylenburgh (1612–1642), Rembrandt's first wife.

Saskia, the well-to-do daughter of a former burgomaster of Leeuwarden, was orphaned at the age of twelve. Rembrandt probably met her through her uncle, the Amsterdam art dealer Hendrick van Uylenburgh, in whose house Rembrandt lived. He was also an important patron and business partner of Rembrandt. After their marriage, Rembrandt and Saskia remained lodged in Uylenburgh's house until they moved in 1635 to a rented home in Amsterdam. In 1633, the year of their engagement, Rembrandt portrayed the wealthy twenty-year-old Saskia in fancy dress, wearing jewels in her hair, a veil, and lots of pearls (no. 72, p. 114). She is positioned

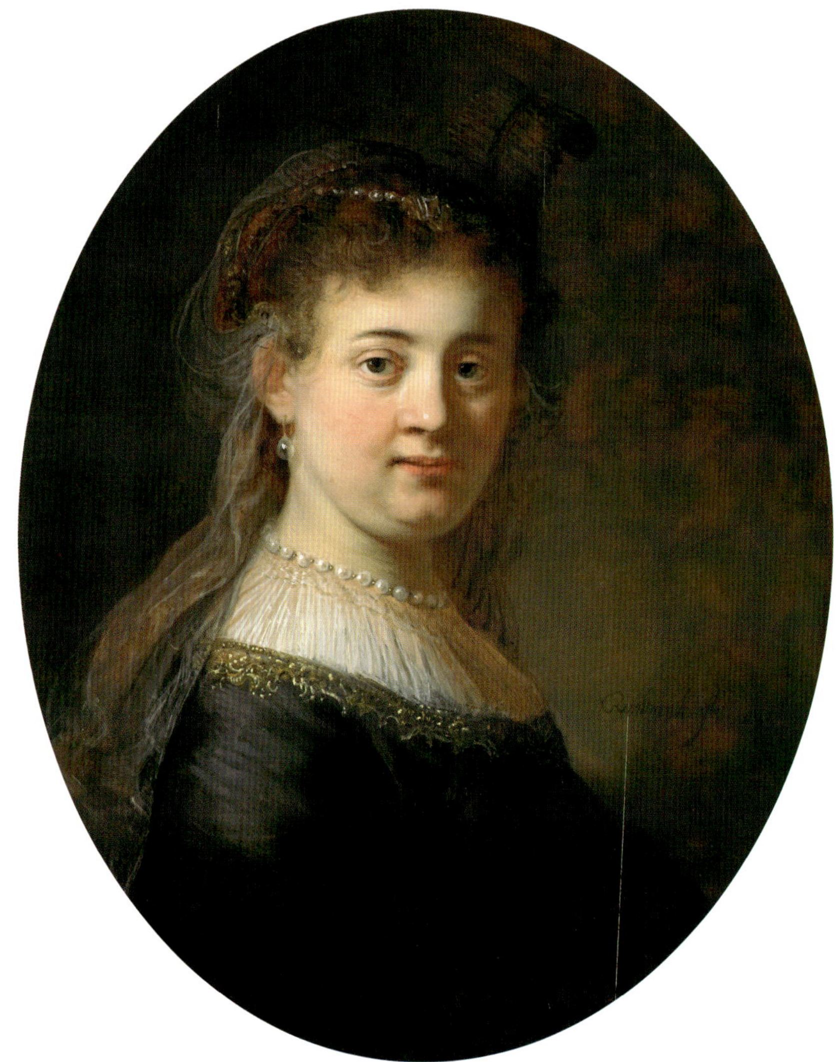

somewhat strangely to the left of center in the painting because the panel, originally rectangular, was made oval later on.

Many affluent Dutch burghers went abroad for extended periods on a journey known as the Grand Tour. Throughout Europe, such a trip was regarded as the best way for young men to round off their educations and as an important part of their introduction to society. France and Italy were seen as the countries with the most to offer cultured young gentlemen. While elsewhere in Europe these travelers were mainly from aristocratic families, in the Republic they also

72 Rembrandt van Rijn (1606–1669) · *Saskia van Uylenburgh (1612–1642), Rembrandt's Wife from 1634* (1633) · Oil on panel · 25½ × 19 inches (oval)

73 Aert de Gelder (1645–1727) · *Ernestus van Beveren (1660–1722), Lord of West Ysselmonde and de Lindt* (1685) · Oil on canvas · 50½ × 41¼ inches

included wealthy merchants and members of the regent class. In these social strata, the Grand Tour was considered a valuable preparation for an administrative career, while for those destined for public office it was an excellent way to further one's knowledge, shape one's character, and acquire the esteemed virtue of "prudentia" (prudence).

Ernestus van Beveren (1660–1722), lord of West Ysselmonde and de Lindt, had just completed a Grand Tour when his fellow townsman Aert de Gelder (1645–1727) portrayed him (no. 73). He was twenty-five years old and had already gained a degree in law from the University of Anjou in 1683. Before long Van Beveren would embark on a career in local politics, serving as alderman, burgomaster, and, from 1704, postmaster of Dordrecht. To give his model a more worthy and timeless character, De Gelder dressed Van Beveren in a heavy black robe trimmed with gold embroidery over a tunic, probably a costume from the artist's studio wardrobe. De Gelder was Rembrandt's last pupil and shared his predilection for imaginary costumes, thickly applied paint, the technique of scratching into the paint with the butt end of a brush, and a preference for yellow-ochre and browns. Throughout his career De Gelder remained faithful to his master's style, and, unlike most of Rembrandt's former pupils, he was apparently unconcerned that by the 1650s this painting style was regarded by many as passé.

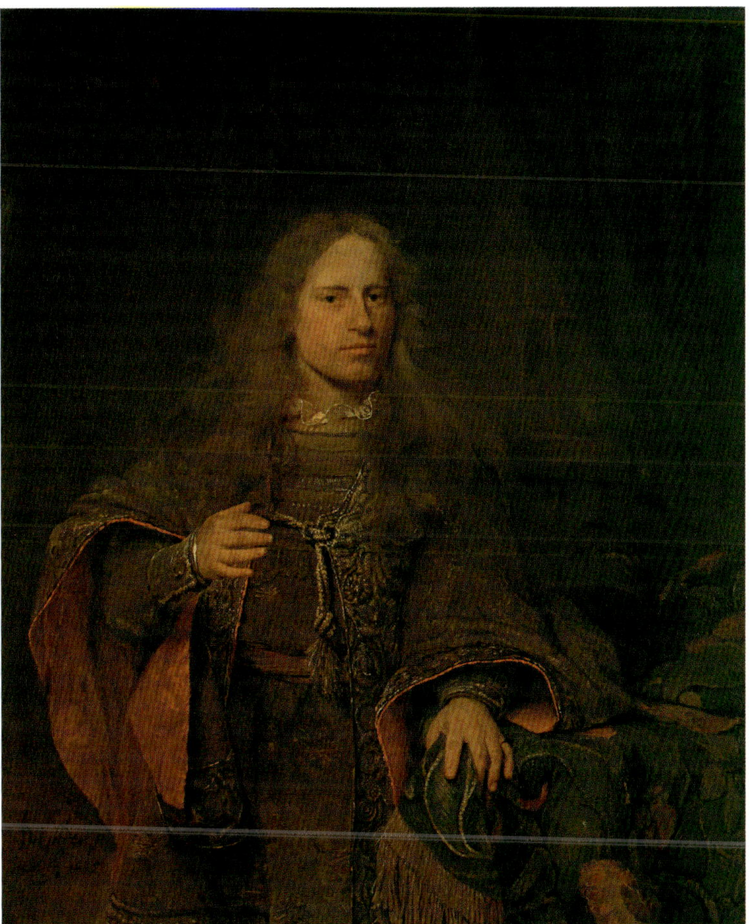

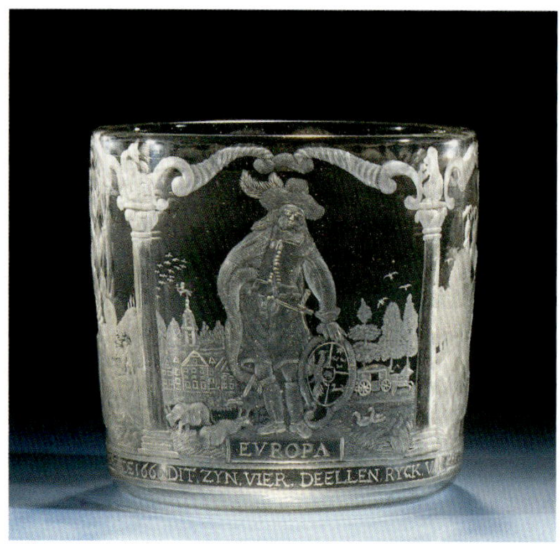


The portrait of the Amsterdam burgomaster Joan Huydecoper (1599–1661) is featured in the engraved decoration of a commemorative glass beaker dated 1660 (no. 74). Wheel-engraved glass was first made in the northern Netherlands around 1650, and this beaker, with its representations of the four continents, is one of the outstanding examples from this early period.

Wheel engraving—embellishing glass with inscriptions or decorations by the grinding action of a wheel—is one of the oldest decorative techniques used on glass. The engraver holds a glass object with both hands against the underside of a rotating disc, usually made of copper. The actual grinding away of the surface of the glass is achieved with the help of an abrasive (finely ground glass bound together with oil), which was either applied directly to the disc or, as is still the case today, trickled onto the glass from above.

In the beaker's elaborate engraved decoration Huydecoper is shown in a feathered hat in front of his country house, Goudesteijn (near the village of Maarssen). His left hand rests on an oval shield bearing his coat of arms, and below him is the indication of the continent he represents, Europe. Asia is personified by a turbaned Arab with a staff in his right hand, set in a landscape with trees, a monkey, and a dromedary. Africa is represented by a warrior wrapped in an animal skin, seen from behind, in a landscape with palms and a score of animals. America is personified in a river landscape by a Native American wearing a feathered headdress and a quiver of arrows on his back, with a bow and arrow in his left hand, and a parrot in his right. Beneath

74 Northern Netherlands · *Beaker with the Portrait of Joan Huydecoper (1599–1661), Burgomaster of Amsterdam* (1660) · Glass · h. 3½ inches, diam. 3½ inches

75 Dirck Dircksz van Santvoort (1610–1680) · *Martinus Alewijn (1634–1684)* (1644) · Oil on canvas · 48¾ × 38¾ inches

76 Dirck Dircksz van Santvoort (1610–1680) · *Clara Alewijn (1635–1670?)* (1644) · Oil on canvas · 48 × 35¾ inches

the figures is a continuous band inscribed (in translation): "Rich in treasures, people, places, are the four parts that one sees; their welfare is in tranquility, the earth prospers in peace, 1660." Possibly, the glass was engraved on the occasion of Huydecoper's fifth election as burgomaster of Amsterdam in 1660, or to commemorate his representation of the city of Amsterdam at the coronation of Charles II in London that year.

Abraham Dircksz Alewijn (1607–1679) was a prosperous Amsterdam merchant trading in cloth and East Indian goods. He and his wife, Geertruid Hooftman, presumably commissioned the portraits (nos. 75 and 76) of their two eldest children, Martinus Alewijn and Clara Alewijn from the Amsterdam painter Dirck Dircksz van Santvoort (1610–1680) to decorate their home. In 1641 they had moved into a grand house on the Herengracht, which can be seen at the extreme left in Jan van der Heyden's Amsterdam cityscape (p. 58). Pastoral portraits of children, usually painted in full figure, were extremely popular with the urban elite in Holland from the 1640s onward. These buyers generally associated landscapes populated with shepherds and pastoral figures with a certain sophistication and the more material aspects of country life, such as investment in property—preferably with a noble title attached. Dirck van Santvoort painted the Alewijn children in 1644 dressed in fantastic garments with attributes (a hunting horn, shepherd's crook, hunting bow, and floral wreath) that symbolize both pastoral and hunting activities. Like the Herengracht house in which they were hung, the portraits would have underscored the prominent social position of the Alewijn family to contemporaries, as the hunt was a pastime of the wealthy upper class and at one time a privilege reserved exclusively for the nobility.

Although the hunt had become a popular theme in Dutch landscape painting by the 16th century, the list of Dutch 17th-century artists who produced hunt paintings is long and indicates a

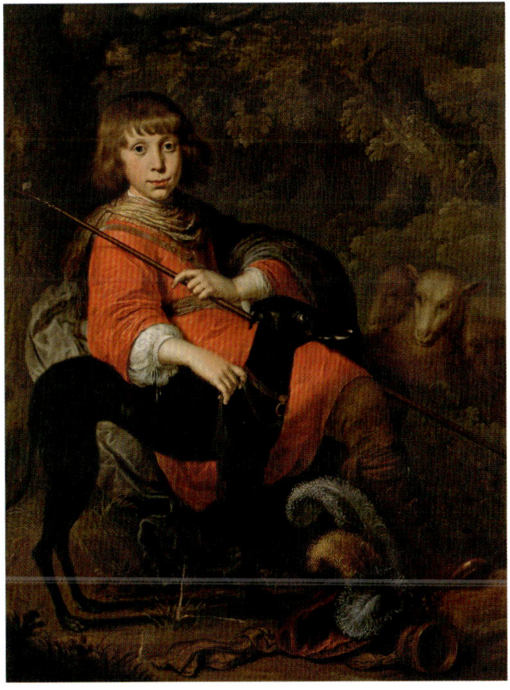

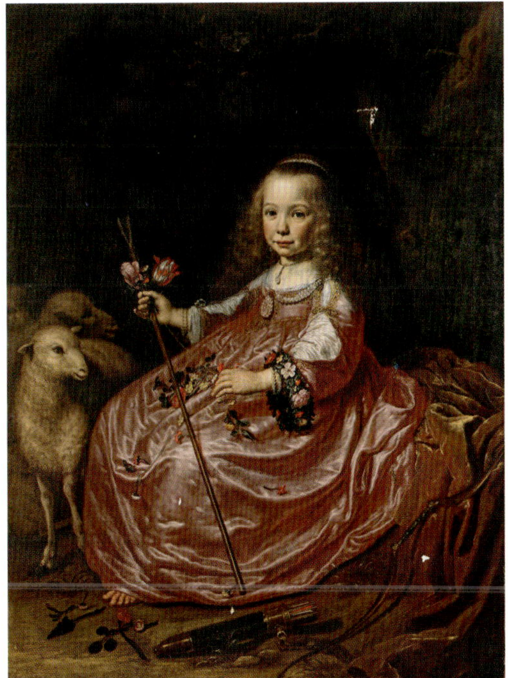

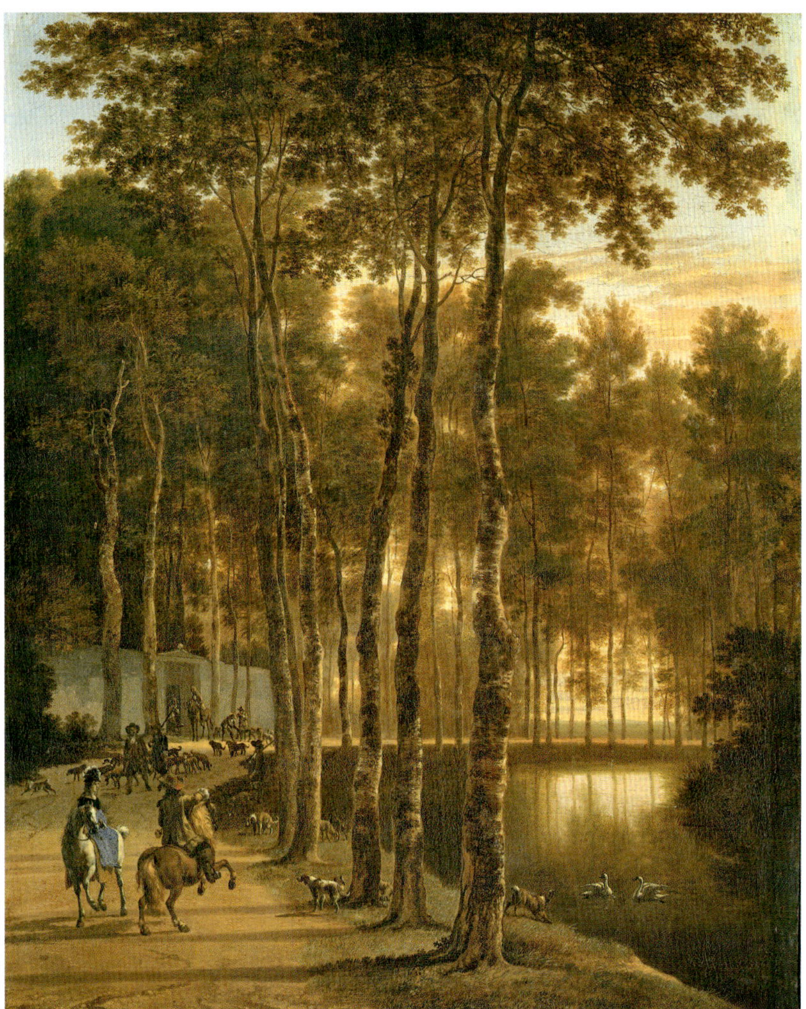

particularly great demand for such works at that time. From the beginning of the century, artists began depicting preparations for or the return from the hunt, rather than representing the event itself. In the composition of *Avenue of Birches* (no. 77), Jan Hackaert portrayed preparations for the hunt in a forest landscape with a clarity and order that would satisfy a contemporary taste for stateliness and elegance.

Hackaert was celebrated for woodland scenes that seem to place the viewer within the painting rather than outside, as a spectator. In this scene, golden light, recalling the warmth of the Italian sun, filters through the foliage of tall, majestic trees and is reflected in the calm waters of the lake. For this work, one of his masterpieces, Hackaert employed one of his favorite

77 Jan Hackaert (c. 1629–before 1685) · *Avenue of Birches* (c. 1660–1685) · Oil on canvas · 26¼ × 21 inches

78 Melchior d'Hondecoeter (1636–1695) · *Birds in a Park* (1686) · Oil on canvas · 44 × 55 inches

compositions: a dramatic head-on view down a long avenue with figures on one side and a row of tall trees on the other. The image of the birches is doubled by their reflection in the water, and their slenderness is further enhanced by the vertical format of the painting.



Paintings of poultry may seem an unlikely decoration for upper-class houses, but in the hands of the specialist Melchior d'Hondecoeter (1636–1695) such was the case. The portrayal of fowl and poultry yards and still lifes featuring birds and attributes of the hunt were a specialty the artist inherited from his father, Gijsbert d'Hondecoeter (1603–1653), originally a master from Antwerp. After moving from his birthplace of Utrecht to Amsterdam in 1663, Melchior d'Hondecoeter made a name for himself with a clientele of wealthy merchants and regents who, from the late 1660s, were decorating newly built canal houses and luxurious country homes. Hondecoeter's stately park landscapes with exotic birds and his monumental hunt still lifes were much in demand, and his ability to represent the feathers and skins of creatures so that they are almost tangible was widely admired. It is said that Hondecoeter had trained a cock to stand still on command to pose for him. Probably in reality it was somewhat more complicated, as one of the objects described in Hondecoeter's inventory at his death was "a small gallow on which birds could be fastened."

Hondecoeter's clientele included the stadholder-king William III who, from the 1670s on, commissioned various large paintings for his palaces. *Birds in a Park* of 1686 (no. 78) features both familiar Dutch domestic fowl and exotic birds. Hondecoeter painted these birds from life, using his own poultry yard. The more exotic species he would have studied in the aviaries at country houses. His patron William III had an extensive menagerie at one of his palaces and several aviaries. Thus Hondecoeter's realistic depictions were an illustration of an aristocratic interest.

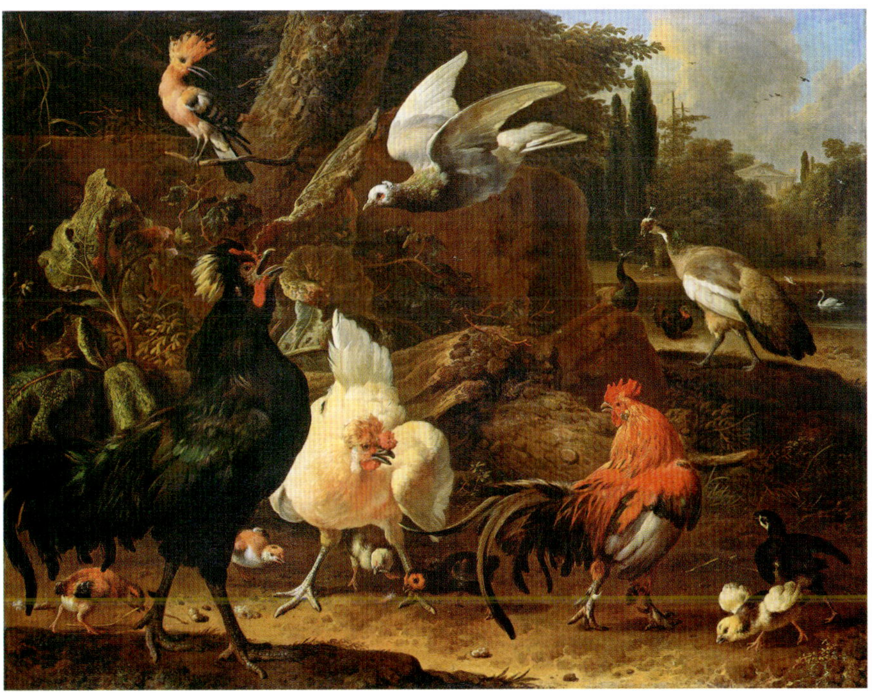

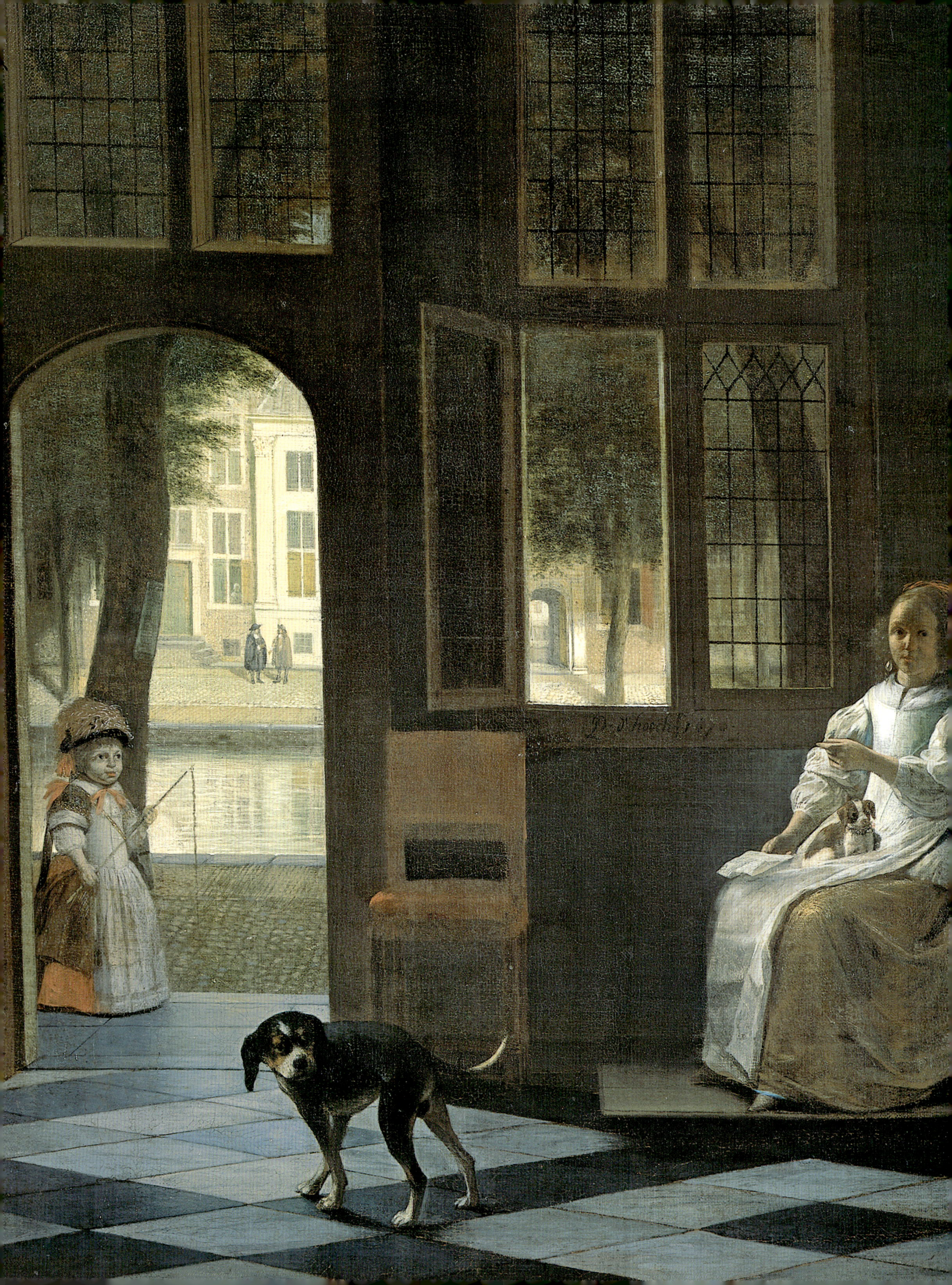

# 7
# GENRE PAINTING

PAINTINGS IN WHICH PEOPLE ARE PORTRAYED going about their everyday activities—in and around the house, in a tavern, at work—are known as genre pieces. (The word *genre* is also used more generally to denote painting types, such as a still life, portrait, history painting, or even a genre piece.) Many genre pieces that appear to have been painted from life were actually done in the artist's studio. In many—but not all—of these seemingly realistic paintings, there are hidden, moral messages which are not easy to decipher. The tremendous popularity of genre pieces in the 17th century suggests that people took considerable pleasure in solving their riddles while reveling in their artistic qualities and amusing scenes. Some portraits of the era also have a genre-like quality, and in these works, too, there is more going on than immediately meets the eye.

Adriaen van Ostade, who painted *The Fishwife* (p. 62), is one of the greatest Dutch painters of peasant genre scenes. A substantial number take place in and around country taverns, populated with smoking and drinking peasants. In *"Travelers at Rest": Peasants outside a Country Inn* (no. 79, p. 122), Van Ostade shows such a group engaged in lively conversation. The viewer's eye is drawn to details like a stoneware jug, whose glaze subtly reflects the daylight though the man who holds it is in shadow, and a clay Gouda pipe, prominently positioned on a wooden bench in the foreground. In the 17th century, smoking was not considered unhealthy but corruptive, a vice to which common people were particularly prone. Many of Van Ostade's paintings were meant to entertain the higher social classes with scenes of disreputable peasant life and behavior that "decent" people should avoid. Earlier in his career the artist had painted peasants as coarse figures with rough manners and a penchant for drunkenness and brawling. They were caricatures, clearly intended to serve as bad examples. With the passing years, he took a much milder view of peasant life. Although Van Ostade's subjects drink and smoke, the somewhat pedantic warning is subordinate to a less layered and more sympathetic portrayal, which would have appealed to the painter's urban clientele.

In *"The Skaters": Peasants in an Interior* of 1650 (no. 80, p. 123), a group crowds around the hearth of a dimly lit tavern, happily conversing, drinking, and smoking. Outside the tavern

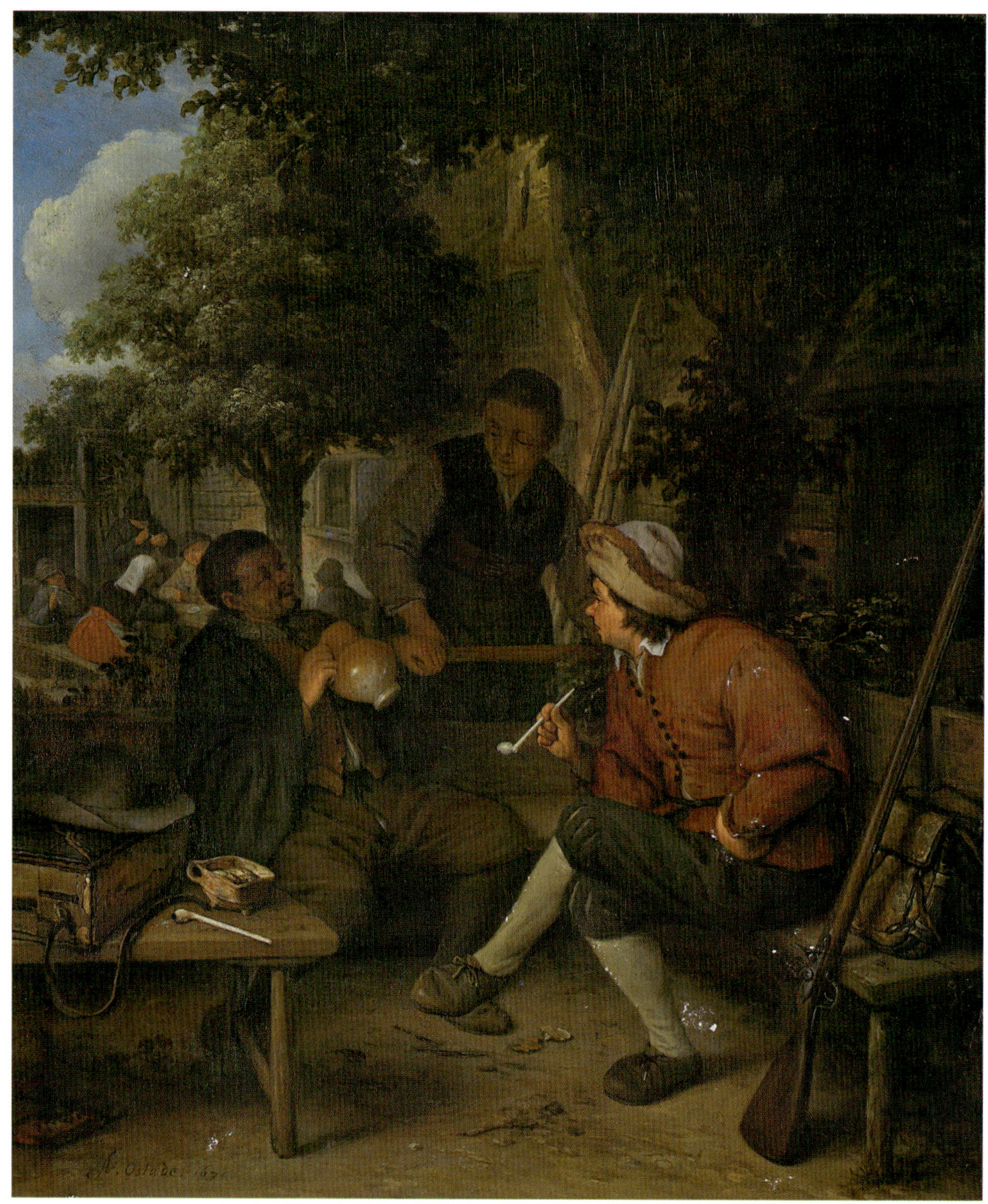

79 Adriaen van Ostade (1610–1685) · *"Travelers at Rest": Peasants outside a Country Inn* (1671) · Oil on panel · 14¼ × 11¾ inches

80 Adriaen van Ostade (1610–1685) · *"The Skaters": Peasants in an Interior* (1650) · Oil on panel · 17¼ × 14 inches

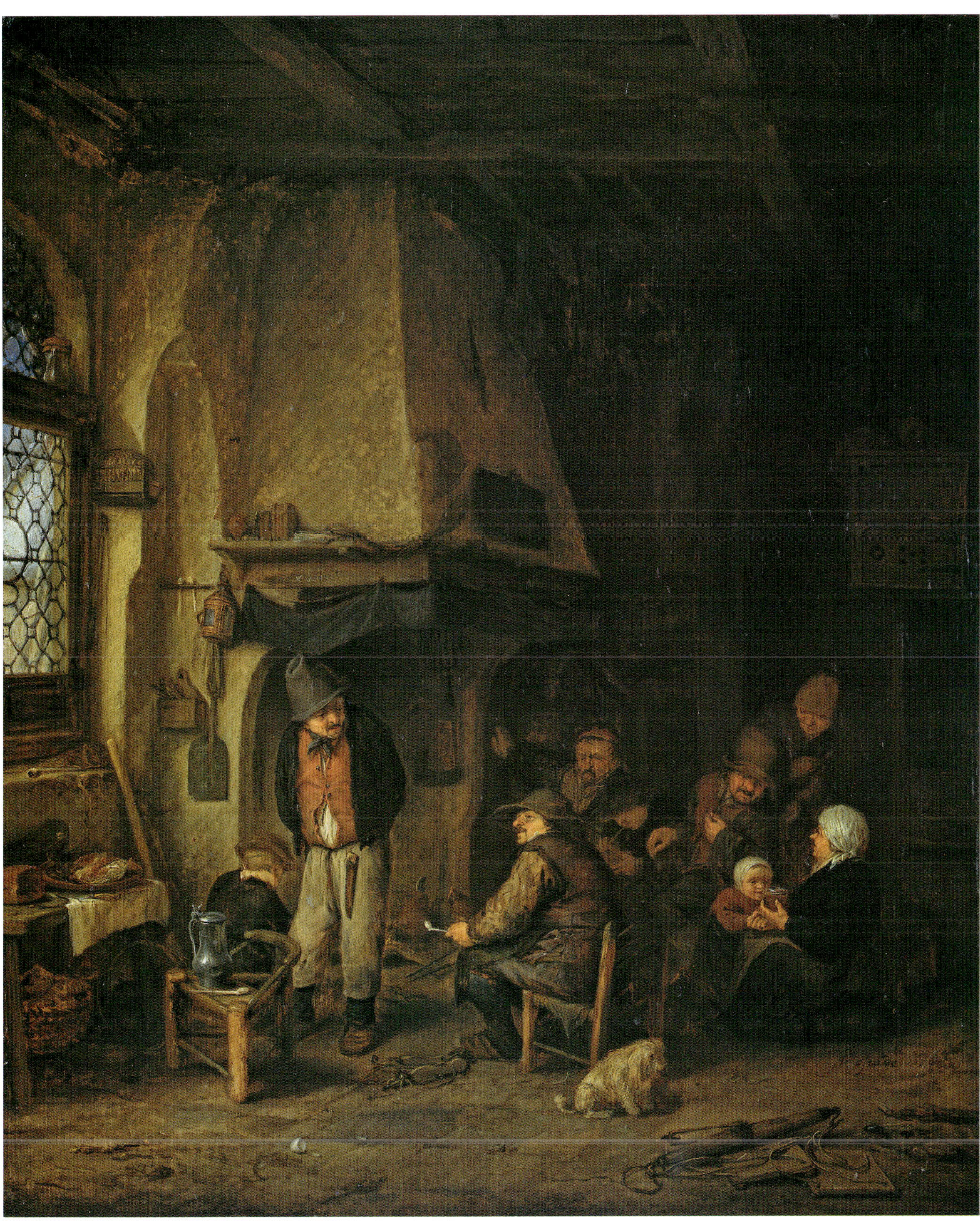

winter apparently has set in, since skates are scattered on the floor—explaining why this painting is traditionally known as *The Skaters.* Van Ostade painted this work in subdued colors: plenty of browns, earthy tints, and discreet reds and greens. He cleverly created sharp contrasts of light and dark, totally obscuring half the interior and reflecting the light, which penetrates through the large window on the left, to fall on only a few areas—notably the face of the foremost peasant and the white head scarves worn by a mother and child. This use of color and contrast of light and dark are reminiscent of Rembrandt's paintings.

Adriaen van Ostade spent his whole life in Haarlem and appears to have been relatively well-off. A member of the local Saint Luke guild of painters, he stood as headman in 1647 and 1661, and in 1662 he was dean. Van Ostade was also a prominent member of the militia. As an artist, he was exceptionally prolific: no fewer than eight hundred paintings and several hundred drawings and watercolors have been preserved. Moreover, in his day he was a renowned etcher, second only to Rembrandt.

Although Rembrandt is known to have drawn several studies of beggars—sketches made in the street and informal etchings—his most fully resolved depiction of the motif is *Beggars Receiving Alms at the Door* of 1648 (no. 81). Rembrandt observed the figures with great precision in the print. It shows an old bearded man wearing a nightcap, leaning on the hatch of a divided door. He places a coin in the outstretched hand of a vagabond woman whose curious baby peers over her back. A man next to the woman plays a hurdy-gurdy (the typical instrument of the itinerant musician), enclosing the knob of the handle with his right hand. His unfocused gaze indicates he is possibly blind. In front of him a boy with hunched shoulders, wearing a large hat, stands watching.

Rembrandt etched the figures meticulously, delineating contours against densely hatched sections behind, sometimes using just a few lines to indicate shapes. The subtle rendering of shadows and the fall of light is applied to great effect. The composition is masterly; nothing distracts from the central event of giving and receiving, the act of charity around which the figures are grouped in a circle. Genre scenes such as this were appreciated in the 17th century as celebrations of charitable virtue and not as personal reflections by artists on the theme of poverty and begging.

Nicolaes Maes (1634–1693) was a student of Rembrandt. His work often communicates an explicit moral message, although his intentions in *Girl at the Window* (no. 82, p. 126) are less obvious than in many of his other genre paintings. A girl leans forward, resting on a pillow placed on a windowsill. Because strong light catches her face and hands, her forward movement from the enclosed space is enhanced, while the rest of her body remains largely obscured, connected to the dark interior. The large, foreshortened red hatch and the horizontal lines of its wooden boards lead the eye to the figure of the daydreaming girl. Her thoughts are far from the everyday housekeeping duties of a maidservant. The painting belongs to the venerable tradition of visual representations of the deadly sin of sloth, and it is the young girl's laziness that Maes presents for our moral judgment.

By contrast, Maes's *Woman Spinning* of about 1657 (no. 83, p. 127) shows an elderly woman busy at her spinning wheel in an orderly domestic space. The act of spinning was commonly

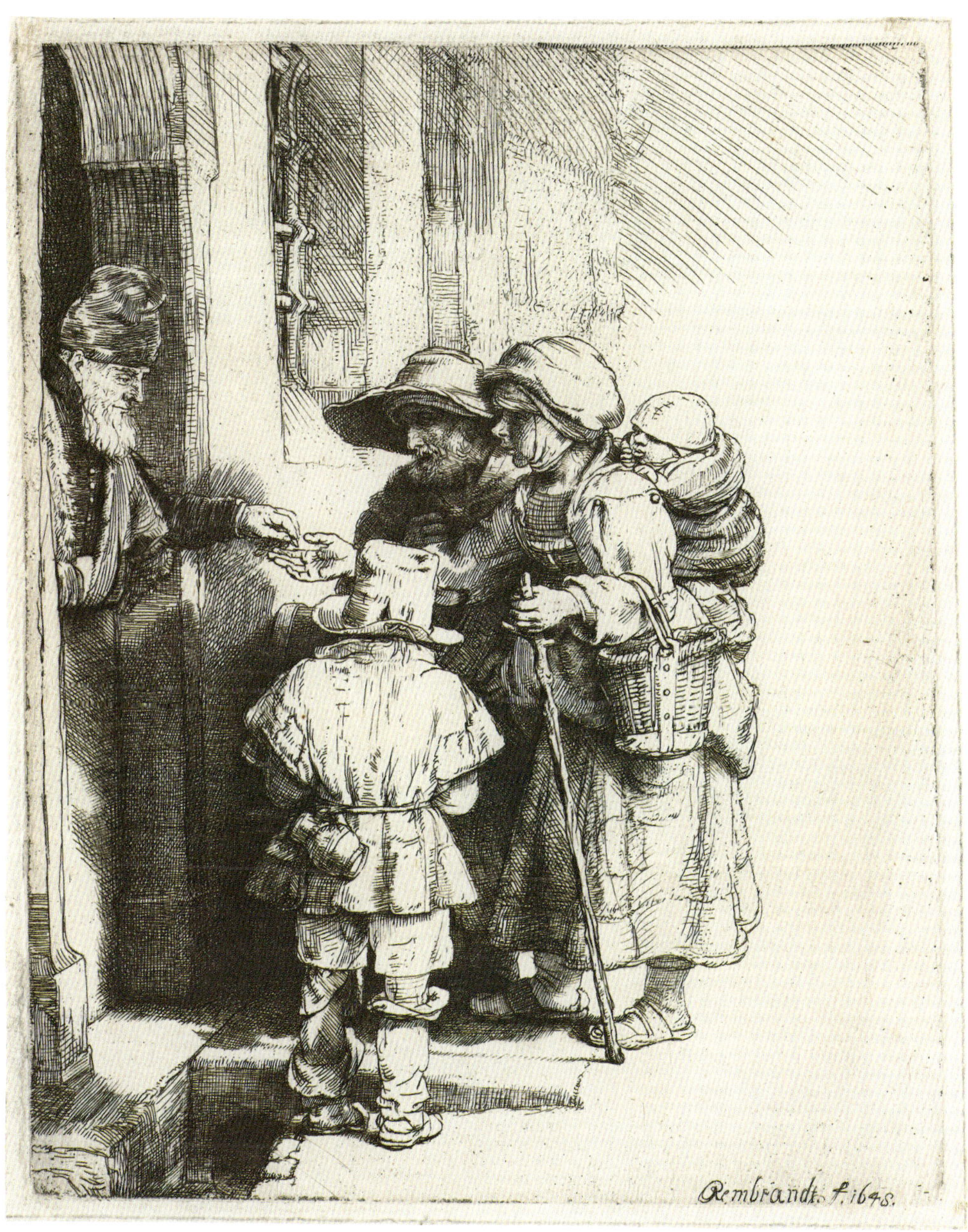


81 Rembrandt van Rijn (1606–1669) · *Beggars Receiving Alms at the Door* (1648) ·
Etching and drypoint · 6½ × 5 inches

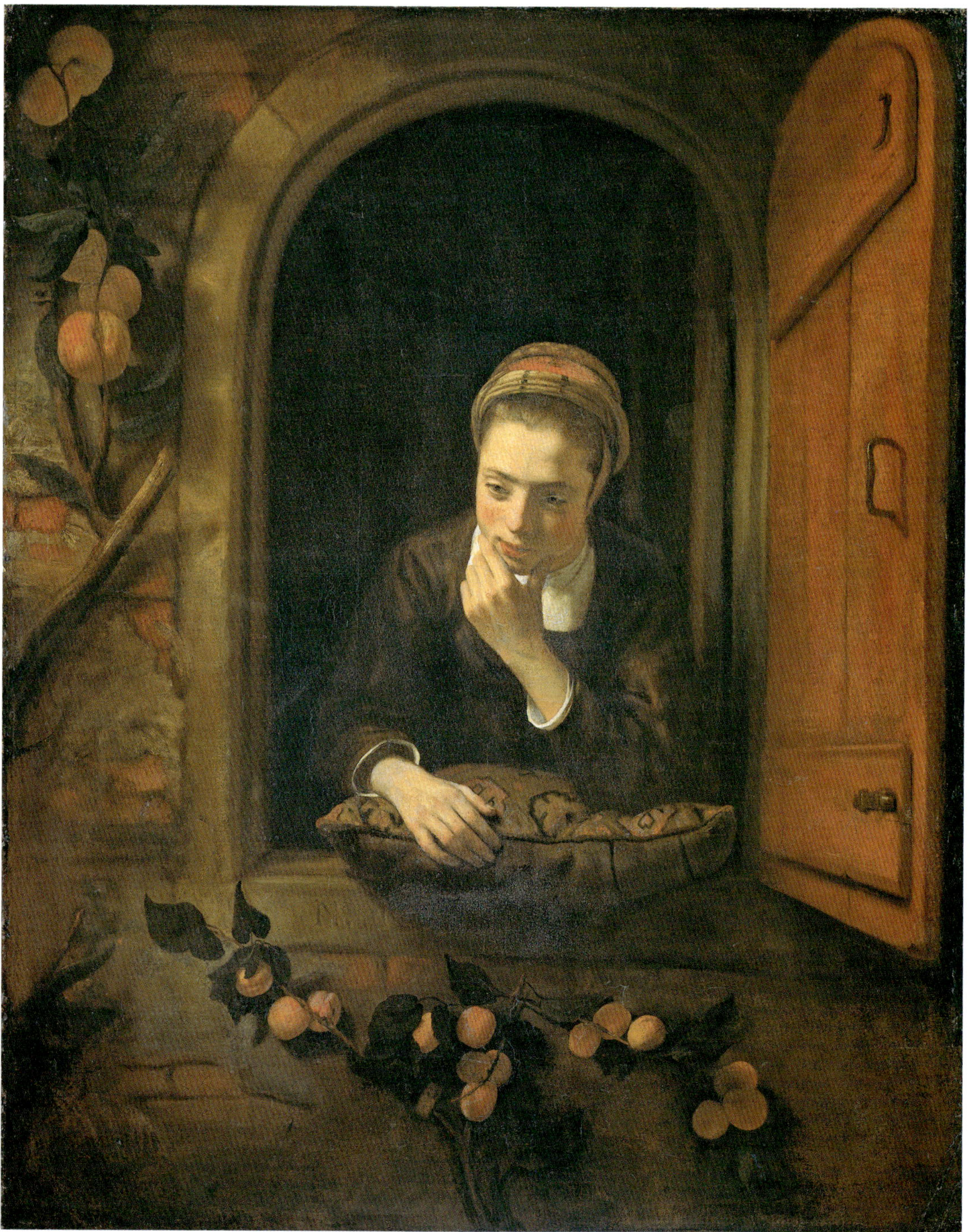

82 Nicolaes Maes (1634–1693) · *Girl at the Window* (c. 1654) · Oil on canvas · 48½ × 37¾ inches

83 Nicolaes Maes (1634–1693) · *Woman Spinning* (c. 1657) · Oil on panel · 16¼ × 13¼ inches

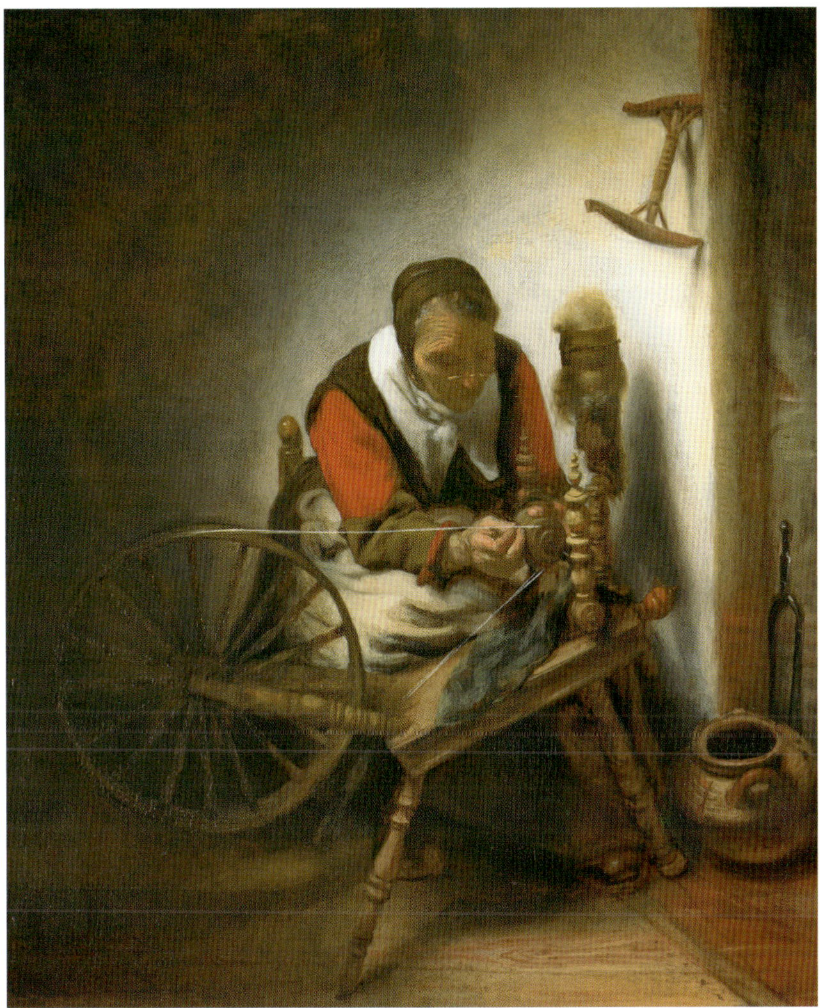

associated with female virtue and diligence. The contemplative nature of the scene, the atmospheric space, and the shadowy sections rich in contrast are reminiscent of Rembrandt's paintings. The saturated colors, especially the deep, shiny black and warm red, are typical of Maes's genre paintings of the 1650s. After 1660 he produced very few such scenes, devoting himself almost exclusively to portrait painting. His style likewise evolved, becoming more elegant, in emulation of the fashion at the French court and in paintings by Flemish artists such as Anthony van Dyck (1599–1641). Ferdinand Bol (1616–1680), a former pupil of Rembrandt who had adopted that same fashionable style, may have influenced Maes's later work. Ultimately the paintings of both men stood quite far off from that of their master.

The *Merry Company* (no. 84, p. 128), dated 1620, is the only known work by Isack Elyas, who probably worked in Haarlem. This seemingly realistic scene of elegantly dressed men and women has been interpreted as a representation of the five senses, based on what is known about the symbolic meaning of such imagery in contemporary prints and emblem literature. The singing lutenist may represent Hearing; the two young men holding glasses, Taste and Touch; the old man holding a strip of paper, Sight (though possibly also Touch); and finally the young girl

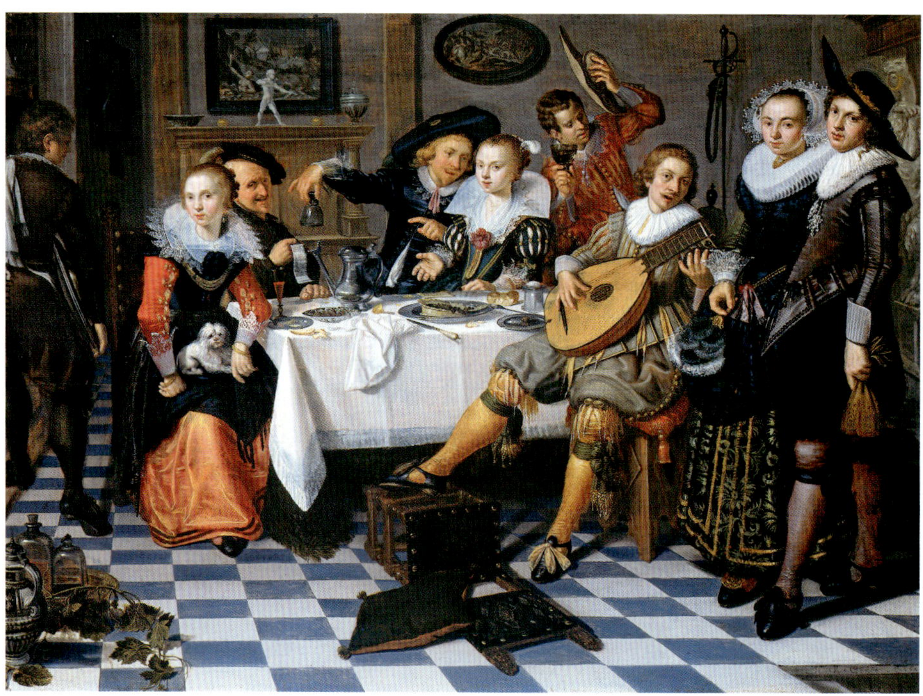

with a lapdog, Smell. A man and woman standing on the extreme right are the only fashionably dressed figures who are not part of the merrymaking. Since the scene may have been intended as a warning against worldly pleasure and frivolity, with their insistent gaze they perhaps invite the young and inexperienced viewer to follow their example and refrain from superficial revelry.

Rembrandt painted *The Music Lesson* (no. 85) in 1626, when he was just twenty years of age. It shows a group of people in a room playing music, but they are hardly ordinary musicians. All are exotically dressed in oriental costumes and extravagant headdresses. The young woman in the foreground reads music from a sheet, singing and beating time, while a young harpist and an older man playing a viola da gamba accompany her. An old woman follows over the girl's shoulder, listening attentively with her hand on her chin. A rich display of books piled high, a violin, and a lute are in the foreground at the company's feet. The meaning of this mysterious scene has not yet been conclusively explained. It is interpreted by some as an allegory of transience, given the presence of common *vanitas* symbols such as musical instruments, a score of books, and several valuables (like the silver beaker on the table). Others think the painting is a reference to love, first and foremost, which was often linked to music. The harmony that is central in both music and marital or family love was an important theme as well in Abraham van den Tempel's portrait of David Leeuw and his family (p. 107).

84 Isack Elyas (active c. 1620) · *Merry Company* (1620) · Oil on panel · 18½ × 24¾ inches

85 Rembrandt van Rijn (1606–1669) · *The Music Lesson* (1626) · Oil on panel · 25 × 19 inches

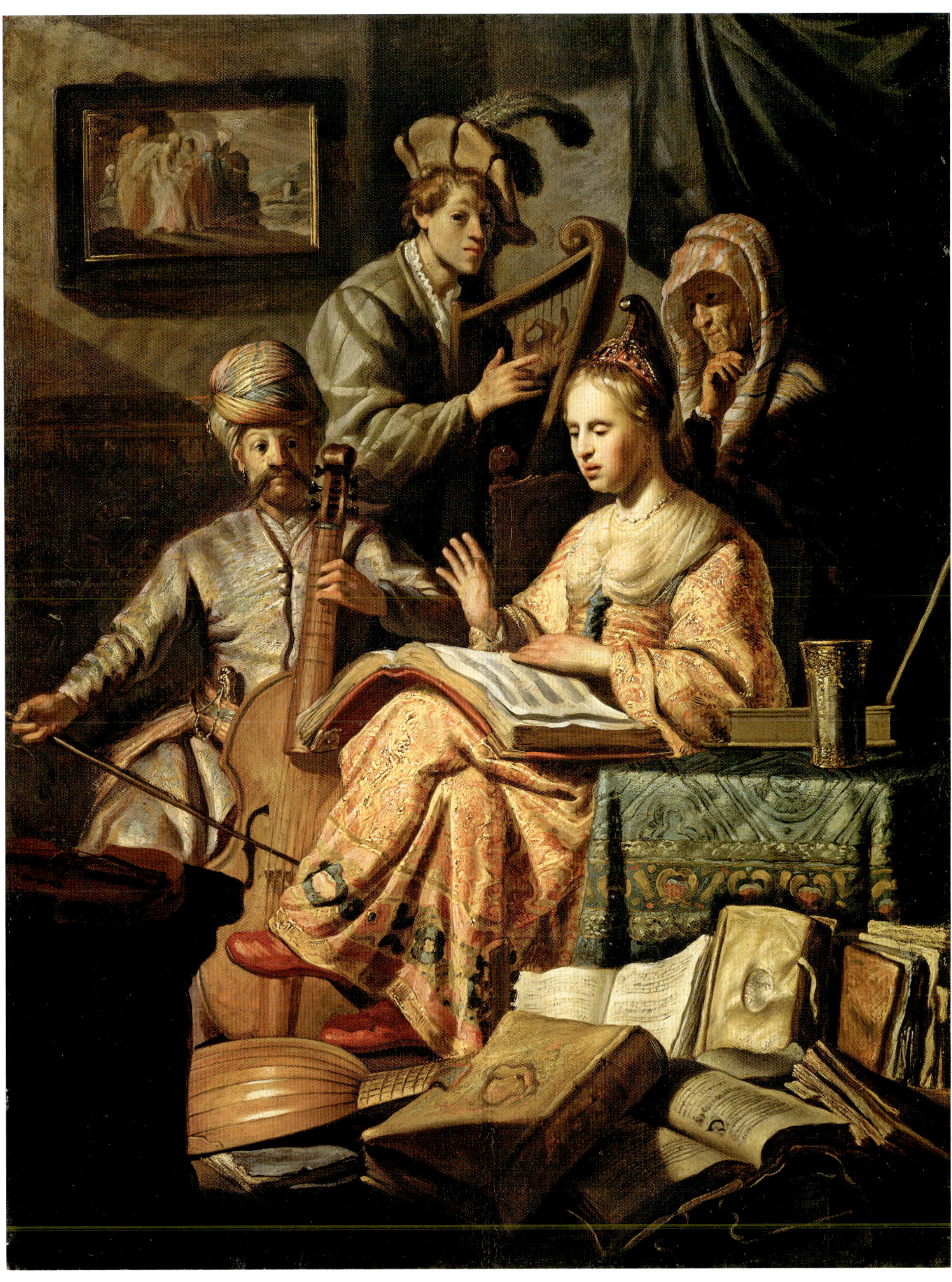

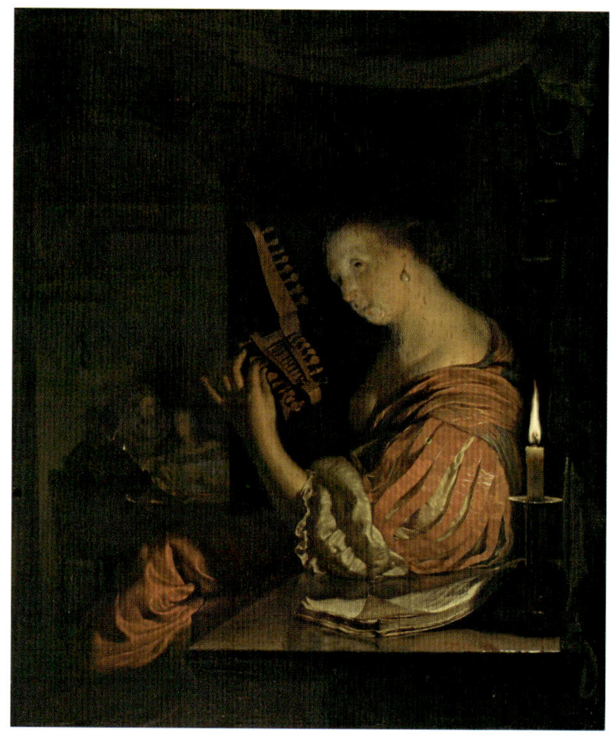

Rembrandt's *Music Lesson* shows he already had considerable technical skill at an early age and could accurately depict the different textures of wood, paper, and fabric. His use of areas of bright light and deep shadow in this composition predict the keen interest in chiaroscuro (contrasts of light and dark) displayed in his later work. But there are differences as well: in this early work Rembrandt's choice of bright colors stands apart from the dark, brownish tonality of his later paintings.

*Tuning the Lute* (no. 86), painted around 1680 by Frans van Mieris I (1635–1681), again illustrates the link between music and love: in the words of the contemporary writer Jacob Cats, "Love makes one sing." The seductive powers of music are the main theme as the elegantly dressed young woman in the painting prepares to make music, perhaps to sing (or to make love?). She plays her lute in an interior lit only by the flame of a burning candle—a common symbol of love. Her left arm rests on an open songbook, with its characteristic oblong format. Behind her, in an adjacent room, three (apparently young) people play cards. The combination of female beauty, music making, and gambling or playing cards is often found in 17th-century brothel scenes, which were a favorite subject of Van Mieris.

86 Frans van Mieris I (1635–1681) · *Tuning the Lute* (c. 1680) · Oil on panel · 8½ × 6¾ inches

87 Gabriel Metsu (1629–1667) · *The Hunter's Present* (c. 1658–1660) · Oil on canvas · 20 × 19 inches

A leading figure in the Leiden school of *fijnschilders* (fine painters), Van Mieris painted many small interior genre scenes, like this work, as well as portraits and historical subjects in an extremely detailed and highly finished manner. Both his style and choice of subjects are closely related to those of his master, Gerard Dou. Like Dou in *Man Smoking a Pipe* (no. 5, p. 26), Van Mieris included a painted curtain in *Tuning the Lute.*

A sexual invitation is the subtext of *The Hunter's Present* (no. 87) by Gabriel Metsu (1629–1667). A man enters a room in which an elegantly dressed lady sits. The partridge he offers her and the rifle and dead duck in the foreground suggest he has just returned from a hunt. But here the hunt referred to is metaphorical. In the 17th century, the gesture of offering game to a woman was a symbolic invitation to a sexual encounter. The partridge refers to the expression "birding" (making love). In this context it is not just any bird the huntsman presents: the partridge was seen as the lustiest of all birds. In popular tradition it was said to break its own eggs so that it would have all the more excuse for mating! The small Cupid on the cupboard and the kicked-out red

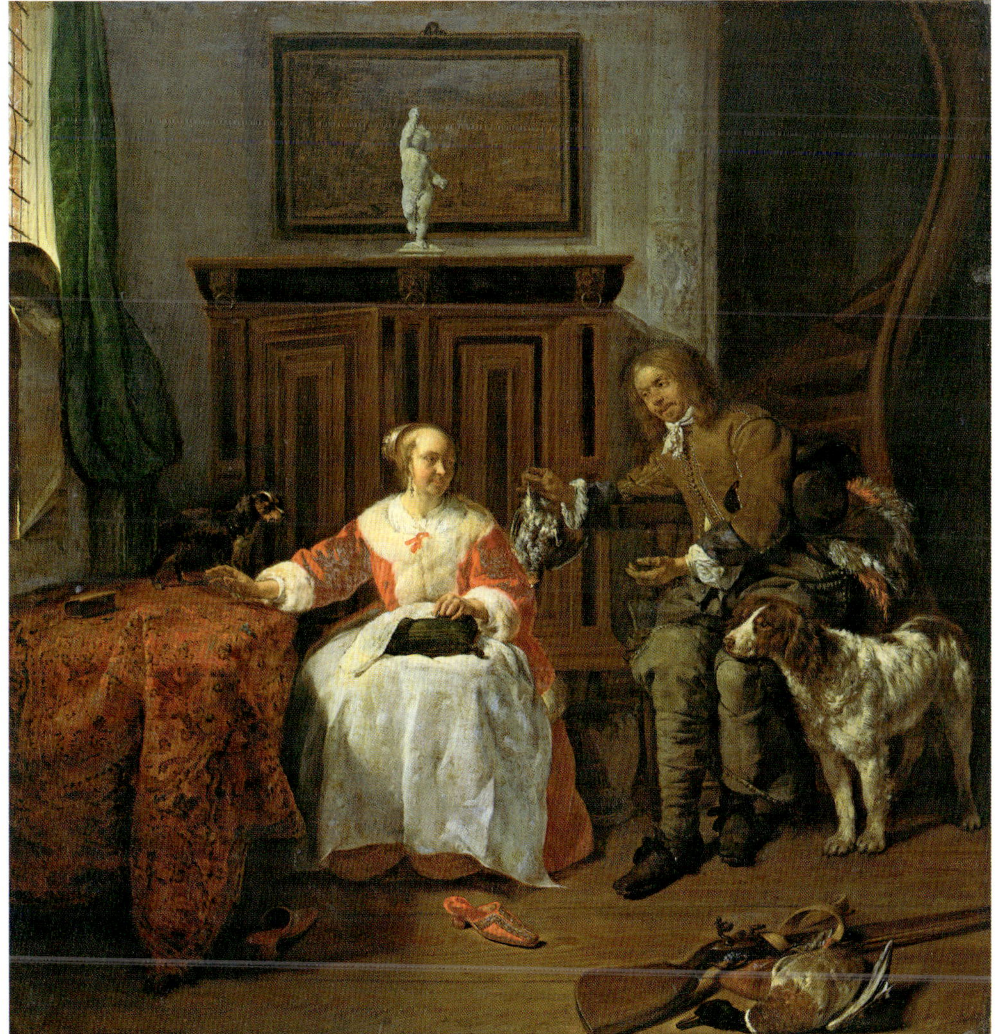

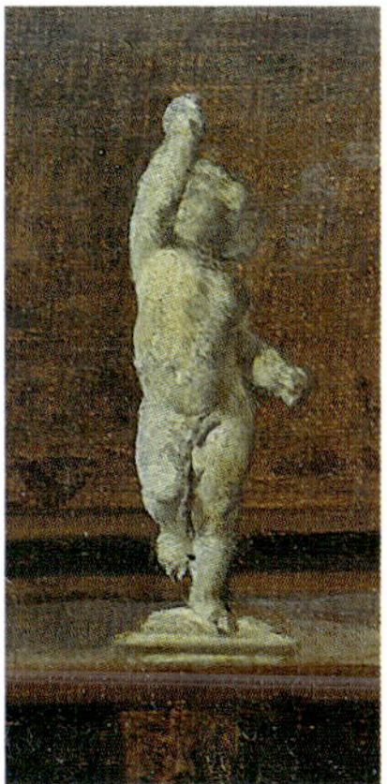

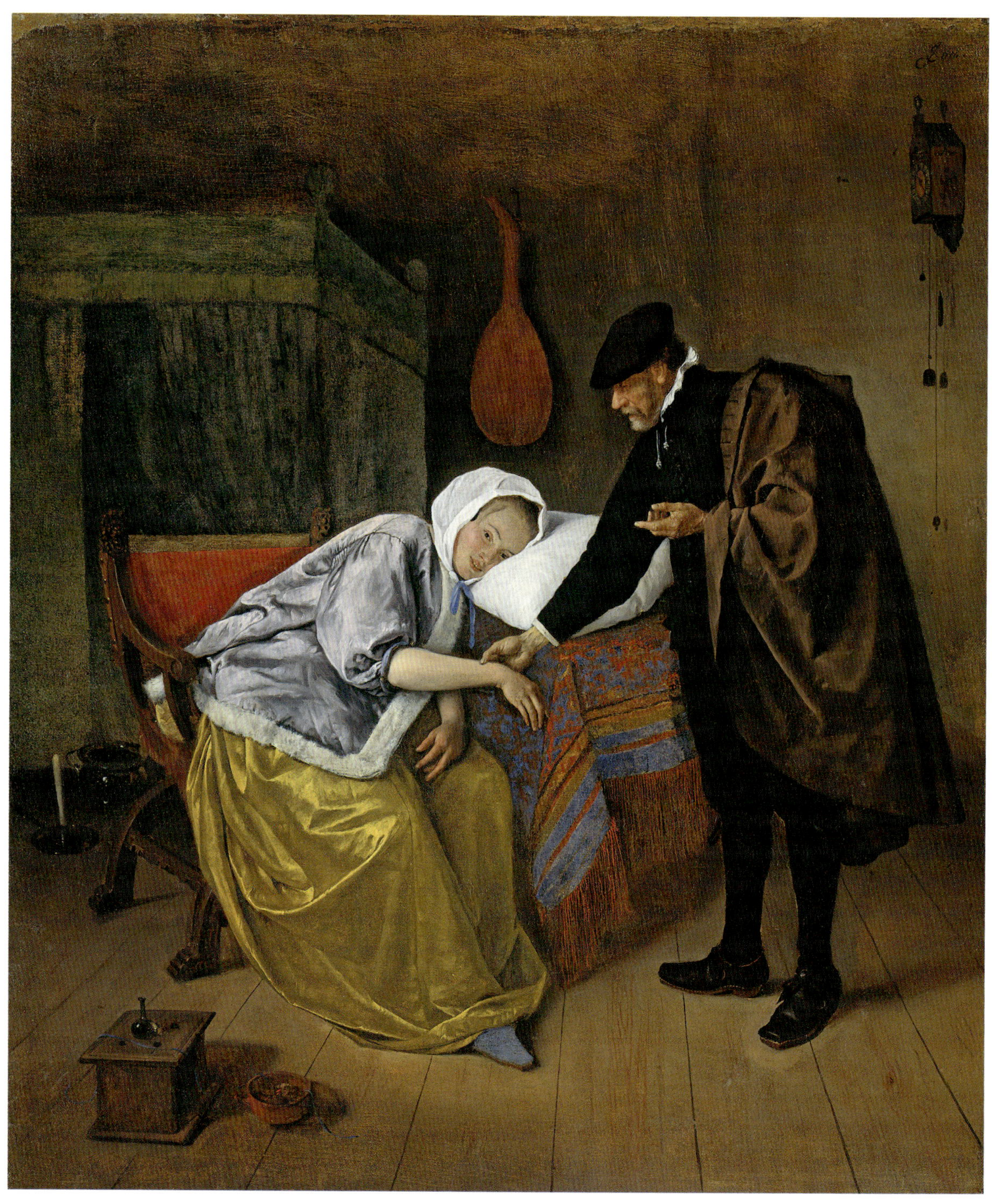

88 Jan Steen (1626–1679) · *The Sick Woman* (c. 1660–1665) · Oil on canvas · 30 × 25 inches

89 Willem Jansz Verstraeten (before 1600–1655) · *Dish with a Doctor in an Interior* (c. 1650) · Faience · diam. 15¼ inches

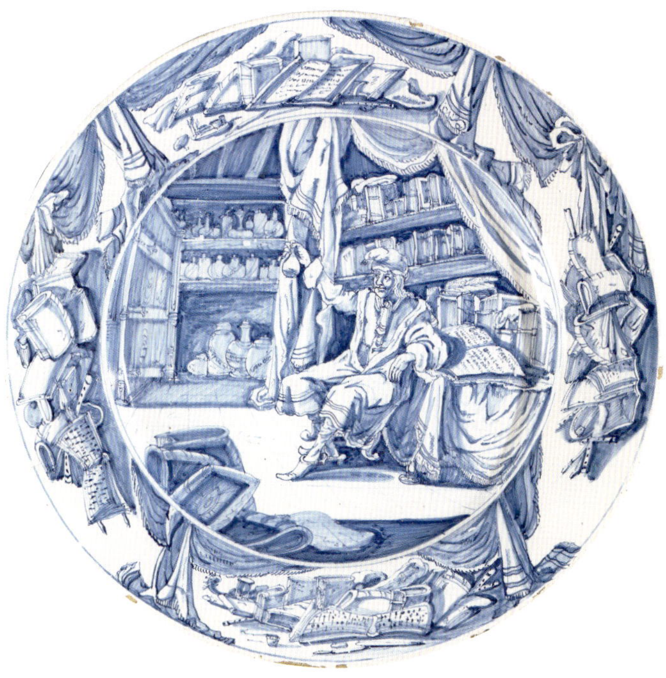

slippers in front of the seated lady are also references to lovemaking and serve to underscore the erotic connotations of the painting.

In Jan Steen's *The Sick Woman* (no. 88), painted between 1660 and 1665, the patient rests listlessly in her chair as the doctor takes her pulse. The diagnosis is clear: the young lady gazing at us with a faint smile and blushing cheeks is not ill, but hopelessly lovesick. The doctor wears clothing that would have been fashionable in the 1560s; only a stage actor playing the role of an incompetent quack would have worn such outdated attire in the early 1660s. Steen included all kinds of clues to what really goes on here: a chamber pot and candle (symbols of lust) sit behind the chair, a lute (symbol of love) hangs beside the bedstead, and in the foreground a flask, probably filled with urine, rests on a foot warmer. Examining slightly heated urine was an outmoded method many charlatan doctors used to determine whether or not a woman was pregnant. The ribbons on the foot warmer allude to the burning of a ribbon soaked in urine, a then-current antidote for morning sickness.

The unusually rich iconography of the faience *Dish with a Doctor in an Interior* of about 1650 (no. 89) recalls the central theme of Steen's painting. A score of musical instruments and songbooks in the ornamented border of the dish suggest that here too love is the illness. The doctor in fancy dress will make his diagnosis by carefully examining a flask of urine. The dish, with its beautiful nuances of blue and skillfully drawn scene, is an excellent example of the high quality of *Hollants porceleyn* (Dutch porcelain) by Willem Jansz Verstraeten (before 1600–1655). The Verstraeten family had immigrated to Holland from the southern Netherlands, changing their name from De la Rue to the Dutch translation of it. After 1625 Willem Jansz Verstraeten and his son, Gerrit Willemsz (d. 1657), were the owners of the only Delftware potteries in Haarlem, one of the earliest Dutch centers of fine ceramics. Their businesses were of great importance to the city's economy and received considerable subsidies from local government.

The interior scenes by Pieter de Hooch (1629–1684), especially the ones he painted from the late 1650s onward, are undoubtedly among the greatest works of 17th-century Dutch art. *Man Handing a Letter to a Woman in the Front Hall of a House* (no. 90), dated 1670, demonstrates how De Hooch was able not only to perfectly reproduce the details of the Dutch home in his carefully constructed compositions, but also, thanks to the incidence of light, give them a convincing atmosphere. The space here is shaped by light: soft, diffuse light that enters from different directions, sharply contrasted with bright sunlight in the distance. The painting shows a daring use of *contre-jour* light, with almost the entire background taken up by windows, obscured by the shadow of a few large trees in front of the house. Beyond the dark contours of the open front door a canal is visible (perhaps the Kloveniersburgwal in Amsterdam), lined with the stately facades of several houses bathed in full, warm light. The open window to the right of the doorway permits a clear, strong shaft of light to enter the room, partly illuminating an elegant lady at the window. She has received a message from a letter carrier and points to a child outside. The interaction between the characters is restrained, giving the scene a certain quietude and a great sense of intimacy. A wonderfully painted dog in the middle turns abruptly, apparently reacting to the messenger's voice. The lady is seated on a low wooden platform known as a *soldertien,* a customary protection against the cold of a marble floor. The pattern of the floor helps to direct our gaze through the open door, lending depth to the brilliantly rendered perspective of the scene. The meticulous execution makes this one of the most attractive of De Hooch's late Amsterdam works.

De Hooch was a pupil of Nicolaes Berchem in Haarlem. In 1652 he moved to Delft where, except for a short stay in Rotterdam, he remained until the early 1660s. He then settled in Amsterdam, where he eventually died in an insane asylum. De Hooch's interiors, with their inclusion of the world beyond through open doors or windows, are among the high points of his career, and they were a source of inspiration for his colleague and fellow townsman in Delft, Johannes Vermeer (1632–1675).

It is genre scenes that best express the unique character of 17th-century Dutch painting. The contemporary demand for these views of daily life, whether intimate domestic interiors or tavern scenes, demonstrates that the citizens of the Dutch Republic were fascinated with their world to an extent that had not been seen in any society before. Together with the other works illustrated here, they effectively convey impressions of life in the Dutch Golden Age and are a lasting legacy of a world seen through the artist's eye.

90 Pieter de Hooch (1629–1684) · *Man Handing a Letter to a Woman in the Front Hall of a House* (1670) · Oil on canvas · 26¾ × 23¼ inches

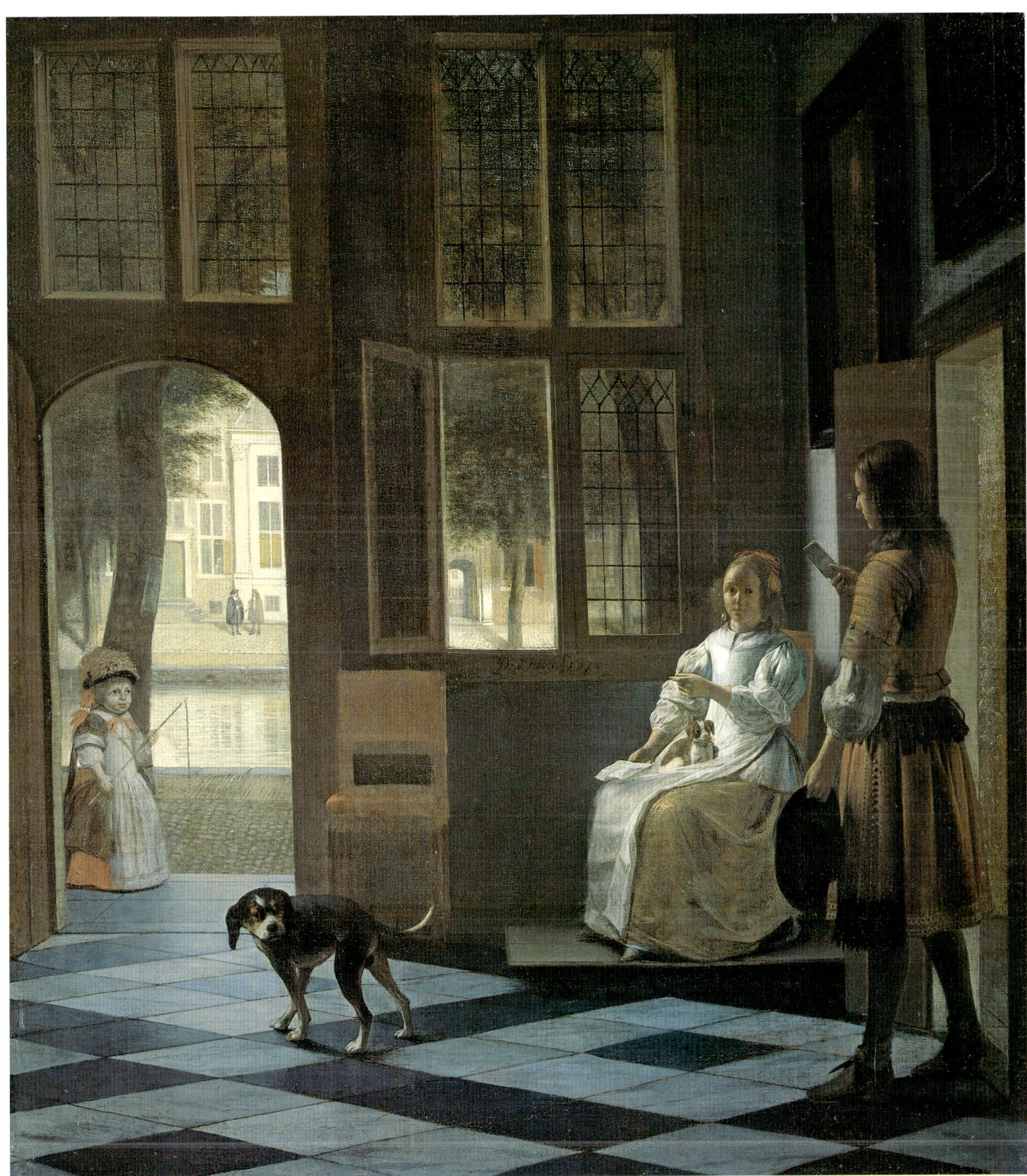

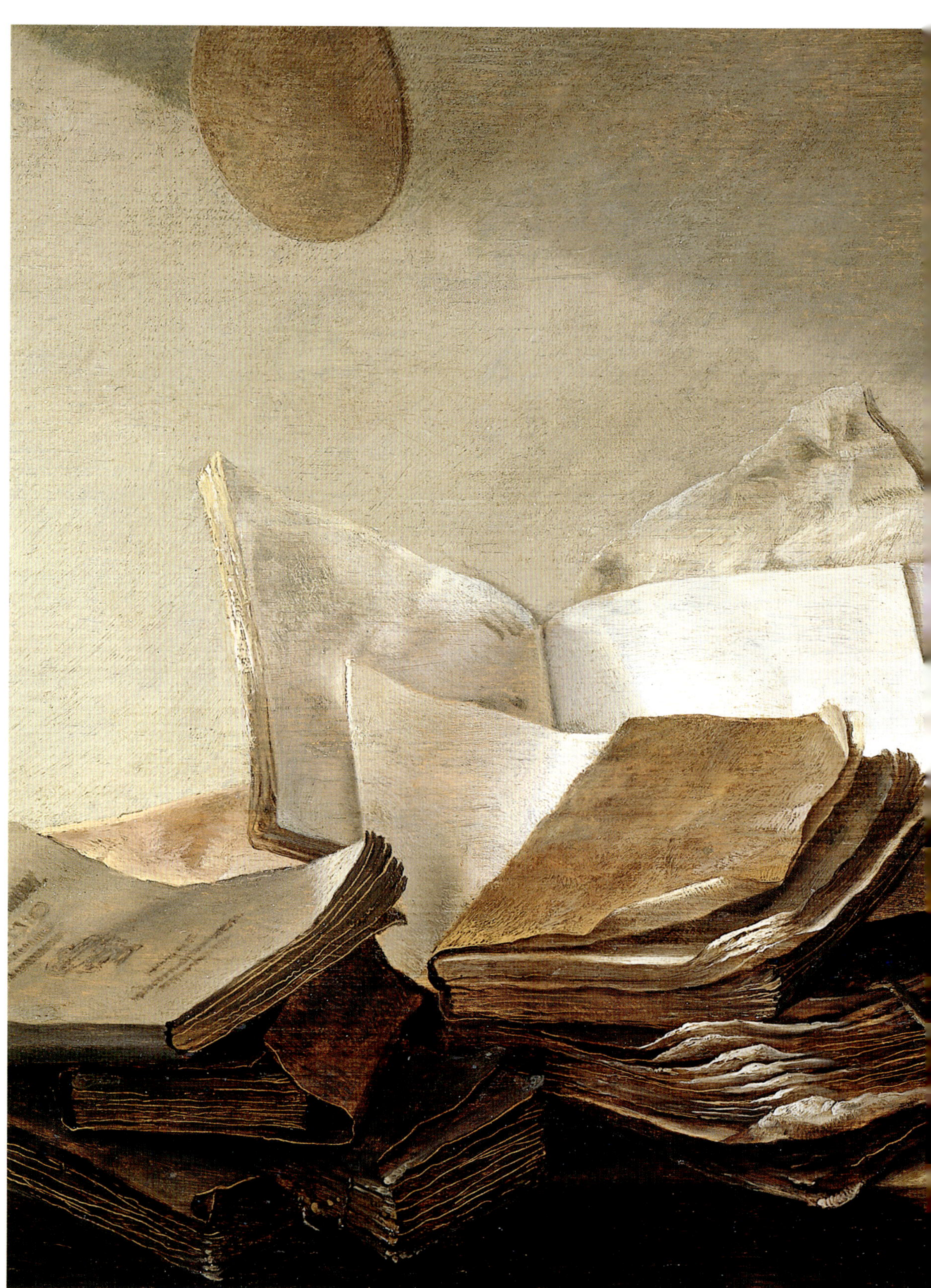

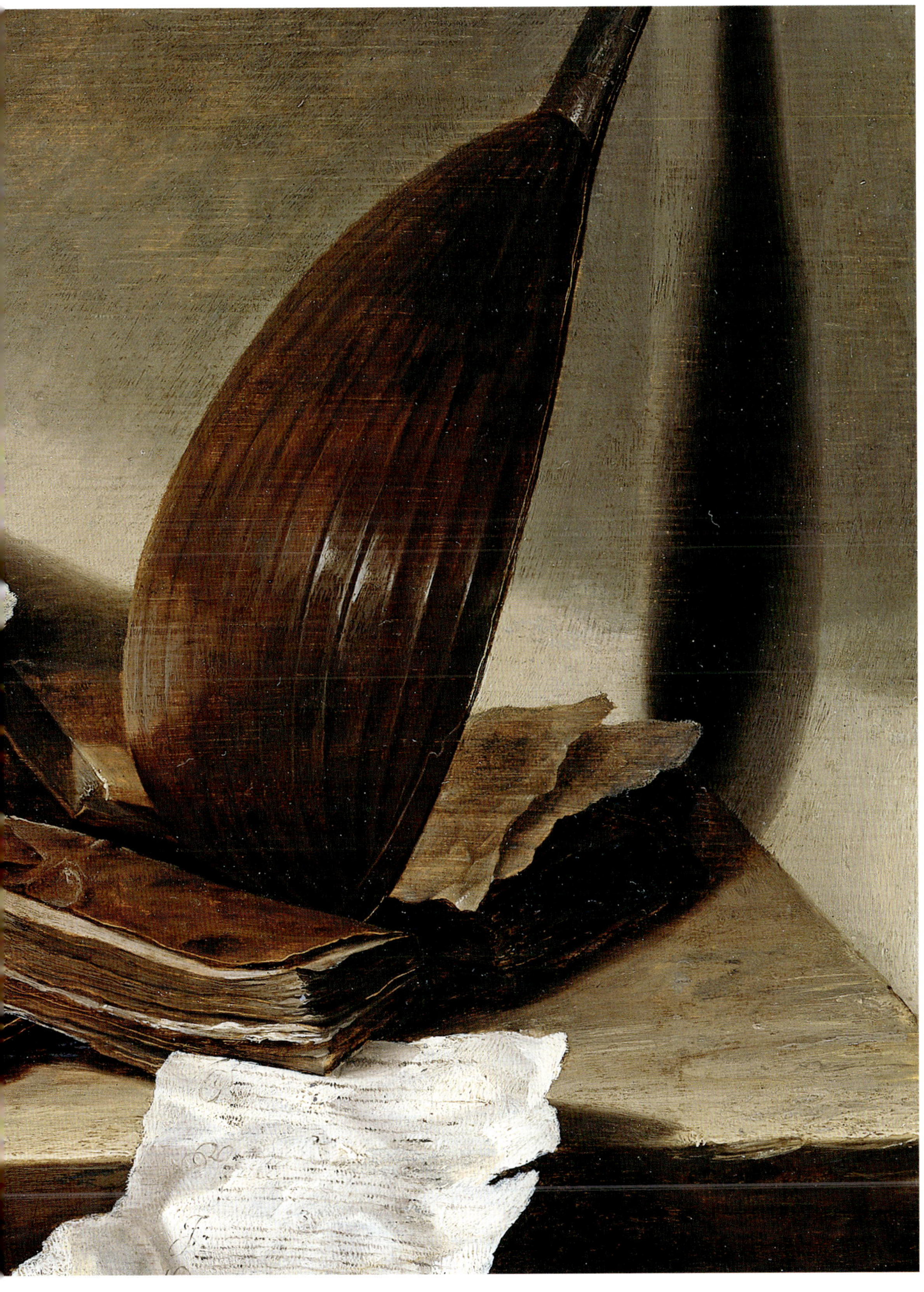

# SUGGESTED READING


## *Dutch 17th-Century History*

Deursen, A.T. van. *Plain Lives in a Golden Age: Popular Culture, Religion, and Society in Seventeenth-Century Holland.* Cambridge, 1991.

Israel, J.I. *The Dutch Primacy in World Trade, 1585–1740.* Oxford, 1989.

———. *The Dutch Republic: Its Rise, Greatness, and Fall, 1477–1806.* Oxford, 1995.

Schama, S. *The Embarrassment of Riches: An Interpretation of Dutch Culture in the Golden Age.* New York, 1987.

Van der Sman, M.C., ed. *Dutch Society in the Age of Vermeer.* Exh. cat. The Hague: Haags Historisch Museum, 1996.

Wheelock, A.K., Jr., and A. Seeff, eds. *The Public and the Private in Dutch Culture of the Golden Age.* Newark, N.J., 2000.

## *Dutch Art of the 17th Century*

Ackley, C.S. *Printmaking in the Age of Rembrandt.* Exh. cat. Boston: Museum of Fine Arts; St. Louis: St. Louis Art Museum, 1980.

Alpers, S. *The Art of Describing: Dutch Art in the Seventeenth Century.* Chicago, 1983.

Bedaux, J.B. *The Reality of Symbols: Studies in the Iconology of Netherlandish Art 1400–1800.* The Hague, 1990.

Blankert, A. *Selected Writings on Dutch Painting: Rembrandt, Van Beke, Vermeer, and Others.* Zwolle, 2004.

———, et al. *Rembrandt: A Genius and His Impact.* Exh. cat. Melbourne: National Gallery of Victoria; Canberra: National Gallery of Australia, 1997.

Broos, B.P.J., et al. *Great Dutch Paintings from America.* Exh. cat. The Hague: Mauritshuis; San Francisco: Fine Arts Museums of San Francisco, 1990.

Buijsen, E., and L.P. Grijp, eds. *Music & Painting in the Golden Age.* Exh. cat. The Hague: Gallery Hoogsteder & Hoogsteder; Antwerp: Hessenhuis, 1994.

Falkenburg, R., et al. *Kunst voor de markt 1500–1700 / Art for the Market 1500–1700.* Netherlands Yearbook for History of Art 50. Zwolle, 2000.

Filedt Kok, J.P., et al. *Netherlandish Art in the Rijksmuseum, 1600–1700.* Zwolle and Amsterdam, 2001.

Franits, W., ed. *Looking at Seventeenth-Century Dutch Art: Realism Reconsidered.* Cambridge, 1997.

Freedberg, D., and J. de Vries, eds. *Art in History, History in Art: Studies in Seventeenth-Century Dutch Culture.* Santa Monica, 1991.

Haak, B. *The Golden Age: Dutch Painters of the Seventeenth Century.* New York, 1996.

Horn, H.J. *The Golden Age Revisited: Arnold Houbraken's "Great Theatre of Netherlandish Painters and Paintresses,"* 2 vols. Doornspijk, 2000.

Jansen, P. Huys, and W. Sumowski. *Rembrandt's Academy.* Exh. cat. The Hague: Gallery Hoogsteder & Hoogsteder, 1992.

Kiers, J., and F. Tissink, eds. *The Glory of the Golden Age: Dutch Art of the 17th Century. Painting, Sculpture, and Decorative Art.* Exh. cat. Amsterdam: Rijksmuseum, 2000.

Kloek, W.T., et al. *Dawn of the Golden Age: Northern Netherlandish Art, 1580–1620.* Exh. cat. Amsterdam: Rijksmuseum, 1993.

Komanecky, M.K., et al. *Copper as Canvas: Two Centuries of Masterpiece Paintings on Copper, 1575–1775.* Exh. cat. Phoenix: Phoenix Art Museum; Kansas City: Nelson-Atkins Museum of Art; The Hague: Mauritshuis, 1998.

Liedtke, W.A. *A View of Delft: Vermeer and His Contemporaries.* Zwolle, 2000.

———, et al. *Vermeer and the Delft School.* Exh. cat. New York: Metropolitan Museum of Art; London: National Gallery, 2001.

Loughman, J., and J.M. Montias. *Public and Private Spaces: Works of Art in Seventeenth-Century Dutch Houses.* Zwolle, 2000.

Montias, J.M. *Artists and Artisans in Delft: A Socio-economic Study of the Seventeenth Century.* Princeton, N.J., 1982.

———. *Art at Auction in 17th-Century Amsterdam.* Amsterdam, 2002.

North, M. *Art and Commerce in the Dutch Golden Age.* New Haven, 1997.

Ploeg, P., van de, et al. *Princely Patrons: The Collection of Frederik Henry of Orange Nassau and Amalia of Solms in The Hague.* Exh. cat. The Hague: Mauritshuis, 1997.

Priem, R. *Dutch Masters from the Rijksmuseum, Amsterdam.* Exh. cat. Melbourne: National Gallery of Victoria, 2005.

———. *The Golden Age: Highlights from the Rijksmuseum, Amsterdam.* Exh. cat. Kobe: Hyogo Prefectural Museum of Art, 2005.

Runia, E., ed. *The Glory of the Golden Age: Dutch Art of the 17th Century, Drawings and Prints.* Exh. cat. Amsterdam: Rijksmuseum, 2000.

Schwartz, G. *The Dutch World of Painting.* Exh. cat. Vancouver: Vancouver Art Gallery, 1986.

Slive, S. *Dutch Painting 1600–1800.* New Haven and London, 1995.

Sluijter, E.-J. *Seductress of Sight: Studies in Dutch Art of the Golden Age.* Zwolle, 2000.

Spicer, J.A., and L. Federle Orr, eds. *Masters of Light: Dutch Painters in Utrecht during the Golden Age.* Exh. cat. San Francisco: Fine Arts Museums of San Francisco; Baltimore: Walters Art Gallery; London: National Gallery, 1997.

Sutton, P. *A Guide to Dutch Art in America.* Grand Rapids, Mich., 1986.

Thiel, P.J.J. van, et al. *All the Paintings of the Rijksmuseum in Amsterdam: A Completely Illustrated Catalogue.* Amsterdam, 1976; *First Supplement: 1976–1991,* Amsterdam / The Hague, 1991.

Thiel, P.J.J. van, and C.J. de Bruyn Kops, eds. *Framing in the Golden Age: Picture and Frame in Seventeenth-Century Holland.* Zwolle, 1995.

Turner, J., ed. *The Grove Dictionary of Art from Rembrandt to Vermeer: 17th-Century Dutch Artists.* New York, 2000.

Weller, D.P., ed. *Sinners & Saints, Darkness and Light: Caravaggio and His Dutch and Flemish Followers.* Exh. cat. Raleigh: North Carolina Museum of Art; Milwaukee: Milwaukee Art Museum; Dayton, Ohio: Dayton Art Institute, 1998.

Westermann, M. *A Worldly Art: The Dutch Republic, 1585–1718.* New York, 1996.

———, et al. *Art & Home: Dutch Interiors in the Age of Rembrandt.* Exh. cat. Denver: Denver Art Museum; Newark: Newark Museum, 2001.

Wright, C. *Paintings in Dutch Museums: An Index of Oil Paintings in Public Collections in the Netherlands by Artists Born before 1870.* London and Totowa, N.J., 1980.

• • • • •

## Ceramics

Dam, J.D. van. *Delffse porceleyne 1620–1850 / Dutch Delftware 1620–1850.* Zwolle, 2004.

———. *Gedateerd Delfts aardewerk / Dated Dutch Delftware.* Zwolle, 1991.

Jörg, C.J.A. *Porcelain and the Dutch China Trade.* The Hague, 1982.

Lemmen, H. van. *Delftware Tiles.* Aylesbury, 1986.

Pluis, J., et al. *De Nederlandse tegel: decors en benamingen, 1570–1930 / The Dutch Tile: Designs and Names, 1570–1930.* Leiden, 1997.

## Glass

Hudig, F. *An Essay on Dutch Glass Engravers, Reprinted from European Glass by Wilfred Buckley, C.B.E.* Plymouth, 1926.

Ritsema van Eck, P.C., and H.M. Zijlstra-Zweens, *Glass in the Rijksmuseum.* 2 vols. Zwolle, 1993–95.

## Silver

Blaauwen, A.L. den. *Nederlands zilver: 1580–1830 / Dutch Silver: 1580–1830.* Exh. cat. Amsterdam: Rijksmuseum; Toledo: Toledo Museum of Art; Boston: Museum of Fine Arts, 1979.

Citroen, K. *Dutch Goldsmiths' and Silversmiths' Marks and Names prior to 1812: A Descriptive and Critical Repertory.* Leiden, 1993.

Frederiks, J.W. *Dutch Silver.* 4 vols. The Hague, 1952–1961.

Hernmarck, C. *The Art of the European Silversmith 1430–1830.* 2 vols. Amsterdam, London, and New York, 1977.

• • • • •

## Architectural Painting

Giltaij, J., and G. Jansen, eds. *Perspectives: Saenredam and the Architectural Painters of the 17th Century.* Exh. cat. Rotterdam: Museum Boijmans Van Beuningen, 1991.

Goossens, E.J., ed. *The Royal Palace of Amsterdam in Paintings of the Golden Age.* Exh. cat. Amsterdam: Royal Palace, 1997.

Liedtke, W.A. *Architectural Painting in Delft: Gerard Houckgeest, Hendrik van Vliet, Emmanuel de Witte.* Doornspijk, 1982.

Wattenmaker, R.J., et al. *The Dutch Cityscape and Its Sources.* Exh. cat. Amsterdam: Amsterdams Historisch Museum; Toronto: Art Gallery of Ontario, 1977.

## Genre

Briganti, G., et al. *The Bamboccianti: Painters of Everyday Life in Seventeenth Century Rome.* Rome, 1983.

Brown, C. *Scenes of Everyday Life: Dutch Genre Painting of the Seventeenth Century.* London and Amsterdam, 1984.

Franits, W. *Dutch Seventeenth-Century Genre Painting: Its Thematic and Stylistic Evolution.* New Haven, 2004.

Giltaij, J., ed. *Senses and Sins: Dutch Painters of Daily Life in the Seventeenth Century.* Exh. cat. Rotterdam: Museum Boijmans Van Beuningen; Frankfurt am Main: Städelsches Kunstinstitut und Städtische Galerie, 2004.

Jongh, E. de, and G. Luijten. *Mirror of Everyday Life: Genre Prints in the Netherlands, 1550–1700.* Exh. cat. Amsterdam: Rijksmuseum, 1997.

Stone-Ferrier, L.A. *Dutch Prints of Daily Life: Mirror of Life or Masks of Morals?* Exh. cat. Lawrence: Spencer Museum of Art; New Haven: Yale University Art Gallery; Austin: Huntington Gallery, 1983.

Sutton, P. ed. *Masters of Seventeenth-Century Dutch Genre Painting.* Exh. cat. Philadelphia: Philadelphia Museum of Art; Berlin: Gemäldegalerie and Staatliche Museen zu Berlin; London: Royal Academy of Arts, 1984.

Sutton, P.C., et al. *Love Letters: Dutch Genre Paintings in the Age of Vermeer.* Exh. cat. Dublin: National Gallery of Ireland; Greenwich: Bruce Museum of Arts, 2003.

Westermann, M. *The Amusements of Jan Steen: Comic Painting in the Seventeenth Century.* Zwolle, 1997.

## History Painting

Blankert, A., et al. *Gods, Saints & Heroes: Dutch Painting in the Age of Rembrandt.* Exh. cat. Washington, D.C.: National Gallery of Art; Detroit: Institute of Arts; Amsterdam: Rijksmuseum, 1980.

———. *Dutch Classicism in Seventeenth-Century Painting.* Exh. cat. Rotterdam: Museum Boijmans Van Beuningen; Frankfurt am Main: Städelsches Kunstinstitut, 1999.

Schoon, P., and S. Paarlberg, eds. *Greek Gods and Heroes in the Age of Rubens and Rembrandt.* Exh. cat. Athens: National Gallery and Netherlands Institute; Dordrecht: Dordrechts Museum, 2000.

## Landscape Painting

Blankert, A. *Dutch 17th-Century Italianate Landscape Painters.* Soest, 1978.

Brown, C., ed. *Dutch Landscape: The Early Years, Haarlem and Amsterdam, 1590–1660.* Exh. cat. London: National Gallery, 1986.

Buijsen, E., ed. *Between Fantasy and Reality: 17th-Century Dutch Landscape Painting.* Exh. cat. Tokyo: Station Gallery; Kasama: Nichido Museum of Art; Kumamoto: Prefectural Museum of Art; Leiden: Stedelijk Museum De Lakenhal, 1992.

Duparc, F.J., and L. Graif. *Italian Recollections: Dutch Painters of the Golden Age.* Exh. cat. Montreal: Montreal Museum of Fine Arts, 1990.

Gibson, W. *Pleasant Places: The Rustic Landscape from Bruegel to Ruisdael.* Berkeley, Los Angeles, and London, 2000.

Harwood, L.B. *Inspired by Italy: Dutch Landscape Painting, 1600–1700.* Exh. cat. London: Dulwich Picture Gallery, 2002.

Stechow, W. *Dutch Landscape Painting of the Seventeenth Century.* London, 1966.

Suchtelen, A. van, ed. *Holland Frozen in Time: The Dutch Winter Landscape in the Golden Age.* Exh. cat. The Hague: Mauritshuis, 2001.

Sutton, P.C., and P.J.J. van Thiel, eds. *Masters of 17th-Century Dutch Landscape Painting.* Exh. cat. Amsterdam: Rijksmuseum; Boston: Museum of Fine Arts; Philadelphia: Philadelphia Museum of Art, 1987.

## Marine Painting

Giltaij, J., and J. Kelch, eds. *Praise of Ships and the Sea: The Dutch Marine Painters of the 17th Century.* Exh. cat. Rotterdam: Museum Boijmans Van Beuningen; Berlin: Staatliche Museen zu Berlin and Gemäldegalerie im Bodemuseum, 1996.

Keyes, G.S., ed. *Mirror of Empire: Dutch Marine Art of the Seventeenth Century.* Exh. cat. Minneapolis: Institute of Arts; Toledo: Toledo Museum of Art; Los Angeles: Los Angeles County Museum of Art, 1990.

Preston, L.R. *The Seventeenth-Century Marine Painters of the Netherlands.* Leigh-on-Sea, 1974.

## Portraiture

Bedaux, J., and R. Ekkart, eds. *Pride and Joy: Children's Portraits in the Netherlands, 1500–1700.* Exh. cat. Haarlem: Frans Hals Museum; Antwerp: Koninklijk Museum voor Schone Kunsten, 2000.

Buvelot, Q., and C. White, eds. *Rembrandt by Himself.* Exh. cat. London: National Gallery; The Hague: Mauritshuis, 1999.

Jongh, E. de, ed. *Faces of the Golden Age: Seventeenth-Century Dutch Portraits.* Exh. cat. Yamaguchi: Prefectural Museum of Art; Kumamoto: Prefectural Museum of Art; Tokyo: Station Gallery; Rotterdam: Kunsthal, 1994.

Lurie, D.J., ed. *17th-Century Dutch Family Portraits.* Exh. cat. Tel Aviv: Museum of Art, 1994.

Kettering, A. McNeil. *The Dutch Arcadia: Pastoral Art and Its Audience in the Golden Age.* Montclair, 1983.

Scholten, F. *Portrait Sculpture / Gebeeldhouwde portretten.* Amsterdam, 1995.

## Still-Life Painting

Bergström, I. *Dutch Still-life Painting in the Seventeenth Century.* London, 1956.

Chong, A., and W. Kloek, eds. *Still-life Paintings from the Netherlands, 1550–1720.* Exh. cat. Amsterdam: Rijksmuseum; Cleveland: Cleveland Museum of Art, 1999.

Helmus, L.M., ed. *Fish Still Lifes by Dutch and Flemish Masters, 1550–1700.* Exh. cat. Utrecht: Centraal Museum; Helsinki: Amos Anderson Art Museum, 2004.

Jongh, E. de, ed. *Still-life in the Age of Rembrandt.* Exh. cat. Auckland: Auckland City Art Gallery; Wellington: National Gallery; Christchurch: Robert McDougall Art Gallery, 1982.

Segal, S. *A Prosperous Past: The Sumptuous Still Life in the Netherlands, 1600–1700.* Exh. cat. Delft: Stedelijk Museum Het Prinsenhof; Cambridge, Mass.: Fogg Art Museum; Fort Worth: Kimbell Art Museum, 1988.

Sullivan, S.A. *The Dutch Gamepiece.* Totowa, N.J., 1984.

Taylor, P. *Dutch Flower Painting, 1600–1720.* New Haven and London, 1995.

Vroom, N.R.A. *A Modest Message as Intimated by the Painters of the "Monochrome Banketje."* 3 vols. Schiedam, 1980.

Wallert, A., ed. *Still Lifes: Techniques and Style, An Examination of Paintings from the Rijksmuseum.* Zwolle, 1999.

Willigen, A. van der, and Fred G. Meijer. *A Dictionary of Dutch and Flemish Still-life Painters Working in Oils, 1525–1725.* Leiden, 2003.

• • • • •

## *Monographs*

Adams, A. Jensen. "The Paintings of Thomas de Keyser (1596/97–1667): A Study in Portraiture in Seventeenth-Century Amsterdam." PhD diss., Cambridge, Mass., 1985.

Bachmann, F. *Aert van der Neer (1604–1677): Life and Work, with a Catalogue Raisonné of Paintings and Drawings.* Doornspijk, 2002.

Baer, R., et al. *Gerrit Dou, 1613–1675: Master Painter in the Age of Rembrandt.* Exh. cat. Washington, D.C.: National Gallery of Art; London: Dulwich Picture Gallery; The Hague: Mauritshuis, 2000.

Bakker, B., et al. *Landscapes of Rembrandt: His Favourite Walks.* Exh. cat. Amsterdam: Gemeentearchief; Paris: Institut Néerlandais, 1998.

Beer, G. de, et al. *Backhuysen aan het roer! Zeeschilder 1630–1708 / Backhuysen at the Helm! Marine Painter 1630–1708.* Exh. cat. Amsterdam: Royal Palace, 2004.

Biesboer, P., ed. *Pieter Claesz: Master of Haarlem Still Life.* Exh. cat. Haarlem: Frans Hals Museum; Zürich: Kunsthaus; Washington, D.C.: National Gallery of Art, 2004.

Brown, C., et al. *Rembrandt: The Master and His Workshop.* 2 vols. Exh. cat. Berlin: Gemäldegalerie SMPK at the Altes Museum; Amsterdam: Rijksmuseum; London: National Gallery, 1991.

Bruyn, J., et al. *A Corpus of Rembrandt Paintings.* 4 vols.: 1, *1625–1631;* 2, *1631–1634;* 3, *1635–1642;* 4, *Self-portraits 1625–1669.* The Hague and Boston, 1982–.

Buvelot, Q., et al. *Frans van Mieris the Elder, 1635–1681.* Exh. cat. The Hague: Mauritshuis; Washington, D.C.: National Gallery of Art, 2005.

Chapman, H. Perry, et al. *Jan Steen: Painter and Storyteller.* Exh. cat. Washington, D.C.: National Gallery of Art; Amsterdam: Rijksmuseum, 1996.

Chong, A., ed. *Rembrandt Creates Rembrandt: Art and Ambition in Leiden, 1629–1631.* Exh. cat. Boston: Isabella Stewart Gardner Museum, 2000.

Grant, M.H. *Rachel Ruysch 1664–1750.* Leigh-on-Sea, 1956.

Helmus, L., ed. *Pieter Saenredam: The Utrecht Works, Paintings and Drawings by the 17th-Century Master of Perspective.* Exh. cat. Utrecht: Centraal Museum; Los Angeles: J. Paul Getty Museum, 2000.

Hinterding, E., et al. *Rembrandt the Printmaker.* Exh. cat. Amsterdam: Rijksmuseum; London: British Museum, 2000.

Kilian, J. *The Paintings of Karel du Jardin, 1626–1678: Catalogue Raisonné.* Amsterdam and Philadelphia, 2005.

Krämer-Noble, M. *Abraham Mignon, 1640–1679.* Leigh-on-Sea, 1973.

Lawrence, C. *Gerrit Adriaensz. Berckheyde (1638–1698), Haarlem Cityscape Painter.* Doornspijk, 1991.

Moltke, J. W. von. *Arent de Gelder: Dordrecht 1645–1727.* Doornspijk, 1994.

———. *Govaert Flinck, 1615–1660.* Amsterdam, 1965.

Naumann, O. *Frans van Mieris the Elder (1635–1681).* 2 vols. Doornspijk, 1981.

Nicolson, B. *Hendrick Terbrugghen.* London, 1958.

Robinson, F.W. *Gabriel Metsu (1629–1667): A Study of His Place in Dutch Genre Painting of the Golden Age.* New York, 1974.

Robinson, W.W. "The Early Works of Nicolaes Maes, 1653 to 1661." PhD diss. Cambridge, Mass., 1996.

Schneeman, L.T. "Hendrick Martensz. Sorgh: A Painter of Rotterdam, with Catalogue Raisonné." PhD diss. Ann Arbor, Mich., 1982.

Schneider, C.P. *Rembrandt's Landscapes.* New Haven and London, 1990.

Schwartz, G., and M.J. Bok. *Pieter Saenredam: The Painter and His Time.* New York, 1989.

Slive, S. *Frans Hals.* 3 vols. New York and London, 1970–74.

———, et al. *Frans Hals.* Exh. cat. Washington, D.C.: National Gallery of Art; London Royal Academy; Haarlem: Frans Hals Museum, 1989.

———. *Jacob van Ruisdael: A Complete Catalogue of His Paintings, Drawings, and Etchings.* New Haven and London, 2001.

Stechow, W., and L.J. Slatkes. *Hendrick Terbrugghen in America.* Exh. cat. Dayton: Dayton Art Institute; Baltimore: Baltimore Museum of Art, 1965.

Strauss, W.L., et al. *The Rembrandt Documents.* New York, 1979.

Sutton, P.C. *Pieter de Hooch: Complete Edition.* Oxford and New York, 1980.

———. *Pieter de Hooch, 1629–1684.* Exh. cat. London: Dulwich Picture Gallery; Hartford: Wadsworth Atheneum, 1998.

Vogelaar, C., et al. *Rembrandt & Lievens in Leiden: "Een jong en edel schildersduo"/"A Pair of Young and Noble Painters."* Exh. cat. Leiden: Stedelijk Museum De Lakenhal, 1991.

Walford, E.J. *Jacob van Ruisdael and the Perception of Landscape.* New Haven and London, 1991.

Wetering, E. van de. *Rembrandt: The Painter at Work.* Amsterdam, 1997.

———, et al. *The Mystery of the Young Rembrandt.* Exh. cat. Kassel: Staatliche Museen; Amsterdam: Museum Het Rembrandthuis, 2001.

Wheelock, A.K., Jr., et al. *Gerard ter Borch.* Exh. cat. Washington, D.C.: National Gallery of Art; Detroit: Detroit Institute of Arts, 2004.

———. *Rembrandt's Late Religious Portraits.* Exh. cat. Washington, D.C.: National Gallery of Art, 2005.

White, C. *Rembrandt As an Etcher: A Study of the Artist at Work.* 2d ed. London and New Haven, 1999.

White, C., and K.G. Boon. *Rembrandt's Etchings: An Illustrated Critical Catalogue.* 2 vols. Amsterdam, London, and New York, 1969.

# INDEX OF ARTISTS AND ILLUSTRATED WORKS

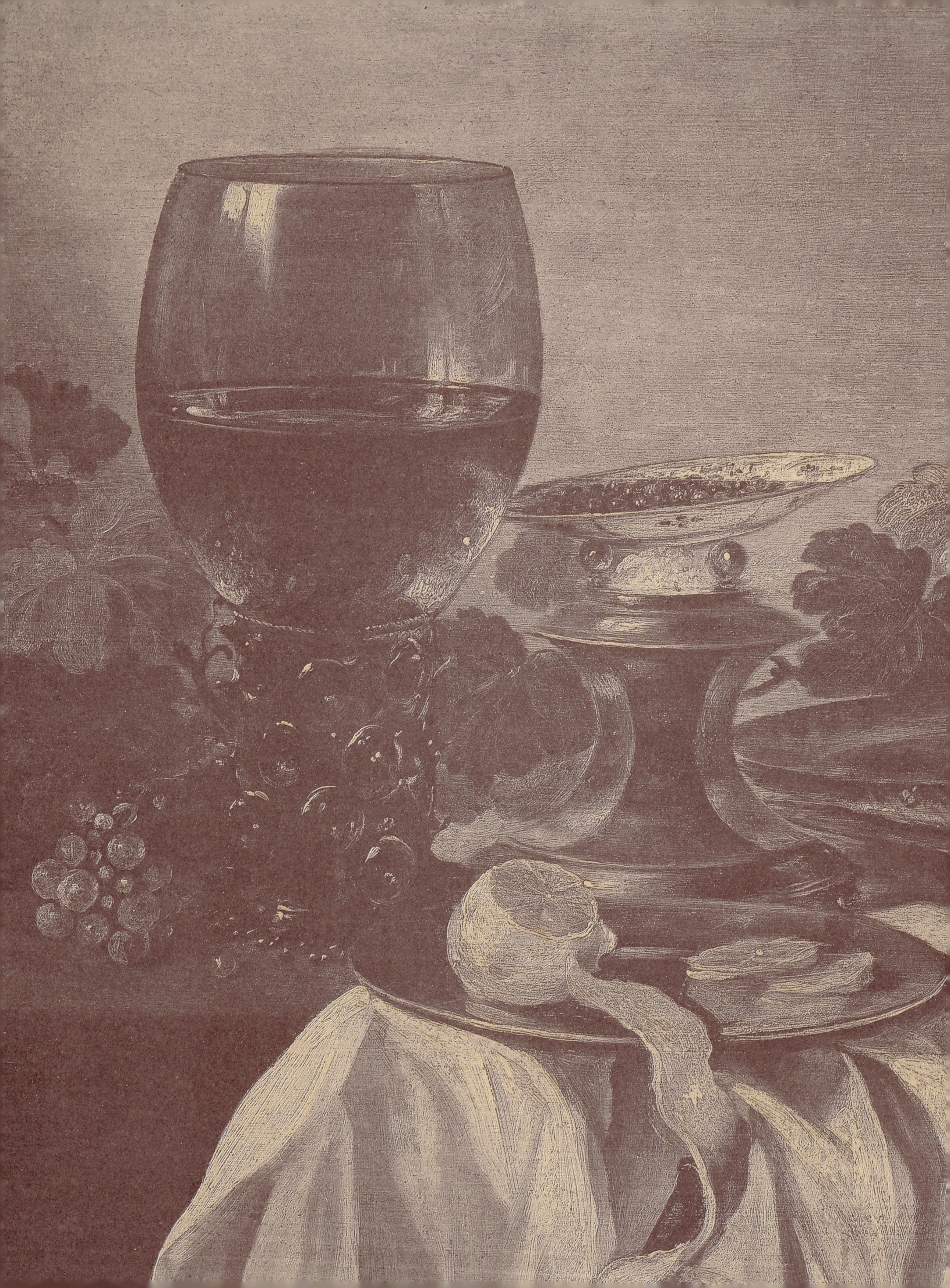